W9-AOP-835

VISUAL QUICKSTART GUIDE

MAYA

Danny Riddell and Andrew S. Britt

Peachpit Press

Visual QuickStart Guide
Maya
Danny Riddell and Andrew S. Britt

Peachpit Press
1249 Eighth Street
Berkeley, CA 94710
510/524-2178
800/283-9444
510/524-2221 (fax)

Find us on the World Wide Web at:
www.peachpit.com

Peachpit Press is a division of Pearson Education.

Copyright © 2002 by Danny Riddell

Editor: Rebecca Gulick
Production Coordinator: Lisa Brazieal
Copyeditor: Elissa Rabellino
Compositor: Owen Wolfson
Indexer: Karin Arrigoni
Cover design: The Visual Group

Notice of Rights

All rights reserved. No part of this book may be reproduced or transmitted in any form by any means, electronic, mechanical, photocopying, recording, or otherwise, without the prior written permission of the publisher. For information on getting permissions for reprints or excerpts, contact permissions@peachpit.com.

Notice of Liability

The information in this book is distributed on an "As Is" basis, without warranty. While every precaution has been taken in the preparation of the book, neither the author nor Peachpit Press, shall have any liability to any person or entity with respect to any loss or damage caused or alleged to be caused directly or indirectly by the instructions contained in this book or by the computer software and hardware products described in it.

Trademarks

Visual QuickStart Guide is a registered trademark of Peachpit Press, a division of Pearson Education.

Throughout this book, trademarks are used. Rather than put a trademark symbol in every occurrence of a trademarked name, we state that we are using the names in an editorial fashion only and to the benefit of the trademark owner with no intention of infringement of the trademark.

ISBN 0-201-77138-1

9 8 7 6 5 4 3 2

Printed and bound in the United States of America

Dedication

Danny Riddell

To my incredible wife, Yee-Ju, and family for inspiring me, believing in me, and challenging me. Without their love, dedication, and support this book would not have been.

Andrew S. Britt

To my wife, Dedra, and my daughter, Katriella, for being there for me in spirit while I was spending time away from them working. The long hours I spent on the book meant long hours for Dedra at home. Her support and understanding made it possible for me to focus on the book.

Acknowledgements

Andrew and Danny would especially like to thank:

Rebecca Gulick, for continually smiling, no matter how much we made her grit her teeth, and for her patience, diligence, and guidance.

Marjorie Baer, for her constant encouragement and leadership.

Elissa Rabellino, for steering our English in the right direction with her fantastic copy-editing.

Lisa Brazieal and Owen Wolfson for formatting and laying out this book.

Jim Wagoner, for his contributions and additions to the book.

In addition, Andrew would like to thank the faculty and students of the Academy of Art College and Ex'pression Center For New Media. I have learned as much as I have taught at these schools.

TABLE OF CONTENTS

TABLE OF CONTENTS

INTRODUCTION

Figure i.1 This voracious prehistoric lizard is just one of the myriad creatures you can bring to life in Maya.

Welcome to *Maya: Visual QuickStart Guide*.

Alias|Wavefront's Maya is the high-end 3D program responsible for bringing to life many of the three-dimensional people, animals, plants, cars, and machines you see in film, videos, and games. Whether you want to create pod races, realistic anatomy, or scenes with an artistic flair, Maya can help you achieve the desired look and feel. Maya's only restriction is your imagination; if you can think it up, you can create it in Maya with precise control over the final imagery (**Figure i.1**).

Maya is an extremely powerful character-animation application. By offering tools for both cartoon and photo-realistic character animators, Maya has become the preferred choice over other 3D character animation programs.

This book introduces you to Maya's interface and features. You'll soon realize, though, that Maya has enough depth to keep you busy learning for years. What really makes Maya a spectacular application is that the average user can learn enough to build incredible worlds relatively quickly. Maya's ease of use for beginners and extreme depth for advanced users have propelled it to the top of the 3D software genre.

Who Is This Book For?

If you want to learn basic 3D concepts, or if you are familiar with other 3D software and want to learn Maya, this book is for you. You should be familiar with computers and other graphics software packages. It's not necessary to have prior 3D knowledge, although that would make it easier learn Maya. This book guides you through the expansive Maya interface and shows you how to animate and render your 3D projects. If you work through this book cover to cover, you will end up with a solid Maya foundation—familiarity with the user interface and the capability to model, texture, and animate 3D content.

Once you have gone through this book and feel comfortable with the Maya basics, you'll be ready to explore Maya's more advanced features, such as particle and dynamic simulations used to create fire, water, and other elements, or real-time rendering for online and game development.

When you have explored Maya modeling, rendering, and animation, you might find that you are better at one than the other. As you work through this book, think about which area seems most interesting to you; it could develop into a hobby or even into a career creating 3D content for movies, product ads, and interactive entertainment.

What You Will Need

You will need to have a copy of Maya for Macintosh or Windows already installed on your computer. See the documentation that comes with the software for instructions on installing Maya.

Maya's incredible power comes at a price in terms of hardware demands. In fact, Maya is the most resource-intensive software we know of. Check out the documentation that comes with Maya for minimum system requirements, or visit Alias|Wavefront's Web site (www.aliaswavefront.com). We recommend beefing up your machine with as much RAM and processor power as you can manage. You will feel the difference. Also, be aware that Maya requires that you use a three-button mouse; in this book we use the phrase *middle mouse button–click* in many of the exercises.

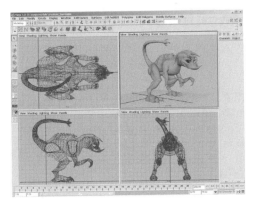

Figure i.2 This is the Maya 4 interface as it appears on Windows.

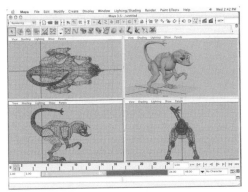

Figure i.3 Here's a look at the interface of Maya 3.5 for Mac OS X.

Maya Versions and Flavors

This book covers Maya 4 for Windows and Maya 3.5 for Mac OS X (**Figures i.2** and **i.3**). We wrote this book using Maya 4 on Windows NT and Windows 2000. Maya 3.5 was not available during most of the book-writing process. Once we got Maya 3.5 for Mac OS X up and running, we saw that there is very little difference between platform versions, at least in the features we cover, although at first glance the two may seem quite different. Any time there is difference in functionality between platforms, we point it out within the text of the section. One interface difference between the Windows and Mac versions is that the Mac version lets you tear off Hotbox menus. In addition, Maya's toolbar is on the left side of the Shelf in the Mac version, and on the left side of the interface in the Windows version. Only Maya 4.0 for Windows has layout-shortcut icons directly under the toolbar, and it comes with some additional primitives in the default Shelf, and shortcuts to the Channel Box and layer editor in the upper right-hand corner of the interface, which the Mac version does not have.

Maya 4 for Windows comes in three flavors: Builder, Complete, and Unlimited. Maya 3.5 for Mac OS X is the same as Maya Complete 3.5 for Windows with updated rendering technology. Let's take a look at the different flavors of Maya for Windows:

Maya Builder is geared specifically for low-polygon modeling and game production. It includes a full complement of polygon-modeling tools for developing real-time Web 3D and game-console content.

continues on next page

MAYA VERSIONS AND FLAVORS

Maya Complete includes all of the tools and features of Maya Builder with the addition of advanced character-animation tools, dynamics (the use of physics to simulate real-world forces), and effects.

Maya Unlimited includes all of the Maya Complete tools and features with the addition of Maya Cloth, Maya Fur, Advanced Modeling Tools, Subdivision Surfaces, Matchmoving, and Maya Batch Renderer.

Because this book is for beginning- to intermediate-level readers, we limit the coverage to the majority of features included in Maya Complete, with the addition of subdivision surfaces, which is available only in the Unlimited version. We don't get into Maya's scripting language, MEL (Maya Embedded Language), because it's beyond the scope of this book.

Additional Resources

There are hundreds of Maya- and 3D-related resources on the Web. One of our favorites is Highend 3D (www.highend3d.com). Highend3d has tutorials and listservs to which many talented 3D artists contribute daily. Some other good 3D tutorial and informational sites are 3D Café (www.3dcafe.com), 3D Ark (www.3dark.com), and AWN (www.awn.com).

VERSIONS AND FLAVORS / ADDITIONAL RESOURCES

MAYA BASICS

Maya's layered user interface is very easy to use and yet lets you access the application's great depth of functionality. This chapter introduces you to that interface and shows you how to set preferences, start a project, and access online help. First, though, it's a good idea to know something about the way Maya works.

About Maya

Maya is a node-based program. A node is a visual representation of an element, such as a surface, texture, or animation curve. Everything in Maya is represented by a node or several connected nodes (**Figure 1.1**). Nodes are made up of many attributes, which are the information that defines the node, such as an object's position or size. You access nodes in the Outliner and Hypergraph (**Figure 1.2**) panels. The advantage of this node-based architecture is that you can precisely control what nodes get connected or disconnected to other nodes, which determines the behavior and look of the object. Maya lets you see all the connections in a scene in the Hypergraph (**Figure 1.3**). The arrows and lines represent the connections. The Hypergraph is covered in more detail later in this chapter.

Figure 1.1 Nodes can be viewed in the Hypergraph or the Outliner. A new node is created for each object.

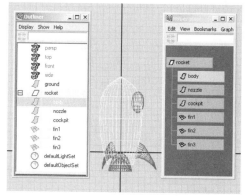

Figure 1.2 A Maya scene file can consist of a limited number of nodes and connections or can have thousands of nodes in more complex scene files.

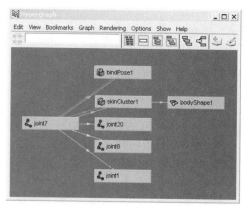

Figure 1.3 Node connections can be seen in the Hypergraph with colored arrows showing the connections between the nodes and the directions of those connections.

ABOUT MAYA

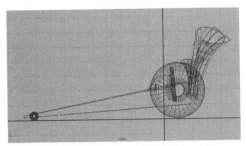

Figure 1.4 Flat, 2D graphics work with the *x* and *y* axes and lack a depth axis that enables images to become three-dimensional.

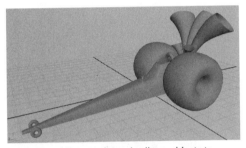

Figure 1.5 Adding another axis allows objects to become three-dimensional. These 3D models can now become accurately represented.

Maya's coordinate system

Traditional animation and graphics applications, like Adobe Photoshop, work in two dimensions, usually *x* and *y* (**Figure 1.4**). An *x* and *y* coordinate system provides height and width but lacks the depth that makes objects three-dimensional. Maya adds a third axis, *z*, which gives objects depth (**Figure 1.5**). The addition of the third axis lets you create proportionally accurate models and animations.

Within the XYZ coordinate system are two kinds of coordinates, *world* and *local*. World coordinates start at the center of the scene in location 0, 0, 0, called the *origin* (**Figure 1.6**). Local coordinates are those around the area of the object.

Objects themselves have what's called *UV coordinate space*. A surface has a U direction and a V direction. In the simple example of a plane, the U direction goes from left to right, and the V direction goes from top to bottom (**Figure 1.7**). It's like latitude and longitude on a world map. Just as you can find a position on earth by the latitude and longitude, you can determine a position on a surface by its U and V coordinates. This becomes especially important when positioning textures on a surface.

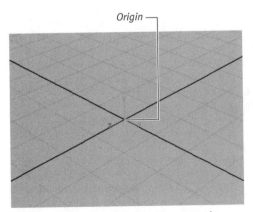

Origin

Figure 1.6 The center point of the Maya scene is called the Origin. All directional values start at 0 from the origin.

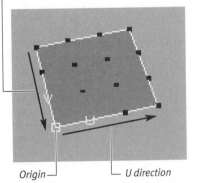

V direction

Origin — — U direction

Figure 1.7 Each surface is described with a U direction and a V direction. You can place curves on surfaces using U and V coordinates.

Maya's Interface

The Maya interface can be daunting at first glance, but it is actually very organized and easy to get around once you familiarize yourself with it (**Figure 1.8**). Along the top of the Maya interface is the main menu bar, which holds all the major Maya commands. There are more menus than would fit in the window, so they are not all visible at once in the menu bar. The menus are grouped into menu sets, which can be accessed from the menu at the far left of the status line.

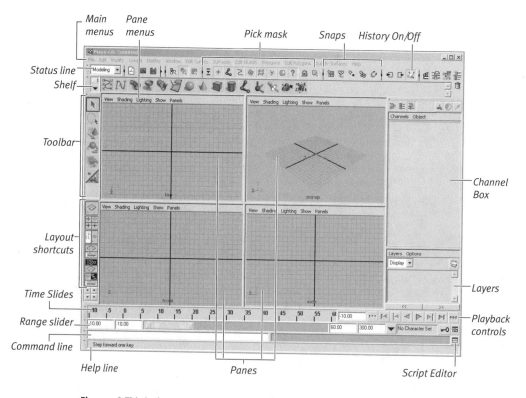

Figure 1.8 This is the Maya interface as it appears by default. Many of the elements seen here can be hidden or customized to suit the task at hand.

MAYA'S INTERFACE

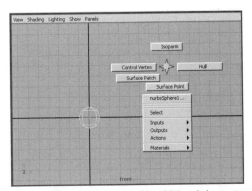

Figure 1.9 A Marking Menu holds additional shortcuts for turning different components on and off.

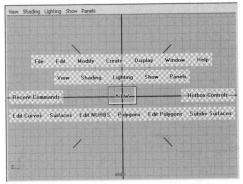

Figure 1.10 The Hotbox is a convenient way to access the menus and commands of the programs. It can be modified to suit a user's workflow in the Hotbox Controls menu.

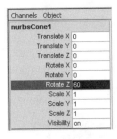

Figure 1.11 Values can be interactively changed by middle mouse button–dragging in a view panel after selecting the attribute's name in the Channel Box.

Figure 1.12 This cone is surrounded by a rotate manipulator. By clicking and dragging the circles, you can make the cone rotate.

The status line is under the main menu bar, and holds many important selection functions. Below that is the *Shelf*, which holds often-used tools. Along the left side of the Windows interface, and to the left of the Shelf on the Mac, is the toolbar, which holds Maya's manipulation tools. You use these tools to select, rotate, move, and scale objects or components.

The default Maya layout opens with four views: Front, Side, Top, and Perspective. The areas that hold these views are called *panes*. The default layout has four panes. At the bottom of the interface are the *Range Slider* and the *Time Slider* that allow you to control your position in time for animation. At the right-hand side of the interface is the *Channel Box*, which holds shortcuts to object attributes.

In addition to the main menubar are menus accessible within individual panes, and *Marking Menus* (**Figure 1.9**). Marking Menus are a convenient way to quickly access tools or commands. They appear when you right-click an object or when you click in one of the five Hotbox regions (see "About the Hotbox," below). Maya is full of menus, and it can take time to truly master them.

One of the best features of Maya is the Hotbox (**Figure 1.10**). The Hotbox holds all the Maya menu sets and appears directly above the mouse pointer when you hold down the (Spacebar). The Hotbox disappears once you release the (Spacebar). The Hotbox can be a great time-saver because you can use it instead of going all the way up to the main menu set to select a command.

To change an object's position, rotation, or scale (collectively known as *transforms*) you can type in values (**Figure 1.11**) or use *manipulators*. Manipulators allow you to change an object's value by clicking and dragging an interactive handle (**Figure 1.12**).

Using the Shelf

The Shelf is a place where you can store often-used tools and commands. You can have multiple Shelf sets to help you organize all your favorite and most frequently used tools (**Figure 1.13**). It is convenient to place tools of the same category into the same Shelf set. For instance, you could create one Shelf that has all the modeling tools you frequently use and another Shelf for all the rendering tools you use. You may have a third Shelf that just holds your 10 or 15 most used tools and commands.

In the Shelf you can add or delete items. You can also show and hide the Shelf to give you more screen space to work with (**Figure 1.14**).

The items you add to a Shelf hold the last setting you used for them. This allows you to add the same tool to the Shelf twice but with different settings. For example, you could add two Create > Primitive > Sphere icons to the Shelf but could adjust one's option to be a full 360 degrees and the other to less than 360, like 240. You could then just click each of these icons to produce the sphere with the amount of degrees you want without having to go back into the options.

To add an object to the Shelf:

◆ Select the menu item you want to add to the Shelf while pressing Ctrl/Control and Shift at the same time.
The tool is added to the Shelf.

To remove an object from the Shelf:

◆ Middle mouse button-drag the icon from the Shelf to the trash.
The tool is removed from the Shelf.

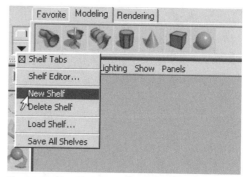

Figure 1.13 The Shelf holds tools and commands. You can customize it, or create additional Shelves, to contain frequently used commands and tools to suit the current task.

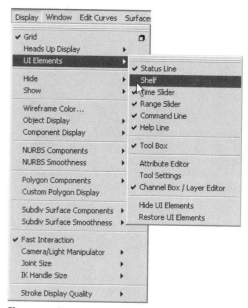

Figure 1.14 Because of the many windows employed in Maya, screen space can quickly become very limited. To save screen space, you can hide many interface elements by deselecting them in the Display > UI Elements submenu.

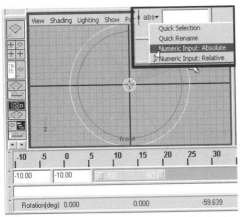

Figure 1.15 The Help Line shows important information about commands and translations. Here, at the bottom of the image, it is showing the rotation of a sphere in degrees.

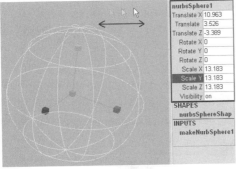

Figure 1.16 The Channel Box, at right, holds information about an object including its position (translate), scale and rotation.

About the Help Line

The Help Line provides information on object transformations and gives you hints on what your next step should be. When you move the mouse pointer over a menu item, text appears in the Help Line, which describes the steps needed to complete the command. If you rotate an object, the Help Line will reflect the change numerically (**Figure 1.15**).

The Numeric Input field to the right of the status line is where you can type precise values for the transformations. This can be useful when you need to have exact positioning for objects, like architectural buildings and product designs. Maya gives you the option to build things by eye or by entering exact position and size figures. When these changes are made, the new values appear in the Help Line.

About the Channel Box

The Channel Box contains a listing of a selected object's *keyable* attributes and is located on the right-hand side of the Maya interface (**Figure 1.16**). If an attribute is keyable, it means that it can be animated. You can change an attribute's value quickly in the Channel Box without having to open another full window, saving screen space. You can enter values in any attribute's field, or you can click on the attribute's name and interactively change its value by middle mouse button-dragging in any view pane.

continues on next page

There are ten default attributes in the Channel Box, which show up when an object is selected (**Figure 1.17**): Translate X, Translate Y, Translate Z, Rotate X, Rotate Y, Rotate Z, Scale X, Scale Y, Scale Z, (which are known collectively as transforms) and Visibility. These attributes can be typed in one at a time, in small sets, or all at once. More attributes can be added to the Channel Box list by using the Channel Control.

Below the transforms are the Shapes and Inputs nodes (**Figure 1.18**). The Shapes section lists the node names that make up the geometry. The Inputs section usually holds attributes that affect the construction history of the selected object.

If more than one object is selected, the Channel Box displays the last object selected, but any value change to an attribute affects all selected objects. You can click and drag across multiple attributes in the Channel Box to select them (**Figure 1.19**). With multiple attributes selected, one value change will change all the selected attributes' values.

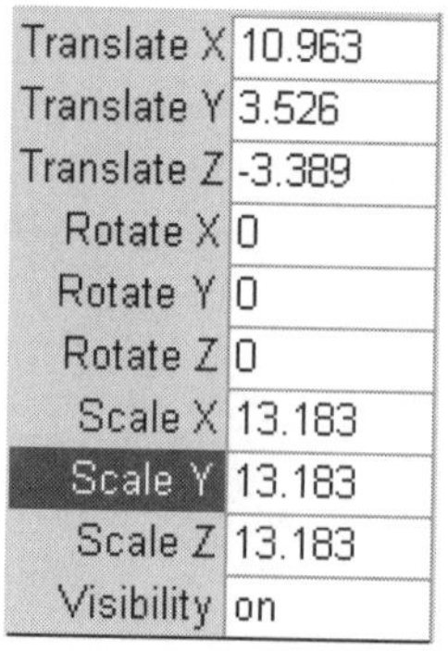

Figure 1.17 The Channel Box has ten default attribute listings for an object, but attributes can be added or subtracted.

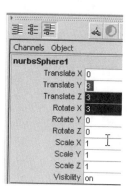

Figure 1.18 Inputs node attributes can be adjusted to change a surface's attributes after it is created.

Figure 1.19 Once multiple attributes in the Channel Box are selected, they can be changed simultaneously.

MAYA'S INTERFACE

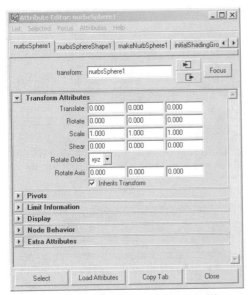

Figure 1.20 The Attribute Editor contains all of the information about the object, or objects that are selected.

About the Attribute Editor

The Attribute Editor is similar to the Channel Box in that its function is to give you access to changeable attributes. Of these two, the Attribute Editor gives a much more detailed representation of the attributes (**Figure 1.20**). In addition to the attributes in the Channel Box, the Attribute Editor contains attributes that are not keyable, that is, they cannot be animated. You can also find information about an object that can't be changed by typing a number in a field.

About the Hotbox

The Hotbox is a collection of menu sets you can access wherever your mouse pointer is, by holding down the [Spacebar]. The Hotbox is divided into five regions named North, South, East, West, and Center (**Figure 1.21**). Each of these regions has a Marking Menu associated with it.

continues on next page

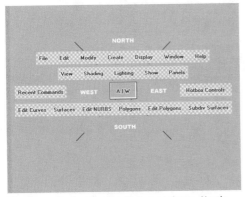

Figure 1.21 Each of the five Hotbox regions—North, South, East, West, and Center—holds a different Marking Menu .

MAYA'S INTERFACE

The default North Marking Menu holds shortcuts to different interface layouts (**Figure 1.22**). The South Marking Menu changes the contents of a pane (**Figure 1.23**)— a Perspective view to an Outliner, for instance (see "About the Outliner," below). The West Marking Menu holds preset selection masks (**Figure 1.24**). Selection masks filter which types of objects can be selected. The East Marking Menu turns user-interface elements on and off (**Figure 1.25**). You could turn off the Shelf to make more screen space, for example. The Center Marking Menu has shortcuts for changing which camera you are viewing the scene through (**Figure 1.26**).

The top row of menus in the Hotbox includes the most commonly used commands. The menus in the second row are the same ones you'll find at the top of each panel. In the third row are the Recent Commands and the Hotbox Controls menus.

The Hotbox Controls allow you to add or remove rows of menus in the hotbox. You can have none but the middle row of menus visible, or choose to have specific menu sets show up. You can even have all of the rows of menus visible at once (**Figure 1.27**).

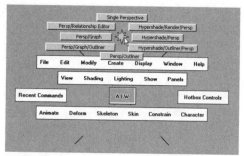

Figure 1.22 In the North region Marking Menu, you can select from different interface layouts.

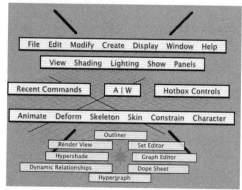

Figure 1.23 The South region Marking Menu allows you to change contents of panes.

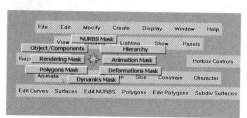

Figure 1.24 You can change object and component selection modes with the Hotbox's West region Marking Menu.

MAYA'S INTERFACE

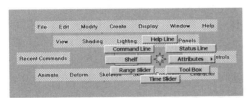

Figure 1.25 You can toggle interface elements on and off with the East region Marking Menu to make more room for modeling and animation.

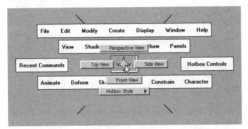

Figure 1.26 You can change views using the Hotbox's Center Marking Menu.

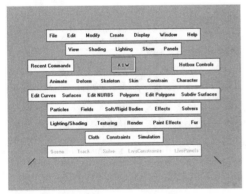

Figure 1.27 This is the Hotbox with all of the menus visible.

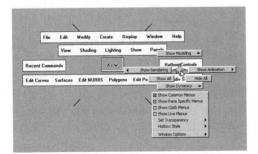

Figure 1.28 You can view one or all of the menu sets inside the Hotbox.

To show all menu sets in the Hotbox:

1. Hold down the [Spacebar].

   The Hotbox appears as long as you continue to hold down the [Spacebar].

2. Click Hotbox Controls.

   A Marking Menu appears over that button (**Figure 1.28**).

3. While still holding down the [Spacebar] and the mouse button, select Show All. Release the mouse button, but continue to hold down the [Spacebar].

   All of the menus appear (Figure 1.27). If you have trouble finding a menu, this is a good way to make it easier.

MAYA'S INTERFACE

11

About the Hypergraph

The Hypergraph window shows how all the nodes in your Maya scene are organized and connected. These connections are very important to the quality of the final animation and rendering. Character setup and movement rely on the proper connections to other nodes in order for character body parts to move naturally as one entity. This organization and connection of individual nodes is called a *hierarchy* (**Figure 1.29**). A scene's hierarchy is shown in the Hypergraph as well as in the Outliner and can be adjusted and deleted within these windows or inside a pane.

Each Maya object type has a specific icon associated with it (**Figure 1.30**). Without these icons each node would look exactly the same. As you get more familiar with Maya you will become more familiar with each object type's icon. For example a curve's icon is ⊠, and a spotlight's icon is ⊠. You can view nodes in the Hypergraph by specific object types (**Figure 1.31**) or show all object types at the same time (**Figure 1.32**). A node in the Hypergraph becomes slanted once it is animated (**Figure 1.33**).

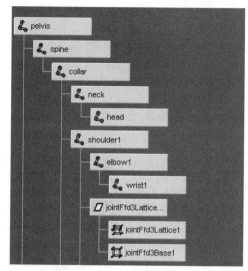

Figure 1.29 Any number of nodes connected together creates a hierarchy. The order of the hierarchy is shown in the Hypergraph and Outliner.

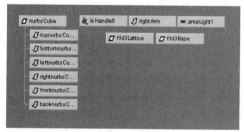

Figure 1.30 Small icons on each node shows its type of object; for example, a surface node has a small blue icon that resembles a simple surface.

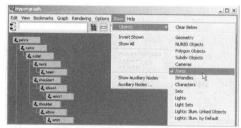

Figure 1.31 You can have the Hypergraph show only one type of node to simplify finding and selecting specific objects. If you are modeling, for example, you may want to show only curves and surfaces and if you are animating you may want to show only joints and IK handles.

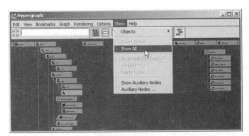

Figure 1.32 The default setting for the Hypergraph is Show All. This view helps illustrate how geometry is connected to a joint, and other hierarchy information.

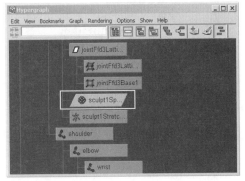

Figure 1.33 Animated nodes become slanted to distinguish them. This can also help you catch any accidental animation set on an object.

Figure 1.34 The upstream and downstream graph of an object reveals additional dependencies of the object. Some of these dependencies may be shading groups, lights, or textures.

Each node in the Hypergraph has *dependencies* connected to it. Dependencies show additional nodes connected to the selected object. An example of this is selecting a newly created sphere, and showing its upstream and downstream connections (**Figure 1.34**). The sphere's shape node, the default shader node, and the connected makeNurbs construction history node become visible. Arrows between the nodes show the directions of the connections. One way you can view a node's dependencies is to click the Show Upstream and Downstream Connections icon ⬚. When you have finished viewing these connections, you can click the Scene Hierarchy icon ⬚ to set the Hypergraph back to showing the scene hierarchy.

continues on next page

Connected nodes can be collapsed to shrink the number of nodes shown at one time and then fully expanded again when needed. A red arrow appears on a collapsed node hierarchy (**Figure 1.35**). To collapse a hierarchy, double-click the topmost node. Double-clicking the top node of a collapsed hierarchy expands the hierarchy one node at a time (**Figure 1.36**). You can expand the entire hierarchy by right mouse button-clicking the topmost node and selecting Expand All from the pop-up menu (**Figure 1.37**).

The Hypergraph is one of the most heavily used windows in Maya. The ability to connect, disconnect, and move nodes around is essential to keeping your scene organized and functional.

Figure 1.35 You can collapse a hierarchy to make more room in the Hypergraph. A collapsed hierarchy is indicated by a red arrow under the top node.

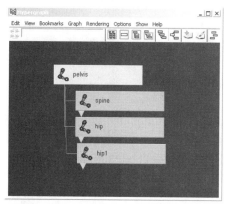

Figure 1.36 A collapsed hierarchy can be expanded one node at a time, which is often useful for temporarily showing a node and then collapsing it again.

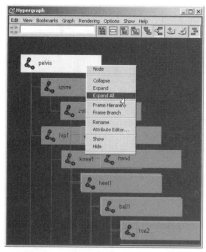

Figure 1.37 When you want to see the whole hierarchy again, you can right mouse click the top node and select Expand All.

MAYA'S INTERFACE

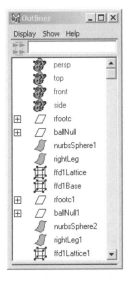

Figure 1.38
The Outliner appears in a slim window, so selecting and moving objects around is easy.

Figure 1.39
In the Outliner, as in the Hypergraph, the user can control which objects are viewed.

Figure 1.40 The four default camera views appear in the Outliner.

About the Outliner

The Outliner is similar to the Hypergraph but shows the hierarchy in a small vertical window (**Figure 1.38**). This makes finding and selecting objects easier. The Outliner's menus hold functions for filtering out specific object types, reducing the number of nodes shown at one time (**Figure 1.39**). You can use the Outliner to change an object's position in the hierarchy as well as to quickly select objects deep down in the hierarchy.

When the Outliner is opened and before any new objects are created, you will see colored listings of the top, front, side, and perspective camera nodes in addition to the defaultLightSet and defaultObjectSet icons (**Figure 1.40**). As each new object is created, a new node becomes visible. Once connections are made to create a hierarchy, a plus sign appears next to the top object in the hierarchy and is used to expand the list of objects within the hierarchy (**Figure 1.41**).

The Outliner is a convenient tool for selecting objects because of its smaller size relative to the Hypergraph. Opening the Outliner takes much less screen space than the Hypergraph, but the Hypergraph gives the user more flexibility of node placement.

Figure 1.41 To see which objects are connected to other objects, click the arrows to expand the hierarchy. Each object in the Outliner has its own icon to indicate its object type.

MAYA'S INTERFACE

Chapter 1

About construction history

As you build surfaces in Maya, the software maintains connections to the original curves or surfaces used to create them. This connection is called *construction history*. The construction history remembers the steps of creation and allows you to change the final object's shape by altering the original curve or surface geometry. This is very useful when you want to tweak a surface without having to build it over again. An example might be drawing a curve that defines the shape of the outside of a vase (**Figure 1.42**) and revolving it to complete the vase shape (**Figure 1.43**). Once the vase is created, the construction history remembers the curve's position and ties it to the shape of the final surface. When you want to change the shape of the vase, you can select part of the original curve and move it, and the final surface will follow the changes of the curve (**Figure 1.44**).

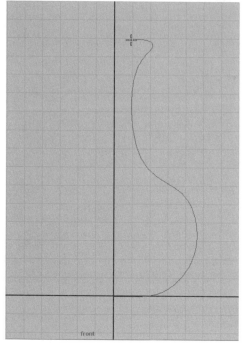

Figure 1.42 Curves can be used to outline a shape that can later be revolved to create a surface.

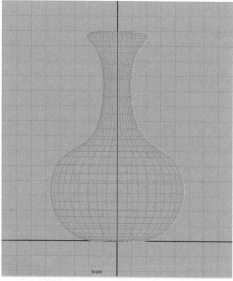

Figure 1.43 One curve can be revolved and then edited to affect the final surface shape after it is created through the object's history.

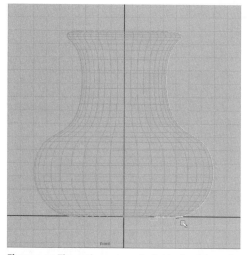

Figure 1.44 The entire curve or individual points on it can be selected and moved to alter the surface shape. The surface is attached to the curve through history and must follow the curve's edits.

MAYA'S INTERFACE

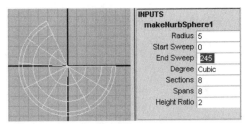

Figure 1.45 An object's primitive surface can be altered after creation through its Inputs node. The Inputs node holds multiple editable attributes specific to each object type.

Most of the *NURBS* (non-uniform rational B-splines) and polygon primitives have construction history attached to their surfaces. The history nodes for the primitives appear in the Channel Box under the Inputs heading. These Inputs nodes are useful for altering common object attributes after the original object creation. An example of this is adjusting the End Sweep of a primitive sphere to take a slice out of the shape (**Figure 1.45**).

To turn the construction history on or off:

◆ Click the Construction History On/Off icon in the Status bar. ⛣ is on and ⛣ is off.

✔ Tip

■ Once the construction history is turned off, each new object created will be without one. If an object has been created without a construction history, you must rebuild the object to have a construction history on it.

To delete an object's construction history:

1. From the Create menu select NURBS Primitive > Sphere to create a sphere or select an object.

2. From the Edit menu select Delete by Type > History.

Beginning a Project

Because of Maya's complexity and the numerous files that may be produced for each project, you need to create a folder set that has multiple folders for specific types of files to help with file organization. You can use Maya's premade folder set, called a *project*, to quickly organize all the files you create (**Figure 1.46**).

Once you create a new project, you can tell Maya where you want your files to go by setting it as the working project. When a project is set, Maya knows which folders to put your renders in and which folders to put your scene files in.

The Maya working file is called a *scene file* and should be saved in the Scenes folder. The best way to create a successful file structure is to first create a new project, set the project, create a new scene, and save the scene in the Scenes folder. The following section describes the process step by step.

To create a new project:

1. From the File menu select Project > New (**Figure 1.47**).

2. Enter a name for the project in the name field at the top of the window.

3. Click Browse, which is next to the Location field and select a folder in which to create the project folders (**Figure 1.48**).

Figure 1.46 Keeping all the different files organized is essential for a steady workflow. Maya has a preset folder set you can use, or you can create your own folders.

Figure 1.47 Creating a new project places a main project folder on your hard drive with multiple folders to organize images, renders, textures, and scene files.

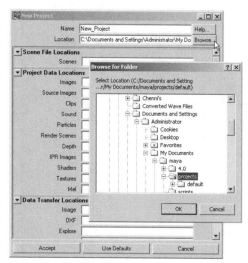

Figure 1.48 Browse to a folder under which you consistently place new project files.

Figure 1.49 Using the default names for the folders helps keep consistency through each new project.

Figure 1.50 Once a project is made and all the folders have been created, you can set the project as current and Maya will place saved files into the correct folders — scene files into the Scenes folder, for instance.

Figure 1.51 Scene files can be used to create separate models or scenes to be imported or opened at a later date. The scene file stores information about textures, models, animation, particles, and all the user settings.

4. Click Use Defaults to use preset folder names.

5. Click Accept.

A project folder is created at the specified location; it has multiple subfolders created with the default folder names (**Figure 1.49**).

In order for Maya to know which folder set you want to store your files in, you must set a project to be associated with your current working files. The final rendered files will go into the set project, so be careful to set the correct project before rendering.

To set a project:

1. Create a project following the steps in the previous section.

2. From the File menu select Project > Set (**Figure 1.50**).

3. Browse and select the folder for the project you want to use.

4. Click OK to set the project.

A Maya working file is called a scene file; it can be saved, opened, and imported into other scene files.

To create a new scene:

◆ From the File menu select New Scene (**Figure 1.51**).

A blank Maya scene is created.

To save a scene:

1. From the File menu select Save Scene.

   The Save window appears the first time a file is saved.

2. Click the pop-up menu next to "Look in" to select a folder in which to save the file (**Figure 1.52**).

   If you have set the project correctly, the pop-up menu should already show the Scenes Folder inside the project folder you have set.

3. Enter a name for the file in the "File name" field, and click Save (**Figure 1.53**).

   The scene is now saved in the Scenes folder.

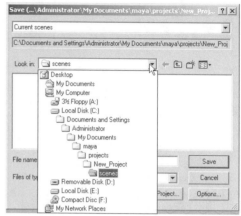

Figure 1.52 If a project has been set, the Save As command will automatically open the scene folder for the set projects, into which you can save the file.

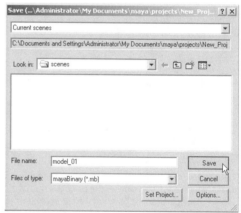

Figure 1.53 It is good practice to name your files in a numbered sequence, as projects often use multiple scene files.

Figure 1.54 Referencing a file into multiple scenes allows the original scene file to be edited; the references files will inherit the changes.

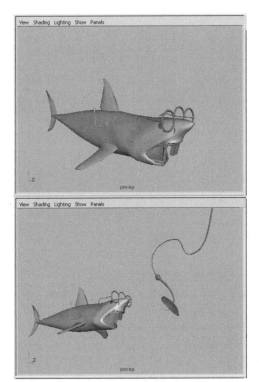

Figure 1.55 Changes made to a referenced file are automatically updated in each scene in which the referenced file is used.

Importing, Exporting, and Referencing

There are two different ways to bring files and geometry into a Maya scene: importing and referencing. When you import a file into Maya, you are permanently merging the file into the current scene. This is recommended if you are working with just one file.

Many times you will want to use the same model in multiple scenes (**Figure 1.54**). You can use referencing to bring a file into multiple scenes at one time. Referencing gives you a chance to edit the original file and have those revisions updated in all the scene files that use the reference. For instance, you can create a character in one file and then reference it into different files for each camera shot. If you later want to make changes to the character, you can open the original character file and make the changes, then save the file. The updates are automatically made to all files that reference the character (**Figure 1.55**).

Referencing can be particularly helpful when more than one person is working on the same project. In this case you could have the modeler create a low-resolution character that the animator can reference into a scene for animation. Then the modeler can be making additions while the animator is creating the character's motion. As model updates are made, the animator sees the model's changes as he or she works.

continues on next page

In addition to importing and referencing, you can also export objects out of a scene. There are two different export options: Export All and Export Selection. The Export All command exports everything in the current scene to a new file. The Export Selection command exports currently selected objects. Using the Export Selection command gives you greater control over what is exported out of the scene. Be aware that Export All will also export the orthographic and Perspective cameras. The scene that the objects are then imported into will have two sets of Front, Top, Side, and Perspective cameras. This can become cumbersome when selecting and rendering the cameras.

Figure 1.56 To export everything in the scene, use the Export All command.

To export an entire scene:

1. From the File menu select Export All (**Figure 1.56**).

   The Export window opens.

2. Navigate to the folder in which you want to place the exported file.

3. Click Export.

   All the file components are exported.

To export selected objects:

1. Select the objects you want to export (**Figure 1.57**).

2. From the File menu select Export Selection (**Figure 1.58**).

   The Export window opens.

3. Navigate to the folder where you want to place the exported file.

4. Click Export.

   The selected objects are exported.

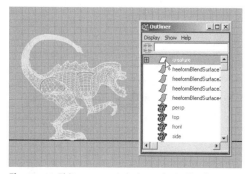

Figure 1.57 This creature is being selected in the Outliner so that it can be exported separately from the rest of the scene.

Figure 1.58 To export only items that are selected in the scene, use the Export Selection command.

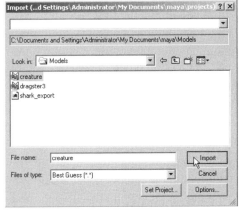

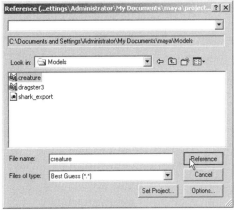

Figure 1.59 Importing a file into another scene combines the imported file into the open file.

Figure 1.60 A creature scene file is being imported into the currently open scene.

Figure 1.61 Select File > Create Reference to bring a file into an existing scene.

Figure 1.62 Browse to the file you would like to reference and click Reference, or double-click the filename, to use it as the reference file.

To import a file:

1. From the File menu select Import (**Figure 1.59**).

   The Import window opens.

2. Navigate to the folder where the file you want to import is located.

3. Click the file to import, and then click Import (**Figure 1.60**).

   The file is imported into the scene.

To reference a file:

1. From the File menu select Create Reference (**Figure 1.61**).

   The Reference window opens.

2. Navigate to the folder where the file you want to import is located.

3. Click the file you want to reference, and then click Reference (**Figure 1.62**).

   The file is referenced into the scene.

IMPORTING, EXPORTING, AND REFERENCING

Setting Maya Preferences

Maya has multiple preferences that can be altered to suit your working style as well as your favorite color scheme. In this section we will only be looking at a few of the most essential preference settings. If you would like to learn more about preferences, refer to the Maya help files.

You can set the number of undos that are allowed. The amount of undos determines how many times you can back out of previous commands.

To change the number of undos:

1. From the Window menu select Settings/Preferences > Preferences (**Figure 1.63**).

   The Preferences window opens.

2. Click Undo under Categories to view the Undo preferences (**Figure 1.64**). The Preferences window opens.

3. The default number of undos is 10. Change the Queue setting to Infinite (**Figure 1.65**).

   Infinite undos will allow you to back out of every command you executed up to the point of the last saved version.

4. Click Save to lock in the changes.

   You now have an unlimited number of undos.

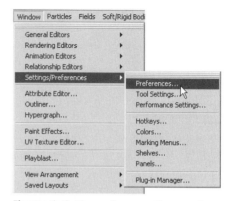

Figure 1.63 Setting preferences allows you to have the configuration you want for your interface each time you start the software.

Figure 1.64 In the Preferences, Undo is selected to change the number of undos allowed.

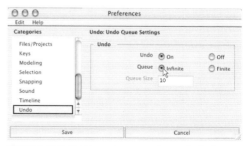

Figure 1.65 In most cases, you want your Undo Queue to be set to Infinite.

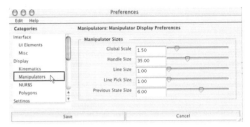

Figure 1.66 Under Manipulators in the Preferences window, you can change this size of the manipulators.

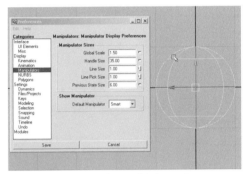

Figure 1.67 Click the sphere, with the Preferences window still open, to select it.

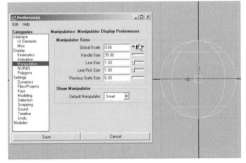

Figure 1.68 Global Scale changes the overall size of the manipulators. Here, they have been made smaller.

The manipulator settings control the look and size of the manipulators. Larger manipulators can often be easier to grab and move.

To change the size of a Maya manipulator:

1. From the Create menu select NURBS Primitive > Sphere.

   A sphere is created at the origin.

2. Select the Move tool by pressing w or clicking the icon in the toolbox.

3. From the Window menu select Settings/Preferences > Preferences.

   The Preferences window opens.

4. Select Manipulators in the Categories list (**Figure 1.66**).

   The Manipulator Display Preferences are displayed to the right.

5. Move the Preferences window so you can view the sphere. Make sure the sphere is selected by clicking it (**Figure 1.67**).

6. In the Manipulator Display Preferences move the Global Scale slider slowly to the left and right. Adjust it until the spacing of the manipulator is to your liking (**Figure 1.68**).

continues on next page

SETTING MAYA PREFERENCES

25

Watch the manipulator on the sphere while adjusting the slider. The overall scale of the manipulator is changed (**Figure 1.69**).

7. Adjust the Handle Size slider back and forth to a position of your liking (**Figure 1.70**).

The handle icons for the manipulator get smaller when you move the slider left and larger when you move the slider to the right (**Figure 1.71**).

To set preferences back to the default set:

◆ In the Preferences window select Edit > Restore Default Settings (Windows) or Restore Factory Settings (Mac) (**Figure 1.72**).

The default settings are restored.

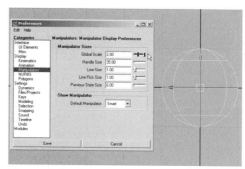

Figure 1.69 Moving the slider to the right scales the manipulator larger, moving the slider to the left shrinks the manipulator's size.

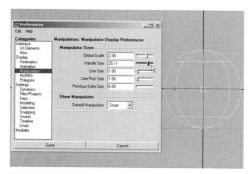

Figure 1.70 The Handle Size setting adjusts the bold part of the manipulators—the arrows, in the case of the Move tool.

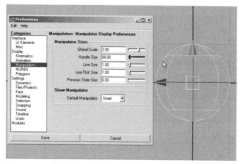

Figure 1.71 The handle icons for the manipulator get smaller when you move the slider left and larger when you move the slider right.

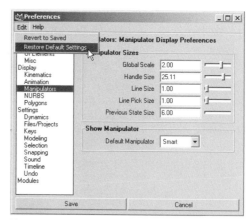

Figure 1.72 You can reset the options to defaults by selecting Edit > Restore Default Settings inside the Preferences window.

SETTING MAYA PREFERENCES

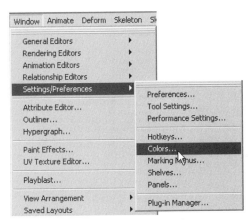

Figure 1.73 You can change the colors of many interface items using the Colors preference settings.

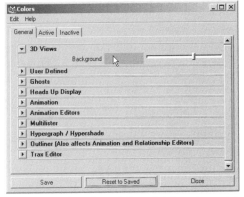

Figure 1.74 In the Colors window, click the color swatch next to Background to open the Color Chooser.

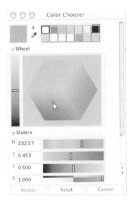

Figure 1.75 Click in the Wheel to pick a color for the background.

To alter your Maya color scheme:

1. From the Window menu select Settings/Preferences > Colors (**Figure 1.73**).
   The Colors window opens.

2. Click the 3D Views arrow ▾ 3D Views to view the Background color slider (**Figure 1.74**).

3. Click the color swatch next to Background to open the Color Chooser.

4. In the Wheel, click the color you would like for your Maya background (**Figure 1.75**).

5. Click Accept to lock in the color.
   Your Maya background becomes the color chosen.

✔ Tip

■ All parts of the interface color scheme can be changed using the same steps.

Keyboard Shortcuts

Any function in Maya can have a keyboard shortcut associated with it. This shortcut is called a *hotkey*. Hotkeys can be huge time-savers, since you can use them instead of having to go to the menu bar to select a function or command. Maya has many default hotkeys, which we recommend keeping until you become more adept with the interface. Later you may find that you use a particular command often and you want to set up a hotkey for it. You create a new hotkey or view the currently set hotkeys as follows.

To create a new hotkey:

1. From the Window menu select Settings/Preferences > Hotkeys (**Figure 1.76**).

   The Hotkey Editor opens.

2. In Categories, click the category name for the command you want to set (**Figure 1.77**).

   The category name is the same as the name of the menu the command is under.

3. Under Commands select the command name you want to create a hotkey for.

   If the command already had a hotkey assigned to it, you would see which key it was in the upper-right corner of the window.

4. In the Hotkey Editor under Assign New Hotkey, choose a Key and a Modifier you would like the command to have (**Figure 1.78**).

   You should remove any current hotkey you don't want the command to have before assigning a new hotkey.

5. Click Assign.

6. Close the Hotkey Editor window.

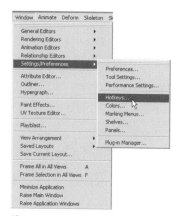

Figure 1.76 Hotkeys can be set to add keyboard shortcuts to nearly any command.

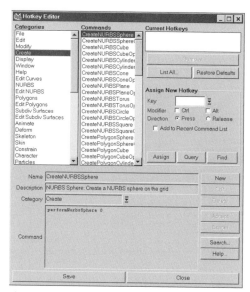

Figure 1.77 In the Hotkey Editor, select the name of the menu and the menu item in the Categories and Commands lists, respectively, to add a shortcut.

Figure 1.78 In the Assign New Hotkey portion of the Hotkey Editor, choose the key and modifier that you want to be a hotkey for the command selected.

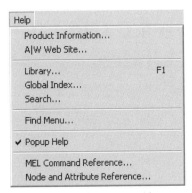

Figure 1.79 The Help menu provides ways to search and browse for information on specific topics.

Maya Help

Maya comes with the manual preloaded in the help files. You can search these files by topic or browse through them page by page. The help files are a good resource to use when you want additional information about a specific topic.

Under the Help menu in the upper right-hand corner of the Maya interface are links to the Maya library, search functions (Windows only), a global index of topics and definitions, and a find-menu feature in case you forget where a menu item is located (**Figure 1.79**).

The Maya library has tutorials, definitions, and references that are easy to navigate, and many of them offer step-by-step instructions.

The Search function allows you to type in a topic on which you would like more information and shows you a list of links categorized by the percentage of relevance to the topic you chose (**Figure 1.80**).

continues on next page

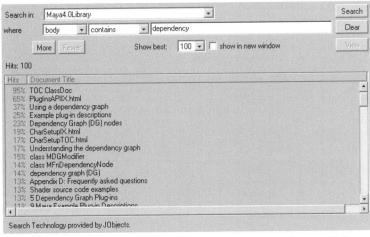

Figure 1.80 The Search window (Windows only) in the Help menu shows multiple listings for additional information on a specified topic.

MAYA HELP

29

Maya's Global Index is similar to an index in the back of a book. You pick the topic you want from an alphabetical listing, and Maya gives you a definition as well as relevant information on the topic (**Figure 1.81**).

The Find a Menu Item feature allows you to type in the name of a topic or function and get the item's menu and path (**Figure 1.82**). This can be a particularly useful tool when you know what a function is called but can't remember what menu it is under.

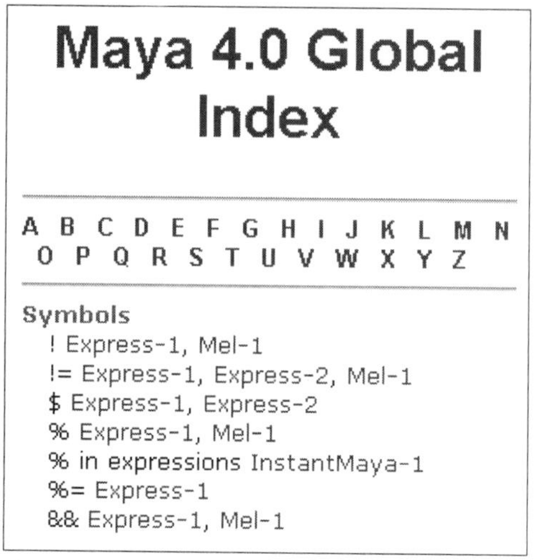

Maya 4.0 Global Index
A B C D E F G H I J K L M N
O P Q R S T U V W X Y Z
Symbols
! Express-1, Mel-1
!= Express-1, Express-2, Mel-1
$ Express-1, Express-2
% Express-1, Mel-1
% in expressions InstantMaya-1
%= Express-1
&& Express-1, Mel-1

Figure 1.81 The Global Index holds command definitions and tutorials for all the Maya help files.

Find a Menu Item
Enter a string to search for:
parent
Use Case Sensitive Search
Edit->Parent
Edit->Unparent
Deform->Edit Wire->Parent Base Wire
Close

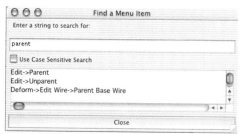

Figure 1.82 The Find a Menu Item feature is a quick way to find every menu in which any given command is located.

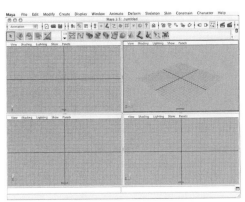

Figure 2.1 The Maya interface can be changed to suit each user.

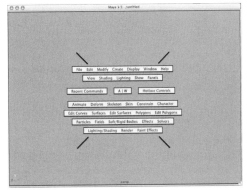

Figure 2.2 The Hotbox is a set of menus that appear where your mouse is when you hold down the Spacebar.

Maya's interface is set up to be fully customizable (**Figure 2.1**). You can change the layout of the interface to best suit your current project as well as your workflow. You can hide each menu and window until you can see only one pane— a panel or window in which to work—and the rest of the interface is hidden. Even when all of the menus are hidden in the interface, you still have full access to them through the Hotbox (**Figure 2.2**). This customizable interface can help speed the workflow of any user.

Along with hiding or showing menus, you can also hide and show specific object types in a pane using the Show menu. Once you are viewing the object types you want in the pane, you can *dolly*, *track*, and *tumble* around the objects to get a better, more three-dimensional view of them. Dollying, tracking, and tumbling are terms also used in film for moving the camera in a specific way or direction.

Maya provides many ways to accomplish the same end result, which helps speed a user's workflow. Each user will use Maya a little differently. If you like to use hotkeys (keyboard shortcuts), there are hotkeys that are associated with the more commonly used commands and can be added to almost any other command for which you would like to have a hotkey.

This chapter discusses the ways you can change the interface and navigate around the scene.

Dollying, Tracking, and Tumbling

Dollying, tracking, and tumbling allow you to change your view of the scene and control how far away or close to the objects you are. You are always looking through some camera, and dollying, tracking, and tumbling are ways to move that camera around the scene. These are some of the most important tools in Maya, because of the need to see objects from every direction and dimension. The point of view from which you see your scene becomes important to alignment and placement of objects.

Tracking a view moves the view up, down, or sideways. You might track a view to see what is currently out of view.

To track a view:

1. Move the mouse over any pane.

2. Hold down [Alt] ([⌘] on a Macintosh) and use the middle mouse button to drag the scene around in the desired direction (**Figure 2.3**).

Dollying a view visually enlarges or shrinks the view. Dollying visually brings objects closer, like zooming in, or farther away, like zooming out.

To dolly a view:

1. Move the mouse over any pane.

2. Hold down [Alt]/[⌘] plus the left and middle mouse buttons, dragging left to shrink the view and right to enlarge the view (**Figure 2.4**).

✔ Tip

- You can Marquee-zoom in by pressing [Ctrl]/[Control] and [Alt]/[⌘] while dragging a Marquee from upper left to lower right. You can zoom out by dragging lower right to upper left.

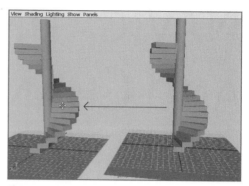

Figure 2.3 Tracking drags the scene up, down, or sideways.

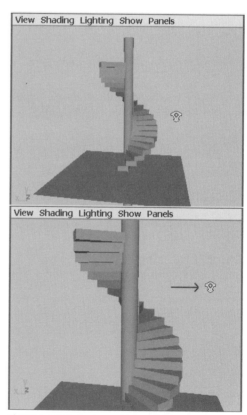

Figure 2.4 Dollying is used to zoom in and out on specific areas of the scene; dollying right (bottom) enlarges the view.

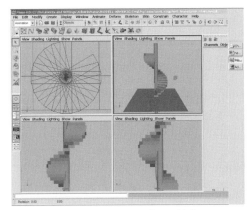

Figure 2.5 This is the Maya interface with four panes visible. Tumbling rotates the view around an object or scene and it only works in the Perspective view.

Tumbling a view visually rotates it around the center of interest. This function is useful for getting the full 3D effect of the objects and the scene. For example, you could tumble around an object to get a view of its front, back, and sides at any angle.

To tumble the view:

1. Move the mouse over the Perspective view.

2. Hold down (Alt)/(⌘) and use the left mouse button to drag and rotate the scene around in the direction desired (**Figure 2.5**).

✔ Tip

■ You can hold (Shift) while tumbling to constrain the tumble direction.

Changing the Layout

There are two windows that are easily confused because their names are so similar, *pane* and *panel*. A pane is conceptually the same as a window pane. If you look inside a window with panes, you might see something different in each pane. The same is true here. A pane can hold a Front, Top, Side, or Perspective view, or a panel.

A panel is a type of Maya window that helps with different Maya functions. For example, the Hypergraph and Outliner are panels that show all of the nodes in a scene, and the Graph Editor is a panel used to edit animation curves. Many of these panels can be opened in their own windows (**Figure 2.6**) or within a specific pane (**Figure 2.7**). One advantage to opening a panel inside a pane is the ability to then tap the (Spacebar) to minimize (**Figure 2.8**) or maximize (**Figure 2.9**) the pane. You can temporarily have access to the pane and then shrink it back down, gaining access to the other panes as well.

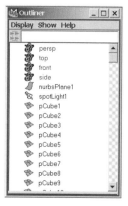

Figure 2.6 The Outliner is open in its own window.

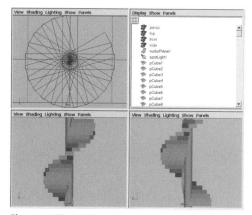

Figure 2.7 The Outliner is in one pane and can be enlarged and shrunk for convenience.

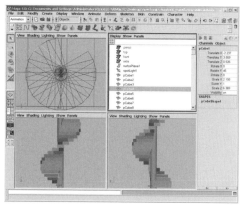

Figure 2.8 Minimizing a pane allows you to view multiple panes at once.

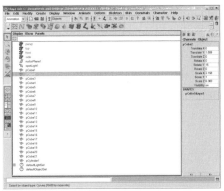

Figure 2.9 Maximizing a pane enlarges the view over any other panes, giving you more workspace within that pane.

Maya's programmers understood that different users would want to work with Maya and its interface layout differently. With this in mind, they have given the user many ways to change Maya's interface and layout. Here when I refer to the layout, I am referring to the number of panes the user is viewing and the specific panels and views that are placed within these panes (**Figure 2.10**).

continues on next page

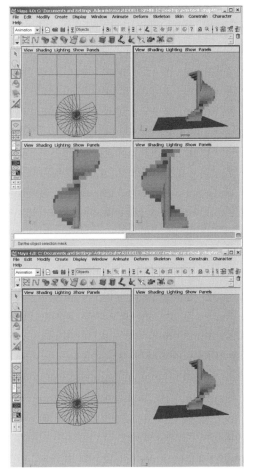

Figure 2.10 Layouts can be sized, saved, and changed to accommodate the user's current needs.

CHANGING THE LAYOUT

When you open Maya for the first time, you
see that its default pane layout is set to four
views: Top, Persp (Perspective), Front, and
Side. The Front, Side, and Top views are
orthographic, meaning that they present a
2D view of the surfaces (**Figure 2.11**). This
allows you to view the surfaces straight on
from the selected view angle. Viewing the
surfaces in an orthographic view can be
important for proper placement and alignment of objects with one another. The three
orthographic views work together to give you
a full and accurate portrayal of where the
objects are relative to the rest of the scene.
Users new to 3D often forget to check their
objects in multiple views, which can cause
placement problems for other objects. Object
placement may look perfect in the Front
view but be completely off in the Side or Top
view. The Perspective view gives you a full
three-dimensional view of your scene (**Figure
2.12**). The combination of all of these views
gives you access to your scene from virtually
any angle.

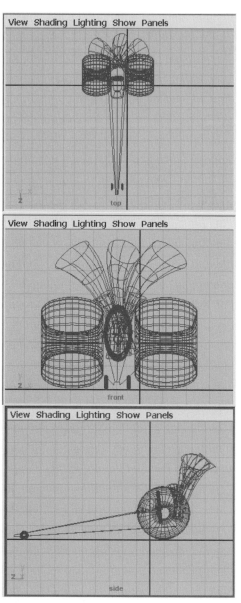

Figure 2.11 Orthographic views are the same as views
you would use when drafting with a pencil. You have
three views that are from a straight-on camera,
making editing and placement easier.

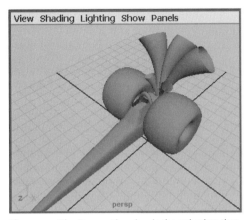

Figure 2.12 The Perspective view is the only view that allows you to tumble around the scene; it gives the user the full 3D effect.

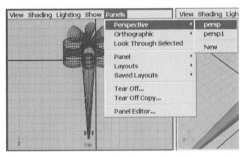

Figure 2.13 Any pane can be changed into a Perspective view by selecting Perspective > persp.

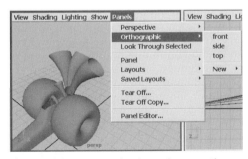

Figure 2.14 Any pane can be changed to any orthographic view such as Front or Top by selecting the Orthographic menu.

Maya allows you to change the layout of the panes, save a new layout, or just change one panel. In this chapter we will be looking at how to perform each of these layout changes.

To change a pane into a Perspective view:

◆ From the Panels menu inside the pane you want to change, select Perspective > persp (**Figure 2.13**).

To change a pane into an orthographic view:

◆ From the Panels menu inside the pane you want to change, select Orthographic > front, side, or top (**Figure 2.14**).

continues on next page

CHANGING THE LAYOUT

Panes don't always have to be view panes like Front or Perspective; they can also be panels used to give you access to other areas and windows within Maya. These panels are often animation windows like the Graph Editor (see Chapter 1) (**Figure 2.15**), or node representations of your scene like the Hypergraph (see Chapter 1) (**Figure 2.16**). As you learn more about Maya, you will learn what each of these panels does to help your workflow.

To change a pane into a non-view panel:

◆ From the Panels menu inside any pane select Panel, and choose the panel name you want—Outliner for example—to change the pane into its respective view (**Figure 2.17**).

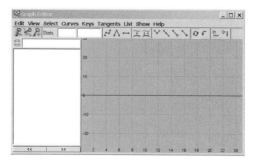

Figure 2.15 The Graph Editor holds all of the animation curves that can be edited. This panel can be embedded in a pane or opened in a window.

Figure 2.16 The Hypergraph holds visual representations of all the objects in the scene and can be embedded in a pane or opened in a window.

Figure 2.17 Many different panels can be embedded inside a pane.

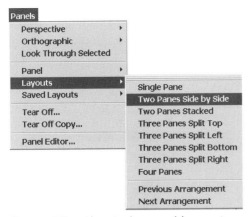

Figure 2.18 Preset layouts give you quick access to the number of panes visible and the panel sets that will go in them.

Figure 2.19 The layout icon (Windows only) shortcuts can be altered after being chosen by holding down the arrows at the bottom of the tool box. You could change a preset pane into a Perspective view with the arrows. The number of arrows varies with the layout selected.

To change the pane layout:

◆ From the Panels menu inside any pane select Layouts, and choose the preset layout name you want—two Panes Side by Side, for example (**Figure 2.18**).

If you select Two Panes Side by Side, you will have only two panels to work with, and they will be laid out one beside the other.

or

Select the icon of the layout you want on the toolbar at the left-hand side of the Maya interface (**Figure 2.19**).

To save a layout:

1. Set up the layout you would like to save and use later.

2. From the Window menu select Save Current Layout

To change your current layout to a saved layout:

◆ From the Panels menu inside any pane select Saved Layouts, and choose the name of the saved layout you would like to use.

CHANGING THE LAYOUT

To edit a layout:

1. From the Panels menu inside any pane select Saved Layouts > Edit Layouts.

2. Under the Layouts tab select the name of the layout you would like to edit (**Figure 2.20**).

3. Under the Edit Layouts tab change the Configuration pop-up menu to the new configuration you would like (**Figure 2.21**).

4. Pull any of the center dividers for the numbered blocks to adjust the blocks' size relative to the size of the other blocks (**Figure 2.22**).

5. Click the close button to close the window. The new layout is now accessible inside the Panels > Saved Layouts menu.

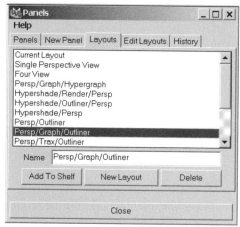

Figure 2.20 You can edit an existing layout or create a new layout under the Layouts tab.

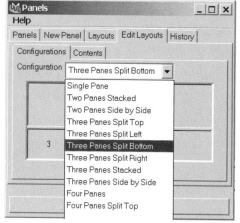

Figure 2.21 You can change the number of panes the layout uses by selecting from the Configuration menu, under the Configuration tab under the Edit Layouts tab.

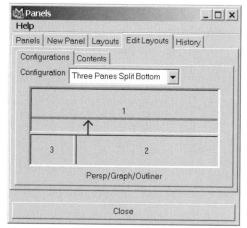

Figure 2.22 It can be helpful to resize the panes now so that each pane will be the size comparable to its use. For instance, you could make the Perspective pane larger so you will always have more working area in that view.

CHANGING THE LAYOUT

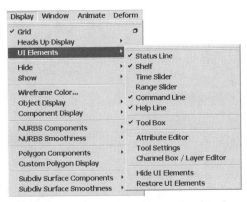

Figure 2.23 Each interface element or related section can be turned on and off to save screen space when the element is not needed.

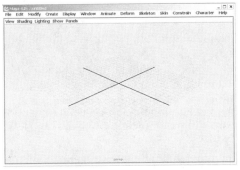

Figure 2.24 A quick way to gain more working space is to use the Hide UI Elements command.

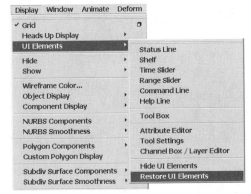

Figure 2.25 You can quickly turn on all interface elements when needed by using the Restore UI Elements command.

To hide or show a UI element:

◆ From the Display menu select UI Elements, and choose the UI elements you would like to hide or show (**Figure 2.23**).

Each UI element name toggles on and off. If it is on, selecting it will turn it off, and vice versa.

To hide all UI elements:

◆ From the Display menu select UI Elements > Hide UI Elements.

All elements become hidden except the main and pane menu bars (**Figure 2.24**).

To show all UI elements:

◆ From the Display menu select UI Elements > Restore UI Elements (**Figure 2.25**).

All UI elements are shown.

CHANGING THE LAYOUT

To hide or show the main and pane menu bars:

◆ Hold down the [Spacebar] anywhere in a pane, and select Hotbox Controls > Window Options > Show Main Menubar or Show Pane Menubars (**Figure 2.26**).

Show Main Menubar and Show Pane Menubars are toggles on and off. If they are on, selecting them will turn them off, and vice versa.

Using the Show menu

The show menu is very useful when you want to isolate a particular type of object, such as curves or lights. This makes it very convenient to show only the object types you want, or to edit and hide all other object types. For example, when you are animating, you may want to show only the character's surface in one pane and only bones in another pane (**Figure 2.27**).

The Show menu allows you to turn all types of objects on and off at once. It also allows you to turn all types of objects on and off individually. It can be useful to turn all objects off first then turn on the one object type you want to isolate (**Figure 2.28**).

The Show menu only visually hides or shows object types; it does not delete the objects. Object types turned off in the Show menu will still be shown in a render.

CHANGING THE LAYOUT

Figure 2.26 The main menu bar and the pane menus must be turned on and off individually.

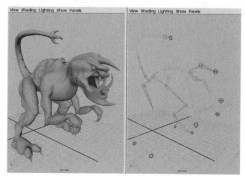

Figure 2.27 You can open two of the same panes, in this case Perspective views, and show different object types in each pane, which makes objects easier to select and visualize.

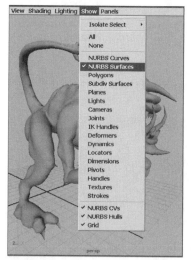

Figure 2.28 Turning all objects off or on in the Show menu helps you to quickly turn on only the relevant object types in the pane.

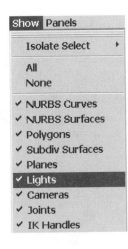

Show Panels

Isolate Select ▶

All
None

✓ NURBS Curves
✓ NURBS Surfaces
✓ Polygons
✓ Subdiv Surfaces
✓ Planes
✓ Lights
✓ Cameras
✓ Joints
✓ IK Handles

Figure 2.29 The Show menu hides and shows all objects of the chosen type. If you choose Lights, then all lights in the view will be hidden.

To hide object types with the Show menu:

◆ From the Show menu inside any pane select the object type you want to hide (**Figure 2.29**).

The object type selected is hidden from view (**Figure 2.30**).

To show hidden object types with the Show menu:

◆ From the Show menu inside any pane select the object type you want to show in the pane (Figure 2.29).

The object type selected becomes visible in the view pane.

You can temporarily enlarge a pane to get a better view of its contents.

To focus a pane to full screen:

1. Move the mouse over the pane you would like to zoom larger (**Figure 2.31**).

2. Tap the [Spacebar] once.

The pane expands to full view, covering any other panes (**Figure 2.32**).

✔ Tip

■ Tap the [Spacebar] again to reset the pane size, uncovering any additional panes.

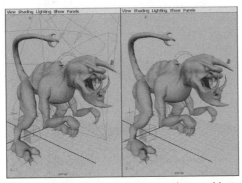

Figure 2.30 There is no way to see or select an object type in a pane while it's hidden through the Show menu.

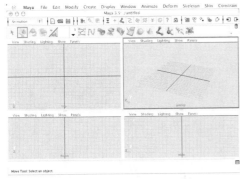

Figure 2.31 The border of the pane turns blue to indicate that it is selected.

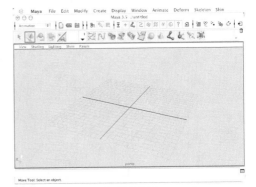

Figure 2.32 Tapping the [Spacebar] zooms the pane; but holding down the [Spacebar] opens the Hotbox. Be careful to use the [Spacebar] correctly.

CHANGING THE LAYOUT

To frame a selected item in a view:

1. Select the item you would like to zoom the camera on by clicking on it.

2. Press f.
   The view zooms to the object (**Figure 2.33**).

✔ Tips

- You can make all of the view panes frame the selected item at the same time by pressing Shift f.

- You can go back and forth from the previous view to the next view with the [and] keys.

To frame all objects in a view:

◆ Press a.
   The view frames all of the objects in the scene (**Figure 2.34**).

✔ Tip

- You can make all of the view panes frame all of the objects at the same time with Shift a.

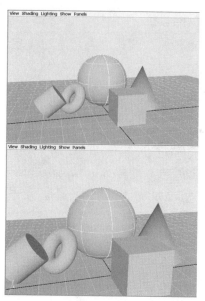

Figure 2.33 Press f to zoom in closer to a selected object.

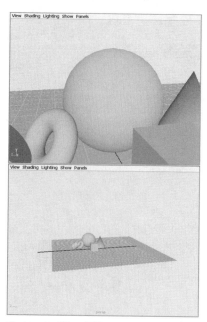

Figure 2.34 When a is pressed, the camera moves from the view on top to the view on bottom. Now all of the objects in the scene are framed within the view.

CHANGING THE LAYOUT

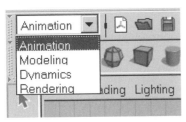

Figure 2.35 Each menu set holds menus specific to the type of process you are working on. If you are in the modeling stage of a project, you can use the Animation menu set to access modeling-related menus.

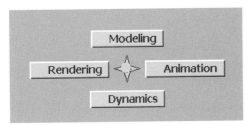

Figure 2.36 Marking Menus can be a good way to change the menu sets when you have hidden the status line or just want to speed your workflow.

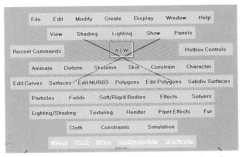

Figure 2.37 The Hotbox can be quickly opened and closed with the ⌴Spacebar⌴.

Maya has four main menu sets: Animation, Modeling, Dynamics, and Rendering. Each of the sets holds menus specific to its topic as well as the common menus: File, Edit, Modify, Create, Display, and Window. The common menus are always accessible from the main menu no matter which menu set you are currently using.

To change the menu set:

◆ On the left-hand side of the status bar use the pop-up menu to select the appropriate menu set (**Figure 2.35**).

or

In any view pane hold down H and the left mouse button to select a menu set from the Marking Menu (**Figure 2.36**).

or

Press F2 for the Animation menu set, F3 for the Modeling menu set, F4 for the Dynamic menu set, and F5 for the Rendering menu set.

To show and hide the Hotbox:

1. Show the Hotbox by holding down the Spacebar (**Figure 2.37**).

2. Hide the Hotbox by releasing the Spacebar.

CHANGING THE LAYOUT

To show and hide specific menu sets in the Hotbox:

1. Show the Hotbox by holding down the [Spacebar] in any pane.

2. Hold down the left mouse button over the Hotbox controls to show the Hotbox controls Marking Menu (**Figure 2.38**).

3. Move the mouse over the menu set name you want to show—Show Animation, in this example.

   This opens an additional Marking Menu.

4. Select the Show/Hide (menu set name) when it appears (**Figure 2.39**).

   The menu set is shown if it was hidden, and hidden if it was shown.

To show all menu sets in the Hotbox:

1. Show the Hotbox by holding down the [Spacebar] in any pane.

2. Hold down the left mouse button over the Hotbox controls to show the Hotbox controls Marking Menu.

3. Select Show All to show all the menu sets in the Hotbox (**Figure 2.40**).

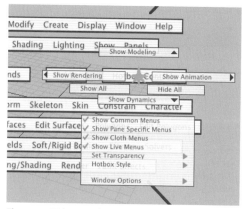

Figure 2.38 You can change the menus that are shown in the Hotbox by using the Hotbox controls Marking Menu.

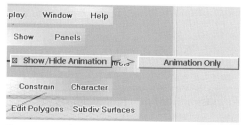

Figure 2.39 Individual menus can be hidden or shown to control the size and accessibility of the Hotbox.

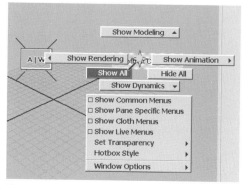

Figure 2.40 One advantage to the Hotbox is that you can turn on all of the menu sets at once, or turn on only one or two.

CHANGING THE LAYOUT

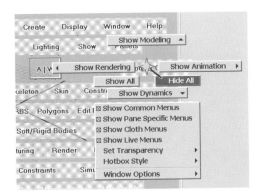

Figure 2.41 You can hide all of the menus in the hotbox.

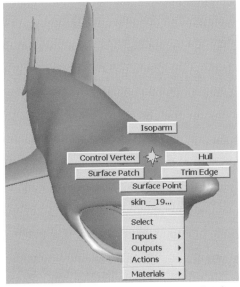

Figure 2.42 Each object has a menu set associated with it called a Marking Menu, which you can get by right mouse-clicking the object.

To hide all menu sets in the Hotbox:

1. Show the Hotbox by holding down the Spacebar in any pane.

2. Hold down the left mouse button over the Hotbox controls to show the Hotbox controls Marking Menu.

3. Select Hide All to hide all the menu sets in the Hotbox (**Figure 2.41**).

   Hiding all of the menus in the Hotbox leaves only the Recent Commands and the Hotbox Controls available. Along with these two menus, all of the Hotbox's Marking Menus are still accessible.

Most objects have a menu specific to their object type called a Marking Menu.

To show an object's Marking Menu:

1. Move your pointer directly over an object.

2. Right mouse-click the object to show its Marking Menu (**Figure 2.42**).

✔ Tips

■ You can quickly drag in the direction of the command you want to select in the Marking Menu without waiting to see the menu appear.

■ In wireframe mode you must click on an isoparm or edge of the object, but in shaded mode you can click anywhere on the object.

To show and hide the grid:

◆ From the Display menu select Grid to toggle the grid on and off.

✔ Tip

■ You can adjust the size, closeness, and colors of the gridlines in the Grid options.

CHANGING THE LAYOUT

The Channel Box is an easy way to adjust many of a selected object's attributes. The Channel Box is on the right side of the interface in the default layout (**Figure 2.43**) but can be retrieved after being hidden, or toggled on and off, using the steps below.

To show or hide the Channel Box:

◆ Click the "Show or hide the Channel Box/Layer Editor" icon 🔳 (Windows only) on the right-hand side of the status line. The status line sits directly below the main menu bar.

or

From the Display menu select UI Elements > Channel Box/Layer Editor (Windows) or UI Elements > Channel Box (Mac) (**Figure 2.44**).

The Channel Box appears on the right-hand side of the Maya interface.

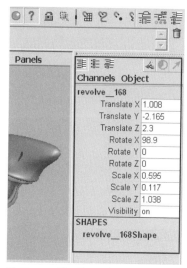

Figure 2.43 The Channel Box can be hidden to save screen space or shown to give the user easy access to keyable object attributes.

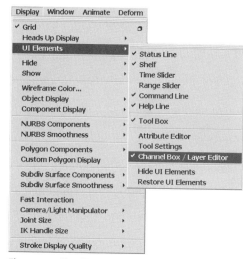

Figure 2.44 The Channel Box and Layer Editor can be shown together (on Windows) to better use screen space.

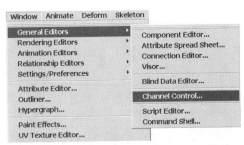

Figure 2.45 Attributes can be taken out of or added to the Channel Box by using the Channel Control.

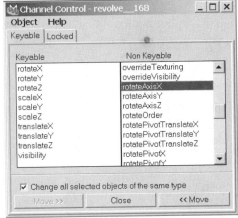

Figure 2.46 The Non Keyable area of the Channel Control window holds attributes that can be added to the Channel Box.

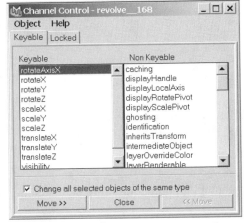

Figure 2.47 You can continue to move more attributes to the Keyable area to be added to the Channel Box.

By default the Channel Box holds the keyable attributes of the selected object. You can add attributes to the Channel Box list.

To add preset attributes to the Channel Box:

1. Create or select an object to add an attribute to.

2. From the Window menu select General Editors > Channel Control (**Figure 2.45**). The Channel Control window opens.

3. Under the Keyable tab select the attribute name in the Non-Keyable area of the Channel Control window (**Figure 2.46**).

4. Click the Move button   << Move   .

5. The attribute is added to the Keyable list of attributes (**Figure 2.47**).

6. Click the Close button to close the Channel Control window.

   The new attribute is shown in the Channel Box (**Figure 2.48**).

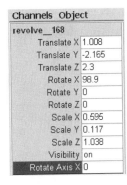

Figure 2.48
The Channel Box reflects the newly added attribute ready for use.

CHANGING THE LAYOUT

The Attribute Editor contains additional attributes not available in the Channel Box. The Channel Box is a great shortcut for accessing many of an object's attributes but is too small to hold all of them. The Attribute Editor remains empty until an object is selected.

To show or hide the Attribute Editor:

1. Click the "Show or hide the Attribute Editor" icon 📜 (Windows only) on the right-hand side of the status line.

   Make a selection to view its attributes.

   or

   From the Display menu select UI Elements > Attribute Editor (**Figure 2.49**).

   The Attribute Editor appears on the right-hand side of the Maya interface.

   or

   Press ⌈Ctrl⌉/⌈Control⌉⌈a⌉.

   The Attribute Editor opens in a new window (**Figure 2.50**).

   or

   From the Window menu select Attribute Editor (**Figure 2.51**).

   The Attribute Editor opens in a new window.

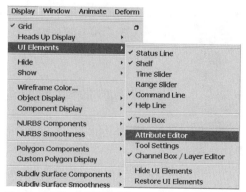

Figure 2.49 The Attribute Editor can be opened from the Display > UI Elements menu.

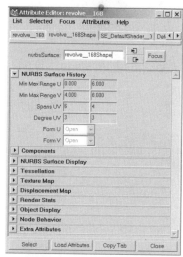

Figure 2.50 When opened in a new window, the Attribute Editor can be moved around and minimized to be out of the way.

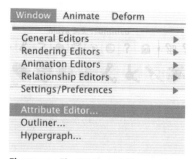

Figure 2.51 The Attribute Editor can be opened in a new window.

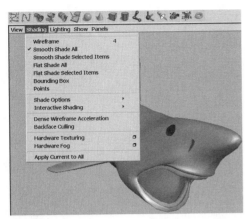

Figure 2.52 The Shading menu controls the display mode for each individual pane.

About Display Options and Smoothness

The display options allow you to change the way the objects are viewed within the pane. You can view your scene in wireframe, smooth-shaded, flat-shaded, bounding-box, or points mode. The display options can be changed according to the current scenario. Bounding box or points can be used to speed interaction when tumbling around a complex scene. Wireframe can be useful for component selection because you can see all the components of the object at once. Smooth shading and flat shading can give you a more complete view of the surface, making modeling a surface easier. Each of the display options is useful for specific situations, so switching between them can be beneficial to your workflow.

The display options also use hardware texturing and lighting. These options allow interactive texturing and lighting, giving you quick feedback while you are texturing and lighting your scene. Most of these settings have a keyboard number shortcut associated with them.

There are three different smoothness levels in which the objects can be displayed: rough, medium, and fine. Objects are displayed rough by default but can be changed using the shortcuts that follow. Rough smoothness can make component selection easier because fewer surface lines are shown. Fine smoothness will give the closest representation of the final surface.

To change the display options from the Shading menu:

◆ From the Shading menu in any pane select Wireframe, one of the Smooth Shade options, one of the Flat Shade options, Bounding Box, or Points (**Figure 2.52**).

Shading and smoothness shortcuts

1 = Rough smoothness (**Figure 2.53**)

2 = Medium smoothness (Figure 2.53)

3 = Fine smoothness (Figure 2.53)

4 = Wireframe mode (**Figure 2.54**)

5 = Shaded mode (**Figure 2.55**)

6 = Hardware Texturing (**Figure 2.56**)

7 = Hardware Lighting (**Figure 2.57**)

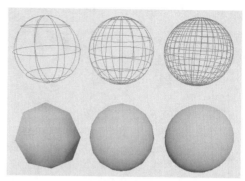

Figure 2.53 Left, rough smoothness shows the object in low resolution. Middle, medium smoothness shows the object with some additional resolution but not too much to obstruct the view of the object. Right, fine smoothness shows the closest representation of the surface's shape.

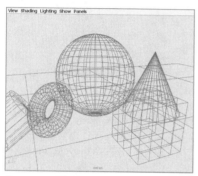

Figure 2.54 Wireframe mode allows you to see through objects and view their geometry on the front and back of the surface.

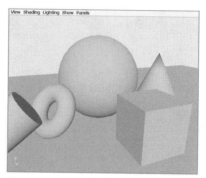

Figure 2.55 Shaded mode presents the surface in gray by default to show its final skin.

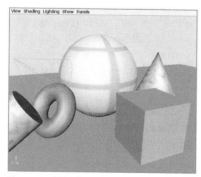

Figure 2.56 Hardware Texturing shows the surface textures within the pane.

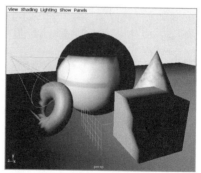

Figure 2.57 Hardware Lighting shows the scene's lighting scenario interactively within the pane. Hardware Lighting can save large amounts of rendering time since you can see the results as soon as you change a light's position.

CREATING
PRIMITIVES AND TEXT

Primitives are the building blocks of 3D modeling. They are premade sets of geometry used to simplify the creation of more complex shapes. Everything in nature, no matter how complex, can be broken down into just a few primitive shapes. Look around the room and try to break down each object into one or two primitive shapes. Is the object built around many cylinders like a metal chair, or is it a squashed cube like a door or a wall? Many objects are a combination of different primitives. An example of this is a bicycle. The bike's wheel is a combination of a cylinder for each spoke and a slim torus defining the tire shape. Other examples of using primitives to build more advanced shapes are creating a detailed face from a simple sphere and creating a building from a few well-placed cubes.

Primitives can be manipulated in many ways, making them an important part of Maya and other 3D programs. Primitives can be stretched, cut, scaled, translated, trimmed, and rebuilt. Because you can change primitives in so many ways, they can be essential tools for your workflow and great time-savers.

There are three major types of primitives in Maya: *NURBS, polygons,* and *subdivisions* (Windows only). It can be difficult at times to decide what type of primitive to use, so this chapter explains some of the strengths and weaknesses of NURBS (**Figure 3.1**) and polygons (**Figure 3.2**). Subdivisions are more advanced and are covered in Chapter 8.

Figure 3.1 The NURBS Primitive Sphere, Cube, Cylinder, Cone, Plane, Torus, Circle, and Square from top to bottom.

Figure 3.2 The Polygon Primitive Sphere, Cube, Cylinder, Cone, Plane, and Torus from top to bottom.

Weighted control points

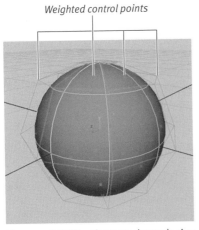

Figure 3.3 NURBS surfaces are changed using weighted control points.

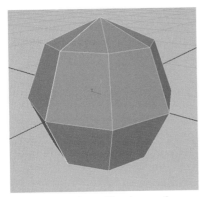

Figure 3.4 A surface with a degree of 1, or setting of linear.

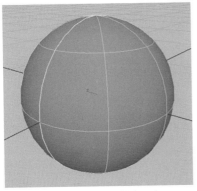

Figure 3.5 A surface with a higher degree produces a smoother surface.

About NURBS

NURBS curves, surfaces, and primitives are an important part of modeling in Maya. NURBS objects can produce long, smooth surfaces such as car hoods or produce sharp angular surfaces such as stop signs. Using NURBS objects allows you to adjust the look of a surface by manipulating just a few weighted control points (**Figure 3.3**).

Each of the NURBS curves and surfaces has a certain degree associated with it that controls the smoothness of the NURBS object. A surface degree of 1, or setting of _linear_, will produce a straight connection between each control point, creating a very angular surface (**Figure 3.4**). As you raise the degree of the NURBS object, you create a smoother curve and surface (**Figure 3.5**). The higher the degree of the curve the more points needed to define it. For more about NURBS degrees see Chapter 7.

continues on next page

NURBS stands for *non-uniform rational B-spline* and describes objects whose shapes are defined by mathematical equations. Luckily for us, the major math is done behind the scenes by Maya. *B-spline* refers to the underlying curve that defines the creation of all NURBS objects. When creating a NURBS object, you use multiple curves to produce a wire representation of what you want the surface to look like. After laying down the shape of the surface using curves, you add a skin over them to create the final surface in a process called *lofting* (**Figure 3.6**).

NURBS objects can be broken down into separate components that work together to define the shape of the NURBS object. Some components are *CVs* (control vertices), *edit points,* and *hulls.* Each of these can be manipulated to help sculpt the surface or define the curves' shapes. For more information on NURBS components see Chapter 7.

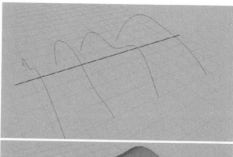

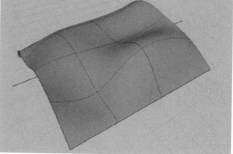

Figure 3.6 The top object has curves only; the bottom object has curves plus a skin.

ABOUT NURBS

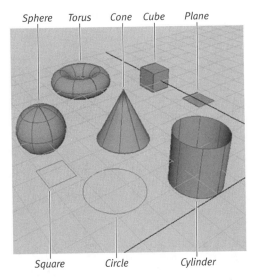

Sphere Torus Cone Cube Plane

Square Circle Cylinder

Figure 3.7 The NURBS primitives are used for starting points for more complex models.

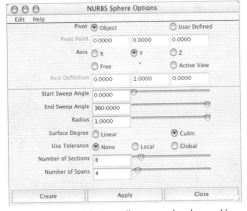

Figure 3.8 A primitive's attributes can be changed in its Options dialog box.

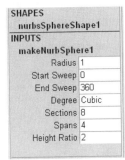

SHAPES
  nurbsSphereShape1
INPUTS
  makeNurbSphere1
  Radius   1
  Start Sweep 0
  End Sweep   360
  Degree   Cubic
  Sections   8
  Spans   4
  Height Ratio 2

Figure 3.9
The construction history allows a surface's attributes to be changed after it's created.

About NURBS Primitives

NURBS primitives are a collection of frequently used, predefined curves and surfaces. There are eight NURBS primitives in Maya: *sphere, cube, cylinder, cone, plane, torus, circle,* and *square* (**Figure 3.7**). NURBS primitives are helpful in speeding workflow because the curves are already drawn for you, and many primitives have already had their curves replaced with surface geometry. These predefined primitive surfaces save you time when creating objects and often give you a head start on creating more detailed shapes. The circle and square primitives are NURBS curves without surfaces attached to them; the other six NURBS primitives are predefined surfaces ready to be placed in the Maya scene or manipulated further.

Each primitive has many attributes that can be set for the object before, or after, it is created. You can change the attributes for each specific primitive in its Options dialog box before the object is created (**Figure 3.8**). Most of these primitives have a construction history attached to their surfaces, allowing the surfaces' properties to be adjusted and fine-tuned after the surfaces are created (**Figure 3.9**). The construction-history attributes appear in the Channel Box under each primitive's makeNurb menu. In this chapter we look at creating NURBS primitives and changing some of their attributes before and after the object is created.

Creating NURBS primitives

NURBS primitives are found in the Create > NURBS Primitives submenu (**Figure 3.10**). You create a primitive by selecting the primitive's name from the submenu. You can also create a NURBS primitive through the Hotbox, as described below. And by simply clicking their icons in the Shelf, you can quickly create the sphere and cone primitives (**Figure 3.11**).

When you create a primitive surface or curve, Maya will place the object's center point at the origin of the scene (the origin is at 0, 0, 0 coordinates). This locates most objects half above and half below the *x-*, *y-*, and *z*-axis lines (**Figure 3.12**). The exception is the cone, whose center point is at its base.

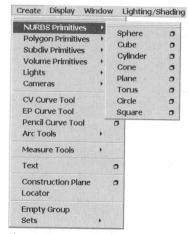

Figure 3.10 NURBS primitives are found in the Create > NURBS Primitives submenu.

Figure 3.11 You can quickly create sphere and cone primitives by clicking their icons in the Shelf.

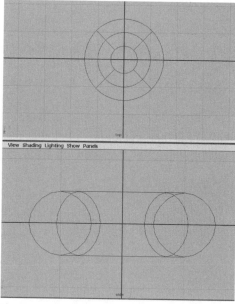

Figure 3.12 Maya places the center point of the primitive at the origin of the scene.

ABOUT NURBS PRIMITIVES

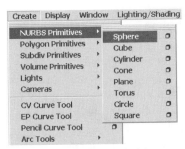

Figure 3.13 Select the name of the primitive you want to create from the NURBS Primitives submenu.

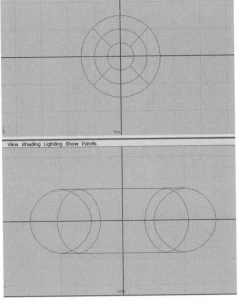

Figure 3.14 The NURBS primitive appears at the origin) of the Maya scene (the sphere is shown).

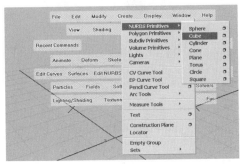

Figure 3.15 You can use the Hotbox to select the NURBS Primitives submenu (the cube is shown).

You can create NURBS primitives by following the steps below.

To create a NURBS primitive using the main menu:

1. From the Create menu select the NURBS Primitives submenu.

2. Select the name of the primitive you want to create (**Figure 3.13**).

   The NURBS primitive appears at the origin of the Maya scene (**Figure 3.14**).

The Hotbox is a great time-saver for creating objects and primitives without having to go up to the main menu. The Hotbox can be displayed from anywhere in the Maya window, making access to the Maya menus even faster.

To create a NURBS primitive using the Hotbox:

1. Hold down [Spacebar] anywhere in the scene to show the Hotbox.

2. From the Create menu in the Hotbox select the NURBS Primitives submenu.

3. Select the name of the primitive you want to create (**Figure 3.15**).

   The NURBS primitive is created at the origin of the Maya scene (**Figure 3.16**).

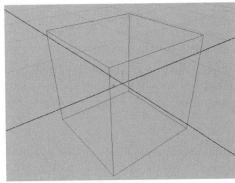

Figure 3.16 The NURBS primitive is created at the origin of the Maya scene (the cube is shown).

The default Shelf in Maya holds shortcut icons for the sphere and cone NURBS primitives (**Figure 3.17**). Selecting these primitives from the Shelf can save two or three steps needed to select the same primitive from the Create menu.

To create a NURBS primitive sphere or cone using the Shelf:

◆ Select the primitive NURBS Sphere  or Cone icon in Shelf 1.

The primitive is created at the origin of the Maya scene (**Figure 3.18**).

✔ Tips

■ If the Shelf is not already open, open it by going to the Display menu and selecting UI Elements > Shelf (**Figure 3.19**).

■ To add primitives or other objects to the Shelf, hold down Shift and Ctrl/Control while selecting the object in the menu. It uses the current options, so, for example, you can have different spheres on your Shelf with different end sweep angles if you change the attributes in the Options before you add it to the Shelf.

■ You can remove items from the Shelf by pressing the middle mouse button while dragging them to the trash can.

Figure 3.17 The default Shelf in Maya holds shortcut icons for the sphere, and cone NURBS primitives.

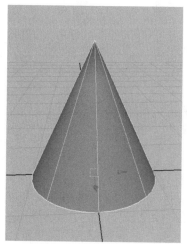

Figure 3.18 Select the primitive NURBS icon in Shelf 1; here the cone has been chosen.

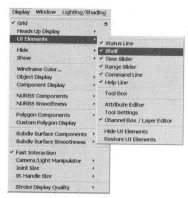

Figure 3.19 You can show the Shelf by selecting UI Elements > Shelf.

ABOUT NURBS PRIMITIVES

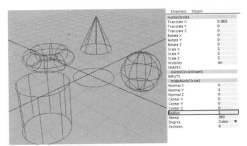

Figure 3.20 The radius attribute makes the object larger and is common to the objects above.

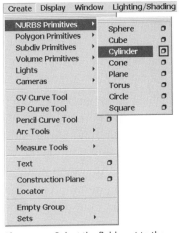

Figure 3.21 Select the field next to the name of the primitive for which you want to set the radius.

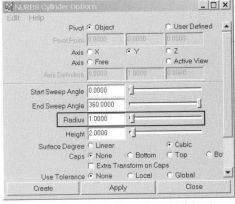

Figure 3.22 Adjust the Radius slider to half the size that you want the diameter of the primitive to be.

Changing Attributes of NURBS Primitives

Each NURBS primitive has a set of attributes associated with it. Some attributes are common to all NURBS primitives, and others are specific to just one or two of the primitives.

All the attributes of the NURBS primitives are changed the same way. This section demonstrates how to change the radius attribute of a NURBS primitive. You can apply the same steps to change other object attributes. The next section defines many of the NURBS primitives' attributes.

The radius attribute is common to the NURBS primitive sphere, cone, cylinder, torus, and circle (**Figure 3.20**).

To set the radius of a NURBS primitive sphere, cone, cylinder, torus, or circle from the Create menu:

1. From the Create menu select the NURBS Primitives submenu.

2. Select the box next to the name of the primitive for which you want to set the radius (**Figure 3.21**).

3. In the Options dialog box that opens, adjust the Radius slider to half the size that you want the diameter of the primitive to be (**Figure 3.22**).

✔ Tip

■ You can type in a value larger than the slider's highest value.

To change the radius of a NURBS primitive after the object is created:

1. Select a primitive NURBS sphere, cone, cylinder, torus, or circle.

2. Select the makeNurb title under the INPUTS heading in the Channel Box (**Figure 3.23**).

3. Click once in the Radius field to select the number there (**Figure 3.24**).

4. Change the number to the size you want the radius to be.

5. Press [Enter] to complete the radius change (**Figure 3.25**).

✔ Tips

- You can also click once on the attribute's name (in our example, Radius) in the Channel Box, and then click and drag the middle mouse button left or right in the view window to interactively change the radius size.

- If the construction history is turned off, the makeNurb node will not be available in the Channel Box.

- The makeNurb history will not be available on a duplicated object unless you go into the Edit > Duplicate options and check Duplicate Upstream Graph.

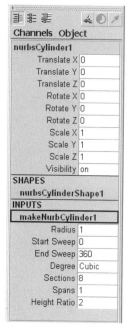

Figure 3.23 Select the makeNurb title under the INPUTS heading in the Channel Box (the cylinder is shown).

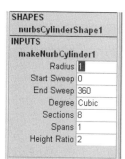

Figure 3.24 Click the Radius field once to select it (cylinder settings are shown).

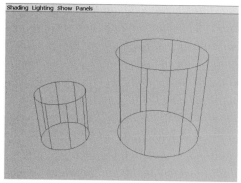

Figure 3.25 Before (left) and after (right) the radius change (the cylinder is shown).

CHANGING ATTRIBUTES OF NURBS PRIMITIVES

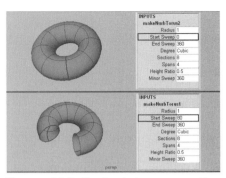

Figure 3.26 Adjusting the start sweep moves the start of the surface away from the surface's end (the torus is shown)—before the change is on top, after the change is on the bottom.

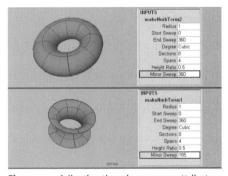

Figure 3.27 Adjusting the minor sweep attribute unfolds the surface along the U direction (the torus is shown)—before the change is on top, after the change is on the bottom.

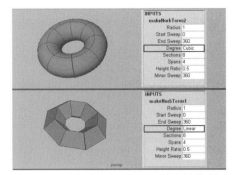

Figure 3.28 If the degree is set to cubic (default), the surface will be curved (top). If the degree attribute is set to linear, the surface will be planar and faceted (bottom).

Here is a list of important NURBS primitive attributes, with their definitions. You set these in the Channel Box or the object's options box.

NURBS Primitive attributes

◆ **Radius**—The radius of an object is half of the object's width. Adjusting the radius scales the object proportionally on all three axes.

◆ **Start Sweep**—Adjusting the start sweep separates the surface away from its end in a clockwise direction, creating a slice of the surface, or a surface of less than 360 degrees (**Figure 3.26**).

◆ **End Sweep**—Adjusting the end sweep has an effect similar to adjusting the start sweep but instead of working in a clockwise direction from the end point, it works from the starting point and opens the surface in a counterclockwise direction, creating a slice of the surface, or a surface of less than 360 degrees.

◆ **Minor Sweep**—The minor sweep attribute is specific to the torus primitive. Adjusting the minor sweep unfolds the surface along the U direction, creating (for a torus) a slice of the surface similar to a spool instead of a full doughnut shape (**Figure 3.27**).

◆ **Degree**—A NURBS primitive can be linear or cubic. If the degree attribute is set to linear, the surface is planar and faceted. If the degree is set to cubic (default), the surface is more curved (**Figure 3.28**).

continues on next page

◆ **Sections**—Adjusting the sections attribute adds more detail to the surface in the U direction, which helps for editing its shape (**Figure 3.29**).

◆ **Spans**—Adjusting the spans attribute adds detail to the surface, which helps for editing its shape (**Figure 3.30**).

◆ **Height Ratio**—This is the ratio of the height in relation to the depth. If the height ratio is set to 2, the height will be twice the size of the depth.

◆ **Length Ratio**—This is the ratio of the length in relation to the depth. If the length ratio is set to 2, the length will be twice the size of the depth.

◆ **Patches U and Patches V**—Patches U and V are specific to the plane and cube primitives. Adjusting these attributes will increase the surface geometry in the U or V direction (**Figure 3.31**).

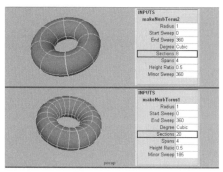

Figure 3.29 Adjusting the sections attribute adds more detail to the surface in the U direction.

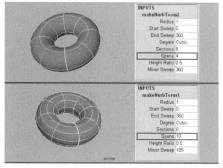

Figure 3.30 Adjusting the spans attribute adds isoparms in the V direction.

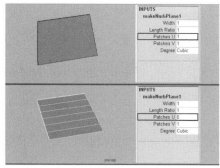

Figure 3.31 Adjusting patches U and patches V attributes increases the surface geometry in the U or V direction.

CHANGING ATTRIBUTES OF NURBS PRIMITIVES

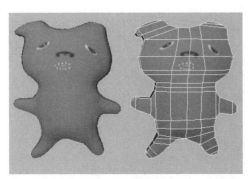

Figure 3.32 A low polygon model renders fast and can be developed quickly (model by Andrew Britt).

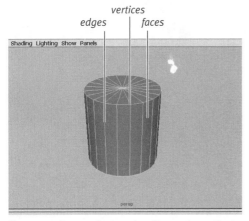

Figure 3.33 Faces, edges, and vertices make up the polygon components.

About Polygons

Polygon meshes are surfaces that give the user a lot of flexibility in modeling because they can be used to produce high-quality, smooth surfaces, as well as low-resolution, fast-rendering surfaces. Games require a small amount of polygons per surface (*low-poly* models) in order for the game engine to render them on the fly. As a result, polygons are the choice for game and Internet developers. A good modeler can create a good-looking, fast-loading model with only a few well-placed polygons (**Figure 3.32**).

Polygons have many components used to manipulate the final look of the surface. *Faces, edges,* and *vertices* make up the polygon components (**Figure 3.33**). All of these components combined together help define the shape of the polygonal object. Each of these components can be manipulated individually, giving the creator precise control of polygon construction.

continues on next page

Polygons, or polys for short, can be created one at a time, slowly adding to the surface's resolution, or you can start with a very simplistic poly object, like a poly primitive (see the next section), and run the Smooth command on it to add more individual polys, increasing the surface's resolution and smoothness (**Figure 3.34**). To learn more about the Smooth command see Chapter 8.

Subdivisions are an important part of a polygonal mesh. The number of subdivisions in the poly surface determines how smooth the final surface will render (**Figure 3.35**). Decreasing the number of subdivisions on a surface will create fewer faces and give the surface a much more angular appearance. The number of poly subdivisions can be set before or after the object is created. You can also subdivide individual polygons, giving you specific control over the final number of polygons created.

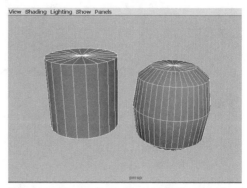

Figure 3.34 You can start with a simplistic poly object, like a poly primitive (left), and run the Smooth command on it to add more individual polys (right).

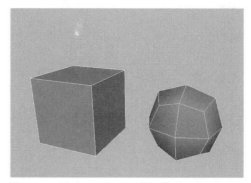

Figure 3.35 The smoothness of the final surface is determined by the number of subdivisions in the poly surface. The default surface is on the left; subdivisions have been added on the right.

ABOUT POLYGONS

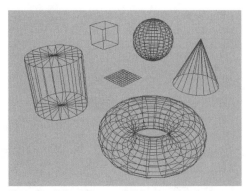

Figure 3.36 The polygon primitives are (clockwise from left), cylinder, cube, sphere, cone, torus, and plane (in the center).

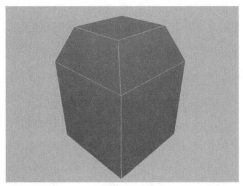

Figure 3.37 Polygon primitives can be extruded, split, subdivided, merged, beveled, and separated, among other things.

About Polygon Primitives

Polygon primitives, like NURBS primitives, are a collection of frequently used predefined surfaces. These predefined primitive surfaces save you time on object creation and often give you a head start on creating more detailed shapes.

There are six polygon primitives in Maya: sphere, cube, cylinder, cone, plane, and torus (**Figure 3.36**). Polygon primitives are helpful in speeding workflow because each individual face that describes the surface is already drawn for you.

Once created, polygon primitives can be extruded, split, subdivided, merged, beveled, and separated, among other things. This allows for fast modeling of objects and precise control over the number of faces used for the surface, so you can control the amount of render time (**Figure 3.37**).

Creating polygon primitives

Polygon primitives are found under the Create menu within the Polygon Primitives submenu. You can also reach the polygon primitives through the Hotbox as described below. By clicking their icons in the Shelf, you can quickly create the poly cube and poly cylinder primitives.

When you create a poly primitive, Maya places the center point of the object at the origin of the scene, as when you create a NURBS primitive.

You can create poly primitives by following the steps below.

To create a polygon primitive using the main menu:

1. From the Create menu select the Polygon Primitives submenu.

2. Select the name of the primitive you want to create (**Figure 3.38**).

   A polygon primitive is created at the origin (0, 0, 0) of the Maya scene (**Figure 3.39**).

The Hotbox is a great time-saver, allowing you to select objects and primitives from a menu without having to go to the main menu. The Hotbox can be displayed from anywhere in the Maya window, making access to the Maya menus even faster.

To create a polygon primitive using the Hotbox:

1. Hold down (Spacebar) anywhere in the scene to show the Hotbox.

2. From the Create menu in the Hotbox select the Polygon Primitives submenu (**Figure 3.40**).

3. Select the name of the primitive you want to create (**Figure 3.41**).

   A polygon primitive is created at the origin of the Maya scene (**Figure 3.42**).

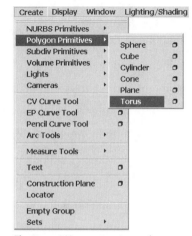

Figure 3.38 You can create a polygon primitive through Create > Polygon Primitives. The torus primitive is selected.

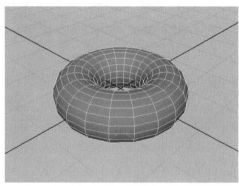

Figure 3.39 A polygon primitive appears at the origin of the Maya scene; the torus is shown.

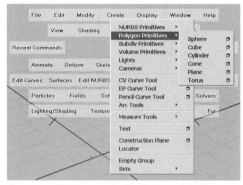

Figure 3.40 You can access the Polygon Primitives submenu using the Hotbox.

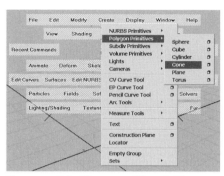

Figure 3.41 Select the name of the primitive you want to create.

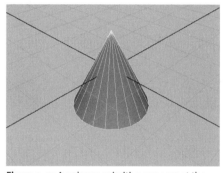

Figure 3.42 A polygon primitive appears at the origin of the Maya scene.

Figure 3.43 Shortcut icons for the cube and cylinder polygon primitives in the default Shelf.

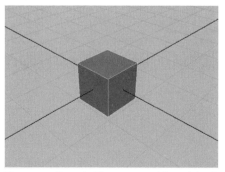

Figure 3.44 The primitive appears at the origin of the Maya scene (the cube is shown).

The default Shelf in Maya holds shortcut icons for the cube and cylinder polygon primitives (**Figure 3.43**). Selecting these primitives from the Shelf can save two or three steps you would take to select the primitive from the Create menu.

To create a polygon cube primitive or cylinder using the Shelf (Windows only):

◆ Select the polygon cube primitive 🔲 or cylinder 🔲 icon in Shelf 1.

   The primitive is created at the origin of the Maya scene (**Figure 3.44**).

✔ Tips

■ If the Shelf is not already open, open it by going to the Display menu and selecting UI Elements > Shelf.

■ To add primitives or other objects to the Shelf, hold down [Shift] and [Ctrl]/[Control], while selecting the primitive in the Create menu.

ABOUT POLYGON PRIMITIVES

Changing a Polygon Primitive's Attributes

Like NURBS primitives, each poly primitive has many attributes that can be set for the object before or after it is created. You can change a primitive's attribute preset in the Options dialog box for each specific primitive before the object is created (**Figure 3.45**). Most of these primitives have a construction history attached to their surface, allowing the surfaces' properties to be fine-tuned after the surface is created (**Figure 3.46**). The construction history attributes appear under each primitive's poly menu in the Channel Box.

All of the polygon primitives' attributes are changed the same way. This section demonstrates how to change the subdivisions height attribute of a polygon primitive. You can apply the same steps to change other object attributes. The next section defines many of the poly primitives' other attributes.

The subdivisions height attribute is common to the all of the polygon primitives. This attribute adjusts the amount of times the height of the surface gets divided. If you raise the number, you are adding polygons to describe the surface along the height of the object (**Figure 3.47**). If you lower the number, you are using fewer polygons to describe the surface along the height of the object (**Figure 3.48**).

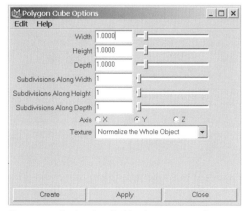

Figure 3.45 Each poly primitive has many attributes that can be set for the object before or after it is created.

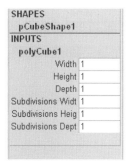

Figure 3.46 Polygon primitives can be fine-tuned after the surface is created by adjusting their poly attributes.

Figure 3.47 If you raise the subdivisions height attribute, you are adding polygons to describe the surface along the height of the object.

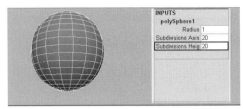

Figure 3.48 If you lower the subdivisions height attribute, you are using fewer polygons to describe the surface along the height of the object.

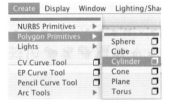

Figure 3.49
Select the box next to the name of the primitive for which you want to set the subdivisions height.

To set the subdivisions height of a polygon primitive from the Create menu:

1. Go to the Create menu, and select the Polygon Primitives submenu.

2. Select the box next to the name of the primitive for which you want to set the subdivisions height (**Figure 3.49**)

3. In the Options dialog box, adjust the Subdivisions Along Height slider to the amount of divisions you want along the height of the surface (**Figure 3.50**).

✔ Tip

■ You can type in a value larger than the slider will go.

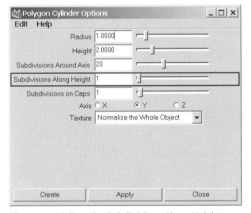

Figure 3.50 Adjust the Subdivisions Along Height slider to the amount of divisions you want along the height of the surface.

To change the subdivisions height of a polygon primitive after the object is created:

1. Select a polygon primitive.

2. Select the poly(object) title under the INPUTS heading in the Channel Box (**Figure 3.51**).

3. Click the Subdivisions Height field to select the number there (**Figure 3.52**).

4. Change the number to the amount of times you want to divide the height.

5. Press ⌨Enter to complete the change (**Figure 3.53**).

✔ Tip

- You can also click the attribute's name (subdivisions height in our example) in the Channel Box, and then click and drag the middle mouse button left or right in the view window to interactively change the subdivisions height value.

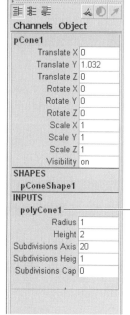

Poly(object)

Figure 3.51 Select the poly(object) title under the INPUTS heading in the Channel Box (the title of a cone is shown).

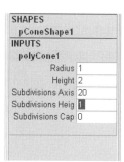

Figure 3.52 Click the Subdivisions Height field to select its contents (the number for the cone is shown).

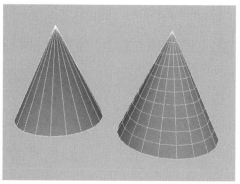

Figure 3.53 Press ⌨Enter to complete the change. The cone with default settings is on the left, the cone with changed subdivisions height is on the right.

CHANGING A POLYGON PRIMITIVE'S ATTRIBUTES

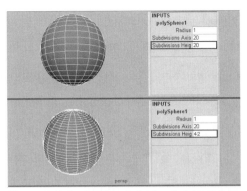

Figure 3.54 Adjusting the subdivisions height attribute will add or subtract polygons in the height (a sphere is shown).

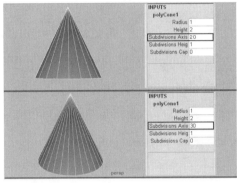

Figure 3.55 Adjusting the subdivisions axis attribute adds or subtracts polygons to the object along the center axis.

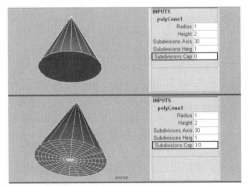

Figure 3.56 Adjusting the subdivisions cap attribute adds or subtracts polygons to or from the object's cap, radiating out from the center.

Below is a definition list of important polygon primitive attributes.

Primitive polygon attributes:

◆ **Subdivisions Height, Width**—These attributes adjust the number of times the height or width of the surface gets divided. Adjusting these attributes adds or subtracts faces in the direction of the axis (**Figure 3.54**).

◆ **Subdivisions Depth**—This attribute adjusts the number of times the depth of the surface gets divided. Adjusting this attribute adds or subtracts faces along the depth of the object.

◆ **Subdivisions Axis**—This attribute adjusts the number of times the surface gets divided along the center axis. Adjusting this attribute adds or subtracts faces to the object in the same way you would add slices to a pizza (**Figure 3.55**).

◆ **Subdivisions Cap**—Two poly primitives have caps, the cone and the cylinder. Caps are pieces of geometry used to cover the round hole(s) of a surface. The cylinder has a cap on the top and bottom of its surface; the cone only has a cap on the bottom of its surface. The subdivisions cap attribute adjusts the number of times the surface's cap gets divided. Adjusting this attribute adds or subtracts faces to the object's cap like a water droplet, sending concentric circles out from the center (**Figure 3.56**).

continues on next page

◆ **Radius**—The radius of an object is half of the object's width. Adjusting the radius scales the object proportionally on multiple axes.

◆ **Section Radius**—This attribute is used only by the torus polygon primitive. Adjusting the section radius fattens or slims the torus's doughnut-like shape (**Figure 3.57**).

◆ **Width, Height, and Depth**—These attributes adjust the object's width, height, or depth.

◆ **Twist**—This attribute is used only by the torus polygon primitive. Adjusting the twist moves the faces around the center axis inside the tube shape from 0 to 360 degrees (**Figure 3.58**).

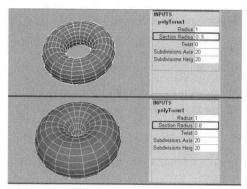

Figure 3.57 Adjusting the section radius fattens or slims the torus's shape.

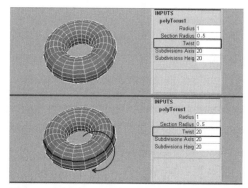

Figure 3.58 Putting a twist on a torus.

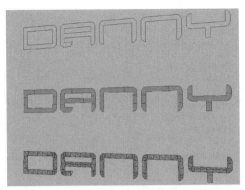

Figure 3.59 There are three types of text: from the top, curves, trims, and polys.

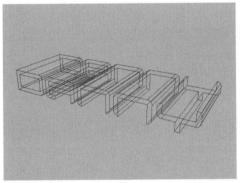

Figure 3.60 Once the 2D text is created, you can do anything to it that you could do to any other curve or surface. This is an example of a loft.

About Text

There are three types of text you can create in Maya: *curves, trims,* and *polys* (**Figure 3.59**). The different text types are all found in the Create > Text Options dialog box. Each of these text types has its place in text creation, and the text type used depends on the application. In this section we will look at the different types of text.

All of the text types in Maya create flat text objects made out of curves, trimmed surfaces (see Chapter 7), or polygons. Although text starts out flat, there are many ways to make it three-dimensional. Once the two-dimensional text is created, you can do anything to it that you could do to any other curve or surface. For instance, if you create text made of curves, you could loft—a function that creates a surface over two or more curves— between a copy and an original (**Figure 3.60**), or you could take text made of polygons and extrude it to make it 3D. See Chapter 7 for more on lofting.

One text type option is Curves. This is a versatile text type because it creates only curves with no surfaces attached to them. You can make the front face of the text planar to create a surface over it, or you can leave the front face open and loft between two copies of the text to make it 3D while leaving a hole for the front face, as in Figure 3.60.

Notice that the text is created in separate selectable pieces. For instance, a letter D would have a curve for the outside of the letter as well as a curve for the center of it.

To create curves-based text:

1. From the Create menu select the box next to Text (**Figure 3.61**).

2. In the Options dialog box click the Text field, and type in new text.

3. Click the arrow next to the Font field and select the font for the text. Click Create (**Figure 3.62**).

4. Make sure Curves is selected for Type (**Figure 3.63**).

5. Click Create to complete the text.

   Text appears in the Maya scene with the bottom-left corner of the text at the origin (**Figure 3.64**).

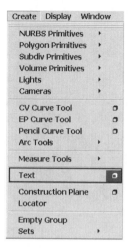

Figure 3.61 Go to the Create menu and select the box next to Text.

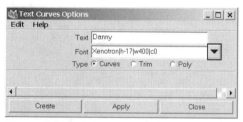

Figure 3.62 Click the arrow next to the Font field, and select the font for the text.

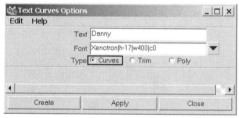

Figure 3.63 Make sure the Curves button is selected for Type.

Figure 3.64 Text is placed in the Maya scene with the bottom-left corner of it at the origin.

Figure 3.65 Trim text type can save you some steps if you are looking for text with surface geometry on the front face of it.

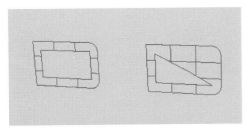

Figure 3.66 You can manipulate the curves components to change an individual letters shape.

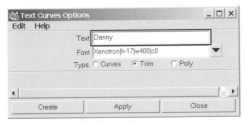

Figure 3.67 Click the Text field, and type in new text.

Figure 3.68 Make sure the Trim button is selected for Type.

Another text-type setting is Trim. Using this text type is the same as selecting the curves and making them planar (see Chapter 7). This text type can save you some steps if you are looking for text with surface geometry on the front face of it (**Figure 3.65**).

With trimmed text you have surfaces attached to curves through history, allowing you to manipulate the curves to change an individual letter's shape (**Figure 3.66**).

To create trimmed text:

1. From the Create menu select the box next to Text.

2. In the Options dialog box click the Text field, and type in new text (**Figure 3.67**).

3. Click the arrow next to the Font field, and select the font for the text. Click OK.

4. Make sure Trim is selected for Type (**Figure 3.68**).

5. Click Create to complete the text.

   Text appears in the Maya scene with the bottom-left corner of the text at the origin, as in **Figure 3.64**.

ABOUT TEXT

The third text type setting is Poly. It's best to use this text type if you want to work the text into other polygon surfaces. With this text type come many options to control the number of polygons used on the text, as well as other helpful text attributes.

The polygons text type also uses surfaces attached to curves through history, allowing you to manipulate the curves to change an individual letter's shape.

To create poly-based text:

1. From the Create menu select the box next to Text.

2. In the Options dialog box click the Text field, and type in new text.

3. Click the arrow next to the Font field, and select the font for the text.

4. Make sure Poly is selected for Type; use the default options for best results (**Figure 3.69**).

5. Click Create to complete the text.

   Text appears in the Maya scene with the bottom-left corner of it at the origin (**Figure 3.70**).

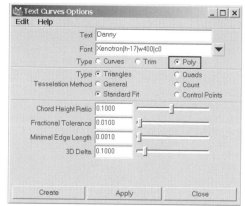

Figure 3.69 Make sure the Poly button is selected for Type.

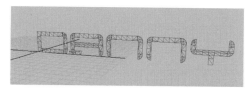

Figure 3.70 Text appears in the Maya scene with the bottom-left corner of it at the origin.

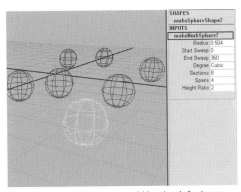

Figure 3.71 nurbsSphere7 would be the default name for the 7th NURBS sphere created in the scene.

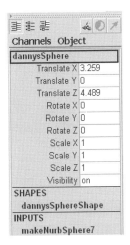

Figure 3.72 Select the object's default name at the top of the Channel Box.

Figure 3.73
Replace the default name with the new name.

Naming Objects

Each time you create an object, Maya gives it a default name. This name is a description of the actual object, followed by the number of times the object type was created. For example, nurbsSphere7 would be the default name for the seventh NURBS sphere created in the scene (**Figure 3.71**). In order to make an object easy to find later, you will want to change its default name to something more descriptive. For example, if you create a sphere for use as a head, then change the name to *head*. This keeps things organized and clear as you continue to add objects to your scene.

To change an object's name:

1. Create an object, or select an existing one by clicking it.

2. Select the object's default name at the top of the Channel Box (**Figure 3.72**).

3. Replace the default name by typing in the new name (**Figure 3.73**).

4. Press (Enter) to complete the name change.

continues on next page

NAMING OBJECTS

✔ Tip

■ You can also change the object's name in the Attribute Editor's transform panel (the first tab) (**Figure 3.74**). Once the object is selected, you can access the Attribute Editor with Ctrl a / Control a.

Every time you create a primitive or other object in Maya, a node is created to represent the object. This node and any connections it might have can be viewed in the Hypergraph. You can also change the name of the object in the Hypergraph. For more information on the Hypergraph, see Chapter 1.

To change an object's name in the Hypergraph:

1. Create an object, or select an existing one.

2. From any view select Panels > Panel > Hypergraph to change the current view into a Hypergraph (**Figure 3.75**).
   This menu is at the top of each view's panel.

3. Press f to zoom in on the object's node.

4. Hold down Ctrl / Control and double-click the node's object name (**Figure 3.76**).

5. Replace the default name with the new name.

6. Press Enter to complete the name change.

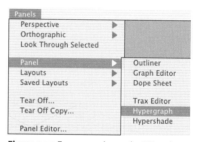

Figure 3.74 You can also change the object's name in the Attribute Editor's transform panel (the first tab).

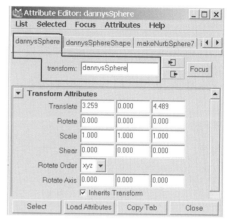

Figure 3.75 From any view select Panels > Panel > Hypergraph to change the current view into a Hypergraph.

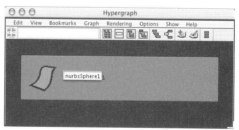

Figure 3.76 Hold down Ctrl / Control, and double-click the node's object name to change it.

NAMING OBJECTS

SELECTION MODES, HIDING, AND TEMPLATING

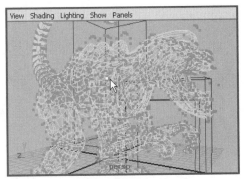

Figure 4.1 A model may have hundreds of points to select. Maya provides helpers for selecting specific points. The component Pick mask is used to select one of the creature's many points.

Any Maya scene might have hundreds of joints, thousands of polygons, and hundreds of thousands of points. This could amount to extreme frustration when trying to select one small point in the middle of huge amounts of geometry (**Figure 4.1**). With a large number of tools that hide, template, layer, and select objects, Maya has taken away much of the frustration involved in the organization and selection of objects.

For the new user, selecting a specific object type or piece of an object, known as a *component,* can be tricky. These objects might be curves, lights, surfaces, or one of an array of other object types. Each of these object types can be turned off using the Pick mask (**Figure 4.2**). The controls in the Pick mask help you mask off object types so you can limit a selection to only the object type you want to select. For example, you can turn off the ability to select everything but curves (**Figure 4.3**). When you try to click anything but a curve, nothing happens. When you click a curve, it is selected. This is a very useful tool, and we will be spending a large amount of this chapter discussing the Pick mask and selection process.

There are times when objects are visually in the way and limit the view of other objects. This is where hiding, templating, and layering come in. These functions allow you to separate out objects so they no longer hinder your view and you can then more easily select the objects you wish.

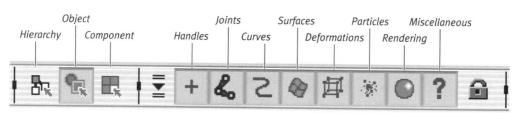

Object — Hierarchy — Component — Handles — Joints — Curves — Surfaces — Deformations — Particles — Rendering — Miscellaneous

Figure 4.2 The controls in the Pick mask determine what objects can be selected at any given time.

Select by object type: Curves (RMB for more info)

Figure 4.3 Individual object types, such as Curves, can be selected in the Pick mask to limit a selection to that object type.

SELECTION MODES, HIDING, AND TEMPLATING

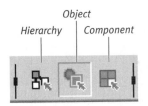

Object

Hierarchy   Component

Figure 4.4
Hierarchy, object,
and component Pick
mask buttons control
whether an object or
an object component
can be selected.

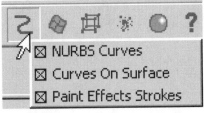

Figure 4.5 Each Pick mask holds additional
masking selections viewable by right mouse
button-clicking its icon.

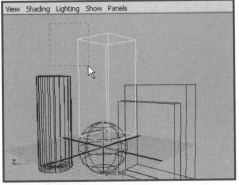

Figure 4.6 Using a marquee can be an easy way to
select multiple objects.

About Selecting Objects and Using the Pick Mask

Most commands in Maya require that you
have an object, or an object component,
selected before a command can be processed.
Selecting an object or component requires
the use of the Pick mask. The Pick mask,
sometimes referred to as the Selection mask,
is used to select an object or component by
type, not just by where you click on the object.

The Pick mask has three modes: *hierarchy,
object,* and *component* (**Figure 4.4**). Each of
these modes also has multiple subsets to
help you mask off everything but the specific
object or component that you want. Under
each of these subsets you can mask off even
more objects to additionally limit your selection. To view the additional subset, right mouse
button-click the icon (**Figure 4.5**). You can
toggle between Object and Component modes
by pressing F8.

This chapter describes the specific function
of each Pick mask mode.

To select an object:

1. Choose the Select by Object Type icon 🐾.

2. Move the mouse over an object.

3. Click the object to select it.
   or
   Draw a marquee that overlaps part of the
   object you want to select (**Figure 4.6**).

4. Release the mouse button to select the
   object(s).

To add objects to a selection:

◆ While holding down (Shift), click each object you want to add to the current selection.

or

While holding down (Shift), draw a marquee that overlaps part of each object you want to add to the selection.

✔ Tip

■ If you overlap a selected object with the marquee, in other words, if you draw a marquee around part of an object that's already been selected, you will deselect it.

To subtract objects from a selection:

◆ While holding (Shift), click each object you want to subtract from the current selection. The objects are subtracted.

or

While holding down (Shift), draw a marquee that overlaps part of each object you want to subtract from the selection.

To invert the selection:

1. Select an object (**Figure 4.7**).

2. From the Edit menu select Invert Selection (**Figure 4.8**).

   Deselected objects become selected, selected objects become deselected (**Figure 4.9**).

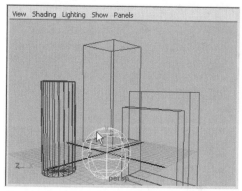

Figure 4.7 Click an object or drag a marquee to make a selection.

Figure 4.8 From the Edit menu select Invert Selection.

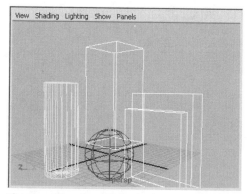

Figure 4.9 When Invert Selection is used, deselected objects become selected, selected objects become deselected.

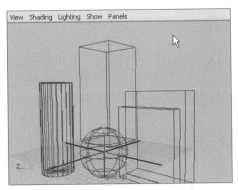

Figure 4.10 Click in the background of a pane to deselect all objects, or (Shift)-click a selected object to deselect it.

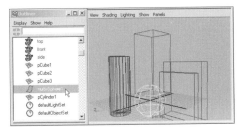

Figure 4.11 Select Outliner from the Window menu, and click the name of the object you want to select.

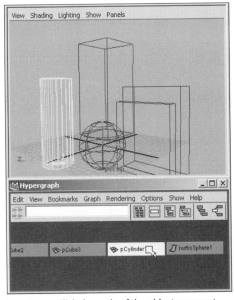

Figure 4.12 Click the node of the object you want to select.

To deselect all objects:

◆ Click once in open space to deselect all objects or (Shift)-click a selected object to deselect it (**Figure 4.10**).

To select an object using the Outliner:

1. From the Window menu select Outliner.

2. Click the name of the object you want to select (**Figure 4.11**).

   The object becomes selected.

To select an object using the Hypergraph:

1. From the Window menu select Hypergraph.

2. Click the node of the object you want to select (**Figure 4.12**).

   The object becomes selected.

Selecting objects using hierarchy mode

Hierarchy mode is used to select objects within a hierarchy. You can select the top node in a hierarchy; a descendent, called a leaf (**Figure 4.13**); or a templated object. There are three major masks in hierarchy mode, defined in **Table 4.1**.

To select the top object in a hierarchy:

1. Create two spheres.

2. Draw a marquee around them to select both of them (**Figure 4.14**).

3. From the Edit menu select Group.
   The two objects become grouped together.

4. From the Window menu select Outliner (**Figure 4.15**).
   The Outliner panel opens.

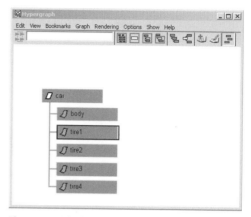

Figure 4.13 A leaf is a node lower down in a hierarchy, such as tire4 in this figure.

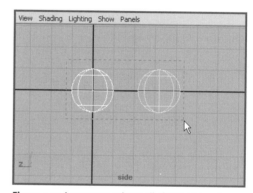

Figure 4.14 A marquee selects all objects it touches; you do not need to box in the entire object.

Table 4.1

Hierarchy Mode Selection Masks

ICON	NAME	FUNCTION
	Root	Selects the top node in a hierarchy
	Leaf	Selects a descendant object
	Template	Selects a templated object. You must select a templated object before untemplating it.

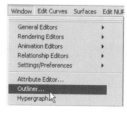

Figure 4.15 The Outliner holds a list of all the nodes in the scene.

Figure 4.16 The plus sign expands the view of all the object names in the hierarchy.

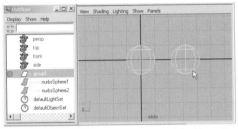

Figure 4.17 The group node at the top of the hierarchy becomes selected no matter which object in the hierarchy you originally selected.

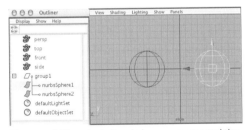

Figure 4.18 The selected node becomes gray, and the top node in the hierarchy becomes green.

5. Click the plus (+) sign to the left of the group name in the Outliner to show the hierarchy (**Figure 4.16**).

6. Set the Pick mask to Select by Hierarchy mode by clicking its icon .

7. Set the submask to Select by Hierarchy: Root by clicking its icon .

8. Click one of the objects.

   The group node at the top of the hierarchy becomes selected (**Figure 4.17**).

To select an object within a hierarchy:

1. Follow steps 1 to 6 of the last task.

2. Set the submask to Select by Hierarchy: Leaf by clicking its icon .

3. Click one of the objects.

   The object clicked, not the group node, becomes selected (**Figure 4.18**). The selected node is shown in gray.

SELECTING OBJECTS AND USING THE PICK MASK

87

Selecting objects using object type mode

Selecting by object type mode ⬚, usually just called *object mode,* selects entire objects. There are eight masks for object mode, described in **Table 4.2.**

This mask is extremely useful when objects that consist of different object types overlap each other in a scene. A good example of this is a character that has already been set up for animation. In this case you might have joints, IK handles, selection handles, and geometry sitting directly on top of each other. This can make the joints behind the geometry difficult to select. By using the object Pick mask, you can turn off all object types except for joints (**Figure 4.19**). Now the only selectable objects are the joints themselves and are much easier to select.

Table 4.2

Object Mode Selection Masks

Icon	Name	Function
+	Handles	Selects selection handles and IK handles
⚡	Joints	Selects skeleton joints
⊃	Curves	Selects NURBS curves, curves on surfaces, and paint effects strokes
⬡	Surfaces	Selects NURBS, polys, and sub-division surfaces as well as planes
⊞	Deformations	Selects lattices, clusters, non-linears, and sculpt objects
☀	Dynamics	Selects particles, emitters, fields, springs, rigid bodies, and constraints
◎	Rendering	Selects lights, cameras, and textures
?	Miscellaneous	Selects IK end effectors, locators, and dimensions

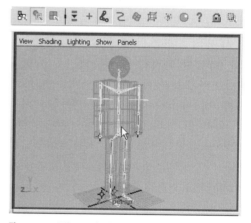

Figure 4.19 When only the Joints Pick mask is selected, joints become the only object type that is selectable.

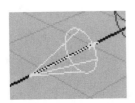

Figure 4.20 Zoom the camera up to an object by pressing ⓕ; press and hold ⓈⓗⓘⓕⓉⓕ to zoom the object in all the views.

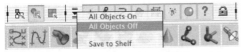

Figure 4.21 Select all objects off in the Pick mask to set the mask to select nothing.

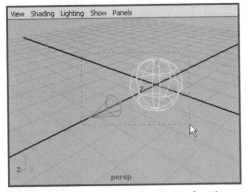

Figure 4.22 Only the sphere, which is a surface, is selected even though the marquee overlaps the spotlight.

To select only surfaces with the Object Pick mask:

1. From the Create menu select NURBS primitive > Sphere.

2. Create a spotlight by clicking its icon in the shelf ▨.

3. Press ⓕ to bring the objects closer to the camera view (**Figure 4.20**).

4. Set the Pick mask to Select by Object Type by clicking the icon ▨.

5. Click the arrow to the right of the Object Pick Mask icon ▤, and select All Objects Off from the pop-up menu (**Figure 4.21**). All object types are turned off in the Pick mask.

6. Set the submask to Select by Object Type: Surfaces by clicking its icon ▨.

7. Drag a marquee around the two objects. Because it is a surface, the sphere becomes selected. The spotlight is not a surface and therefore is not selected (**Figure 4.22**).

✔ Tip

■ The same steps can be used to mask any object types.

Selecting parts of objects with component mode

Every Maya object is made up of different components. Components define the final shape of a curve or surface. For example, a curve is made up of hulls, CVs, and edit points (**Figure 4.23**). The positions of each of these determines the look of the curve. Each object's components can be selected and edited individually using component mode. (For more information on curve and surface components, see Chapter 7.)

The nine major masks in component mode are defined in **Table 4.3**.

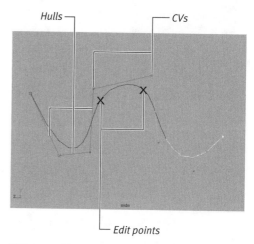

Hulls — CVs

Edit points

Figure 4.23 There are three main selectable components of a curve: hulls, CVs, and edit points.

Table 4.3

	Component Mode Selection Masks	
ICON	**NAME**	**FUNCTION**
▪	Points	Selects NURBS CVs, poly vertices, subdiv vertices, lattice points, and particles
•	Parameter Points	Selects NURBS edit points, curve points, surface points, and subdiv uvs
�	Lines	Selects NURBS isoparms and trim edges, poly and subdiv edges, and springs
◈	Faces	Selects NURBS patches, and poly and subdiv faces
⌁	Hulls	Selects NURBS hulls
◉	Pivots	Selects rotate, scale, and joint pivots
+	Handles	Selects selection handles
?	Local Rotation	Selects local rotation axes and image planes

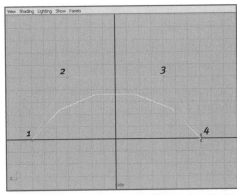

Figure 4.24 Click the four CVs to create the curve.

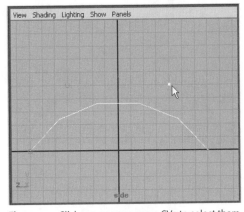

Figure 4.25 Click one or more curve CVs to select them.

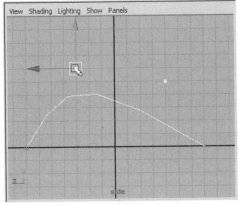

Figure 4.26 CVs can be moved to re-form the curve.

To select and move a curve's CVs

1. Draw a curve using the CV Curve tool ⧉ or open a file that uses curves (**Figure 4.24**).

2. Click the Select by Component icon ⧉ in the Pick mask.

3. Click the arrow next to the Set the Component Type icon ⧉ and select All Components Off from the menu.

4. Click the Points Submask icon ⧉.

5. Select the curve to show its points.

6. Click one or more curve CVs to select them (**Figure 4.25**).

7. Click the Move icon ⧉ in the toolbar. The Move tool manipulator appears.

8. Click and drag the move tool manipulator to move the CVs (**Figure 4.26**).

The Pick mask has preset shortcuts that when pressed set it to specific settings.

Pick mask shortcuts

F8 —Toggles between object and component modes.

F9 —Sets the Pick mask to select vertices (**Figure 4.27**).

F10 —Sets the Pick mask to select edges (**Figure 4.28**).

F11 —Sets the Pick mask to select faces (**Figure 4.29**).

F12 —Sets the Pick mask to select UVs (**Figure 4.30**).

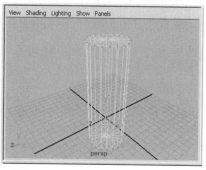

Figure 4.27 Press F9 to have the Pick mask change to select vertices without selecting other common components.

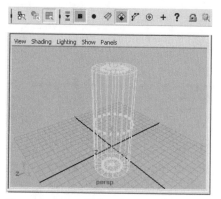

Figure 4.29 Press F11 to have the Pick mask change to select faces without selecting other common components.

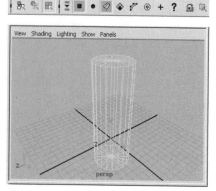

Figure 4.28 Press F10 to have the Pick mask change to select edges without selecting other common components.

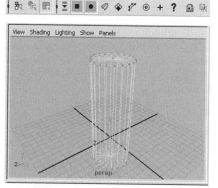

Figure 4.30 Press F12 to have the Pick mask change to select UVs without selecting other common components.

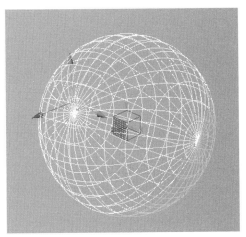

Figure 4.31 Select the points you would like to use for a saved selection.

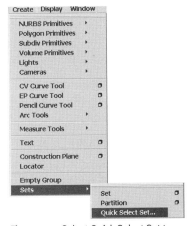

Figure 4.32 Select Quick Select Set to lock in your selection for future use.

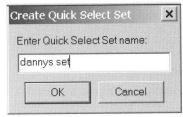

Figure 4.33 Give your selection set a descriptive name to make later use easier.

Often you want to select the same group of points or same objects over and over again. Making the selection more than once can be a tedious and unnecessary process. You can save time by saving and naming the selection for use later; this function is called a Quick Select Set. Once you have made the selection, a Quick Select Set can be used over and over to reselect the same objects and components.

To create a Quick Select Set:

1. In component mode select multiple points (**Figure 4.31**), or in object mode select multiple objects.

2. From the Create menu (Windows) or Edit menu (Mac) select Sets > Quick Select Set (**Figure 4.32**).
   The Create Quick Select Set dialog box opens.

3. Enter a set name in the "Enter Quick Select Set name" field (**Figure 4.33**).

4. Click OK.
   The named selection is now available from the Edit > Quick Select Sets > [set name] menu (**Figure 4.34**).

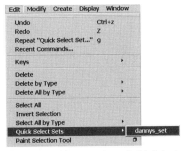

Figure 4.34 After creating a Quick Select Set, you can remake the selection by choosing Edit > Quick Select Sets > [set name].

SELECTING OBJECTS AND USING THE PICK MASK

To hide a selected object:

1. Select an object to hide (**Figure 4.35**).

2. From the Display menu choose Hide > Hide Selection (**Figure 4.36**), or press Ctrl / Control h.

   The selected object becomes hidden from view (**Figure 4.37**).

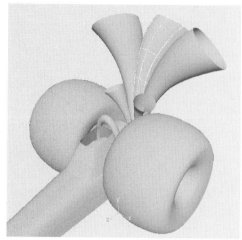

Figure 4.35 Select one or more objects to hide.

Figure 4.36 Hide the selection by choosing Display > Hide > Hide Selection.

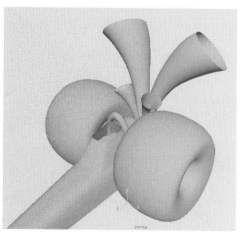

Figure 4.37 The selection becomes totally hidden from view. You can show all objects at once or show the last object hidden.

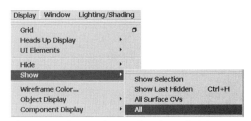

Figure 4.38 Choose Show > All to show all objects that have been hidden.

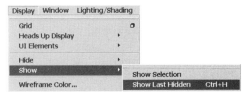

Figure 4.39 Choose Show > Show Last Hidden to have the last object hidden appear.

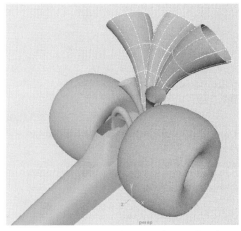

Figure 4.40 Any selected object can be templated. Templated objects appear gray until selected.

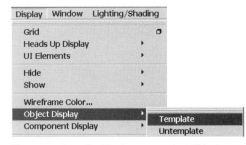

Figure 4.41 From the Display menu select Object Display > Template.

To show all hidden objects:

◆ From the Display menu choose Show > All (**Figure 4.38**).

All hidden objects become visible.

To show the last hidden object:

◆ From the Display menu choose Show > Show Last Hidden (**Figure 4.39**), or press Ctrl/Control Shift h.

The last object hidden becomes visible.

Templating an object allows you to see its placement without the object getting in the way of other selections. Templating an object turns the object gray, and it becomes selectable only with the Select Template Pick mask.

To template an object:

1. Select the objects you want to template (**Figure 4.40**).

2. From the Display menu select Object Display > Template (**Figure 4.41**).

3. The object becomes grayed out (**Figure 4.42**) and is only selectable with the Hierarchy: Select Template Selection mask.

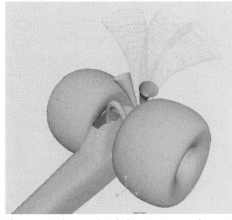

Figure 4.42 The templated objects are gray when not selected and pink when selected with the Template Selection mask.

To untemplate an object

1. Set the Pick mask to hierarchy mode and click the template icon 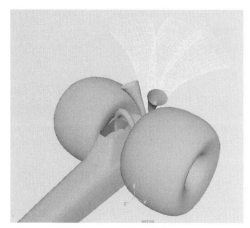 to select templates.

2. Select the templated objects you want to untemplate (**Figure 4.43**).

   The selected templated objects become light pink.

3. From the Display menu select Object Display > Untemplate (**Figure 4.44**).

   The objects become untemplated.

Figure 4.43 To select a templated object you must set the Hierarchy Pick mask to select Template.

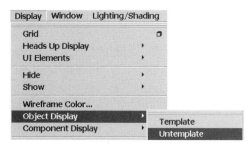

Figure 4.44 To Untemplate an object, select Object Display > Untemplate.

Figure 4.45 You can create additional layers in the Layers menu.

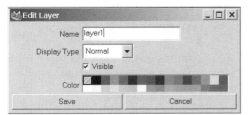

Figure 4.46 The Edit Layer dialog box holds the Name, Display Type, and Color options.

Figure 4.47 Select a descriptive name for the layer.

About Layers

Layers are used to separate objects so they can be viewed and edited separately. Each layer can have a color associated with it, which makes objects on that layer easily recognizable. A layer can be hidden, shown, templated, or referenced. Objects can be moved from layer to layer as needed, and new layers can be created at any time.

To create a layer, rename it, and color-code it:

1. Open the Channel Box, and click the Layer Editor icon 🔳 (Windows), or press and hold the mouse in the east region of the Channel Box and select Layer Bar (Mac).

2. From the Layers menu in the Layer Editor select Create Layer (**Figure 4.45**), or click the Create Layer icon 📄 (Windows only).

   A new layer is created called layer1.

3. Double-click on layer1 to open the Edit Layer dialog box (**Figure 4.46**).

4. Type a descriptive name for the layer in the Name field (**Figure 4.47**).

   On the Mac, press OK to close the window. On Windows, keep the window open.

5. Choose Normal (Windows), or hold down the mouse over the arrow in the layer bar to the left of the layer name, and choose Standard from the pop-up menu (Mac).

   The Display Type pop-up menu allows you to have the objects on the layer be viewed normal (or standard), as a template, or as a reference.

   continues on next page

6. Select a color swatch (**Figure 4.48**).

On Windows, you select a color swatch inside the layer dialog box. On the Mac, double-click on a swatch to the left of the layer name.

The wireframe of each object on the layer will display in the selected color.

7. Click Save.

✔ Tips

■ By default, new objects created are still on the default layer, not the newly created layer. To have each new object be placed on the current layer, choose Use Current Layer from the Layer Options menu (Windows only) (**Figure 4.49**).

■ You can make each new layer the current layer by choosing Make New Layers Current from the Layer Options menu (Windows only).

■ You can delete a layer by right mouse button-clicking on the layer and selecting Delete from the menu.

To move an object to a different layer:

1. Select the objects you want to move to a new layer (**Figure 4.50**).

2. Right mouse button–click on the layer to which you want to move the objects, and choose Add Selected Objects from the menu (**Figure 4.51**).

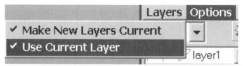

Figure 4.48 Select a color swatch for the objects on the layer. The wireframes of any objects on the layer will become the color of the selected swatch.

Figure 4.49 To have each new object be placed on the current layer, choose Use Current Layer from the Layer Options menu.

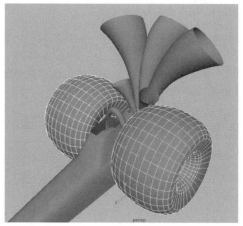

Figure 4.50 Select the objects you want to move to a new layer.

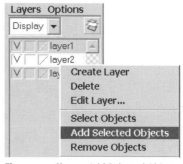

Figure 4.51 Choose Add Selected Objects to move objects to a different layer.

ABOUT LAYERS

Transforming Objects and Components

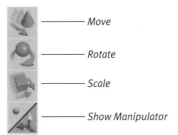

——— Move

——— Rotate

——— Scale

——— Show Manipulator

Figure 5.1 Maya's manipulation tools.

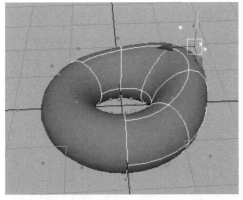

Figure 5.2 The Move tool's translation manipulator is used to move objects and components around the scene.

Maya gives you many ways to move, rotate, and scale objects around the scene, and many shortcuts for completing these common tasks. To move an object, referred to as *translating* an object, you can type in the coordinates in the Channel Box or use one of the many manipulation tools (**Figure 5.1**) to drag the object freely around the scene or constrain it to an axis.

With the same tools you would use to manipulate objects around the scene, you can also manipulate parts of the object, known as *components*. Each type of object has its own components that can be translated (**Figure 5.2**), rotated, and/or scaled to change their look and position, in turn changing the appearance of the object.

Its developers have done a great job of making Maya easy to learn on a surface level while still giving access to more advanced features as your knowledge base grows. The duplication options are a good example. You can duplicate an object multiple times by setting the number of copies, or you can determine exactly where the copies will be placed in the scene as you get more used to changing the options.

Moving, Rotating, and Scaling Objects

Maya provides multiple tools for moving, rotating, and scaling objects and components. Each of these tools has axes that you can grab and move. These axes are called *manipulators* (**Figure 5.3**). The manipulators are used to translate (move), rotate, or scale the object. Manipulators make it easy to constrain objects along a particular axis—click and drag the colored line for the axis along which you want to constrain the object. The colors stay consistent for each tool. RGB colors coincide with the *x-y-z* axes (**Figure 5.4**): On the manipulators the *x*-axis is colored red, the *y*-axis is colored green, and the *z*-axis is colored blue. If you forget the specific color of each axis, look at the view axis in the lower left-hand corner
of each pane (**Figure 5.5**). The axis that is selected on the manipulator is always yellow.

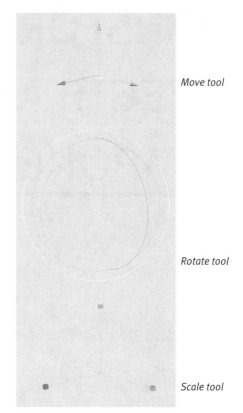

Move tool

Rotate tool

Scale tool

Figure 5.3 The Move, Rotate, and Scale manipulators.

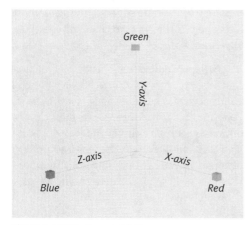

Figure 5.4 RGB colors match the *x-y-z* axes.

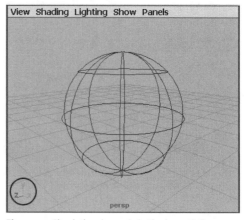

Figure 5.5 Check the view axis in the lower-left corner of each pane to be reminded which color goes with which axis.

Figure 5.6 You can freely translate an object by selecting the center of the Move tool's manipulators, scale proportionally with the center of the Scale tool's manipulator, or click and drag anywhere in the sphere of the Rotate tool to rotate freely.

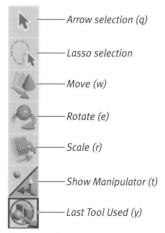

— Arrow selection (q)

— Lasso selection

— Move (w)

— Rotate (e)

— Scale (r)

— Show Manipulator (t)

— Last Tool Used (y)

Figure 5.7 The manipulation tools and their shortcuts.

In addition to constraining an object along an axis, you can freely manipulate the object by clicking and dragging the square in the middle of the Move and Scale tool manipulators, or by clicking and dragging the light blue ring on the outside of the Rotate manipulator (**Figure 5.6**).

Each of the tools in the toolbar, with the exception of the Lasso tool, has a shortcut associated with it. These shortcuts are easy to remember because they coincide with the ⓠⓦⓔⓡⓣⓨ keys on the keyboard. You can just press a tool's key to turn on its manipulator.

The ⓠⓦⓔⓡⓣⓨ keys and the manipulators they turn on are (**Figure 5.7**):

ⓠ Arrow Selection tool

ⓦ Move tool

ⓔ Rotate tool

ⓡ Scale tool

ⓣ Show manipulator

ⓨ Last tool used

✔ Tip

■ Be aware that these keys will not work if the Caps Lock key is on. In Maya, capitals are different hotkeys with different functions mapped to them. For example, the Move, Rotate, and Scale tools are ⓦ, ⓔ, and ⓡ, respectively. As capitals, Ⓦ keyframes translation, Ⓔ keyframes rotation, and Ⓡ keyframes scaling.

MOVING, ROTATING, AND SCALING OBJECTS

To translate an object or component using the Move tool:

1. Select an object or component by clicking it.

2. Press ⓦ or click the Move tool icon 🔲 in the toolbar.

   The Move manipulator is now visible on the object or component (**Figure 5.8**).

3. With the left mouse button, click and drag the arrow in the direction in which you want the object to move (**Figure 5.9**).

   This translates the object along the selected axis.

   or

   Hold down Shift, and middle mouse button-click and drag in the direction in which you want the object to move (**Figure 5.10**).

   Doing this selects the appropriate manipulator axis and translates the object in that direction. This is particularly useful if you just created an object at the origin but moved the camera away from the grid. You can pull the object into your camera view if you know the direction of the origin.

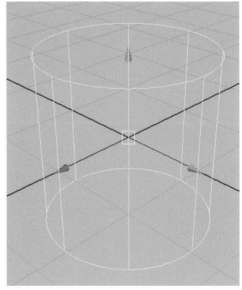

Figure 5.8 The Move manipulator is used to move the object around the scene.

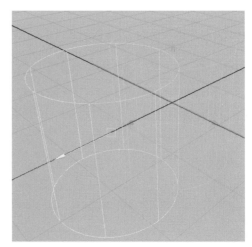

Figure 5.9 Click and drag the axis you want the object constrained to so that you keep control of the exact position of the surface. This is particularly useful in the perspective view.

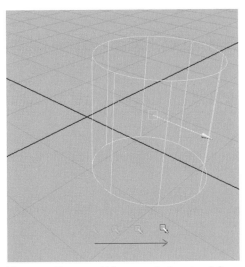

Figure 5.10 You can middle mouse button-drag left and right to interactively change values. Here, a translation value is changed.

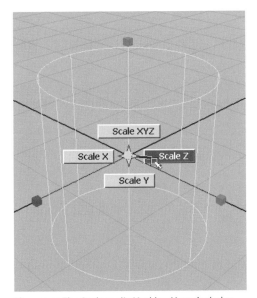

Figure 5.11 The Scale tool's Marking Menu includes shortcuts for scaling proportionally and along an axis.

✔ Tips

- You can also hold down ⌧ to activate grid snap, and middle mouse button–dragging anywhere on the grid will snap the object to that location.

- You can use the ⊞ and ⊟ keys to enlarge or shrink the size of the manipulators.

- From anywhere in a view pane you can hold down the key for the Move (ⓦ), Rotate (ⓔ), or Scale (ⓡ) tool and press the left mouse button to bring up that tool's Marking Menu (**Figure 5.11**).

To scale an object or component:

1. Select an object or component by clicking it.

2. Press r or click the Scale tool icon 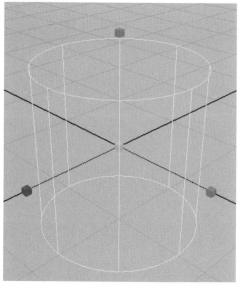 in the toolbar.

   The Scale manipulator is now visible on the object or component (**Figure 5.12**).

3. With the left mouse button click the small square of the axis on which you want to scale the object or component, and drag in the direction in which you want the object to scale (**Figure 5.13**).

   or

   Click and drag with the middle mouse button anywhere in the pane toward the direction in which you want the object to scale (**Figure 5.14**).

   This selects the appropriate manipulator axis and scales the object in that direction.

Figure 5.12 The Scale tool's manipulator is used to scale the object proportionally or along a single axis.

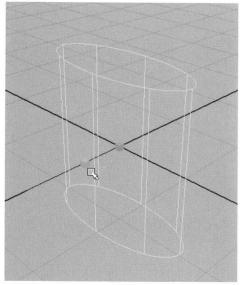

Figure 5.13 Click and drag a Scale tool's axis to scale it along a particular axis.

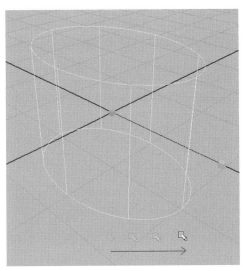

Figure 5.14 This cylinder is being scaled along the x axis by clicking and dragging with the middle mouse button.

To rotate an object or component:

1. Select an object or component by clicking it.

2. Press ⒺⒺ or click the Rotate tool icon 🔄 in the toolbar.

   The Rotate manipulator is now visible on the object or component (**Figure 5.15**).

3. Click with the left mouse button on the circle of the axis you want to rotate the object or component around, and drag in the direction in which you want the object to rotate (**Figure 5.16**).

   continues on next page

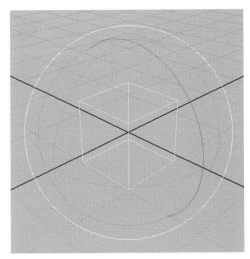

Figure 5.15 The Rotate manipulator is used to rotate the surface on one or more axes

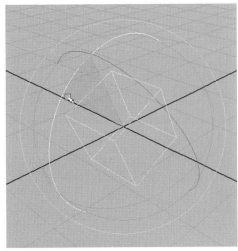

Figure 5.16 Click and drag the axis circle to which you want the object constrained. A gray pie slice shows you how many degrees you have rotated the object.

✔ Tips

- You can click anywhere within the Rotate manipulator sphere, and click and drag to rotate the object without being constrained to any axis.

- Once the axis you want to use is yellow on the manipulator, you can middle mouse button–click and drag anywhere in the pane to rotate it around that axis without touching the axis or the object.

- The light blue outer ring rotates the object or component around an axis that always faces the camera view (**Figure 5.17**).

To translate, rotate, or scale an object or component using the Channel Box:

1. Select an object or component by clicking it.

2. In the Channel Box, click once in the field next to the attribute you want to change (**Figure 5.18**).

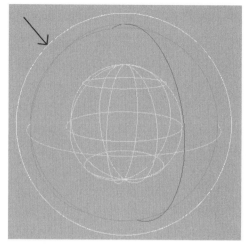

Figure 5.17 The light blue outer ring rotates the object or component.

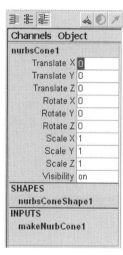

Figure 5.18 Click the field name of the attribute you want to change (Translate X is shown).

MOVING, ROTATING, AND SCALING OBJECTS

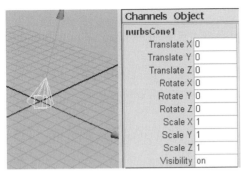

Figure 5.19 The position of the cone with Translate X set to 0.

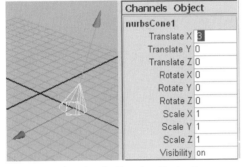

Figure 5.20 Changing the Translate X value to 3 moves the cone 3 units in the positive *x* direction.

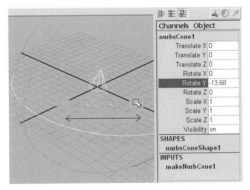

Figure 5.21 Interactively change values with the middle mouse button anywhere in a pane.

3. Type a new value in the selected field.

The object reflects the value change (**Figures 5.19** and **5.20**).

or

Move the mouse over a view pane. Hold down the middle mouse button and drag left or right to interactively change the value of the selected attribute (**Figure 5.21**).

Duplication Options

Maya provides shortcuts for modeling objects with repetitive geometry. A good example of this is making a staircase. You could use one elongated cube and one duplicate action to produce the whole staircase in a minimum number of steps (**Figure 5.22**).

As you can see, it's possible to use the Duplicate tool for simple duplication of an object, or for complex duplications that include rotations, translations, and scales of the object. In addition to its mentioned uses, the Duplicate option holds other valuable tools: mirroring and instancing objects.

An important option of duplication is the ability to duplicate objects with their history Inputs nodes (**Figure 5.23**), or without them. It's important to be aware that the history duplication is off by default. The Duplicate Input Connections checkbox in the Duplicate Options window controls this feature.

Mirroring and instancing objects

The duplication window allows you to create mirrored duplicate objects, producing a reverse copy of the original. Body parts are good candidates for mirroring (**Figure 5.24**). Eyes, ears, arms, and legs each have a nearly identical version of themselves on the other side of the body, but in reverse. This option gives you the ability to model one ear, and then with one click create the second ear in its exact position.

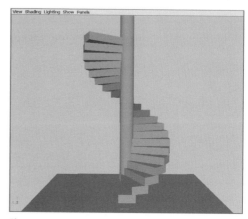

Figure 5.22 This staircase was made with two objects and one duplication.

INPUTS	
makeNurbSphere1	
Radius	0.504
Start Sweep	0
End Sweep	360
Degree	Cubic
Sections	8
Spans	4
Height Ratio	2

Figure 5.23
The sphere's Inputs node holds its editable history attributes.

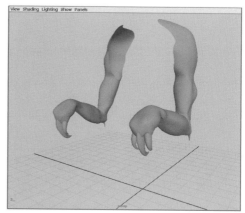

Figure 5.24 A mirrored arm can save time in modeling a second arm.

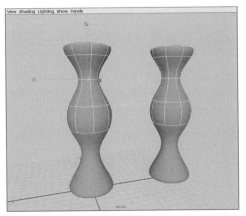

Figure 5.25 The instanced objects will mimic the edits of the first object interactively.

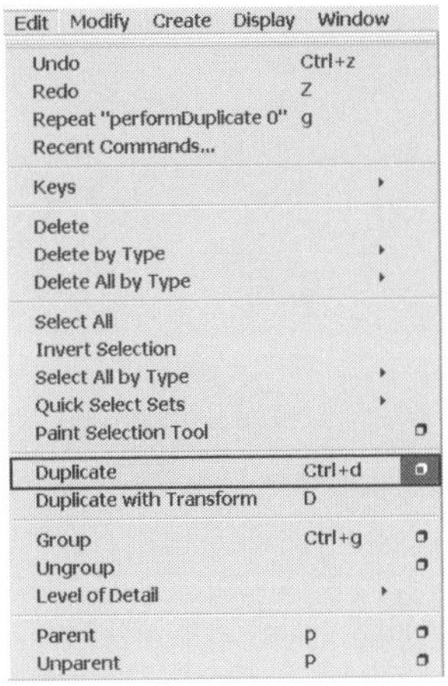

In addition to duplicating multiple objects and mirroring objects, you can create an instance of an object. Instancing an object creates a duplicate that maintains a connection to the shape of the original (**Figure 5.25**). Why is this so great? The beauty of this is that you can then edit the original and have each of the instanced objects follow the edits interactively. For example, if you are creating a building that has multiple pillars that are to be identical, you could create one pillar and instance it the number of times that you want additional pillars. If you later decide that you want to change the look of the pillars, you just have to edit one and the rest will automatically update.

To duplicate an object:

1. Select an object by clicking it.

2. From the Edit menu select the box next to Duplicate (**Figure 5.26**).

   This opens the Duplicate Options window.

3. Enter the amount of duplicates desired in the Number of Copies field (**Figure 5.27**).

4. Click Duplicate ⬚ Duplicate ⬚ .

   The number of copies specified are duplicated and placed on top of each other.

Figure 5.26
From the Edit menu select the box next to Duplicate to open the Duplicate Options window.

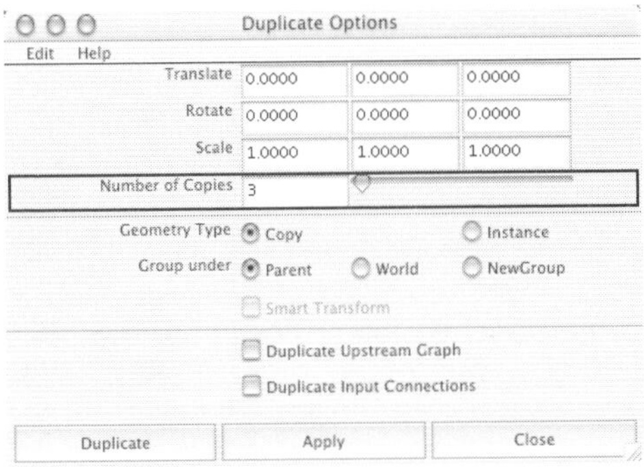

Figure 5.27 Enter the amount of duplicates desired in the Number of Copies field.

DUPLICATION OPTIONS

To duplicate an object with rotation:

1. Select an object by clicking it.

2. From the Edit menu select the box next to Duplicate.

   This opens the Duplicate Options window.

3. Select a rotation amount that each additional copy will make, and type it in the Rotate field of the axis you want to rotate around (**Figure 5.28**). The fields are, left to right: *x*-axis, *y*-axis, and *z*-axis.

   If you have used a sphere, you will only notice a rotation in wireframe mode.

4. Click the Duplicate button to duplicate the object.

✔ Tip

■ You can use the same technique for translating or scaling a copy.

Now that you have the general idea of how to duplicate an object, let's put the options into action and create a simple staircase. We will use the same technique that we used for creating a simple copy with rotation, but now we will use the Translate, Rotate, and Scale options together.

The important part to having a successful duplication with translation is placing the pivot point in the correct position for the objects to rotate around (**Figure 5.29**).

To create a simple staircase:

1. From the Create menu select Poly Primitive > Cube.

   A cube is created at the origin.

2. Type .5 in the Translate Y field in the Channel Box and press ⌑Enter⌑ (**Figure 5.30**).

   This moves the cube up so its base sits on the grid.

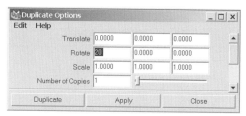

Figure 5.28 Enter the amount of rotation desired in the first field of the Rotate attribute. The first field is the rotate *x* field.

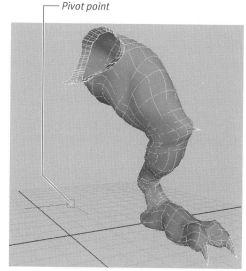

Figure 5.29 The pivot-point placement is used to determine the placement of a duplicated surface.

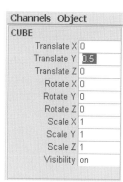

Figure 5.30 Type .5 in the Translate Y field to move the cube's bottom to sit on the grid.

DUPLICATION OPTIONS

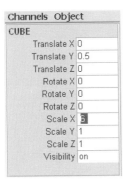

Figure 5.31 Type 6 in the Scale X field to scale the x-axis of the object 6 units.

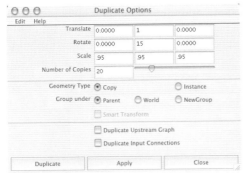

Figure 5.32 The pivot point determines the point in space that the staircase will rotate around.

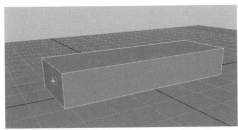

Figure 5.33 Set the duplicate options as shown to properly duplicate the cube.

3. Type 6 in the Scale X field in the Channel Box and press Enter (**Figure 5.31**).

This widens the cube.

4. Press w or click the Move tool icon in the toolbar.

5. Press Insert (Home) on the keyboard to go into pivot-point edit mode.

6. Move the pivot-point to the far-left edge of the cube, constraining in the x direction (**Figure 5.32**).

7. Press Insert / Home again to get out of pivot-point edit mode.

8. From the Edit menu select the box next to Duplicate to open the Duplicate Options window.

9. Set the duplicate options as follows (**Figure 5.33**):

Translate to 0, 1, 0. This moves each new duplicate up the y-axis 1 unit. Our cube is 1 unit high, so each copy will sit on top of the previous one.

Rotate to 0, 15, 0. This rotates each duplicate 15 degrees more than the previous one around the y-axis.

Scale to .95, .95, .95. This scales each duplicate proportionately 95 percent of the size of the last. The staircase will get smaller as it goes higher.

continues on next page

DUPLICATION OPTIONS

10. Enter 20 in the Number of Copies field. This will create 20 new steps.

11. Select Duplicate.

The number of copies specified are duplicated and placed on top of each other after being rotated and scaled (**Figure 5.34**).

✔ Tips

■ It is a good idea to check your options before duplicating. Your options will keep the previous settings unless you reset them. With the Duplicate Options window open, select Edit > Reset Settings and the options will return to default.

■ Move the pivot point farther down the *x*-axis before duplicating to make room for a pole in the center (**Figure 5.35**).

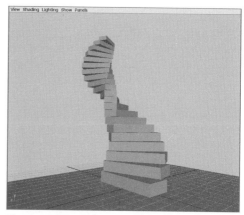

Figure 5.34 A staircase can be built with the click of a button if the proper duplicate options are set.

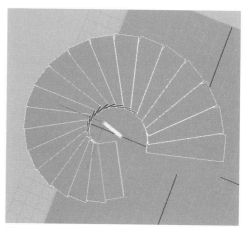

Figure 5.35 Move the pivot point farther away from the original object to add variation to the center of the staircase.

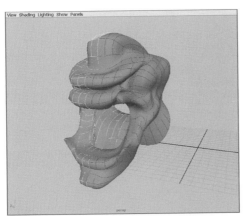

Figure 5.36 You can create half a face and mirror it to complete the rest of the face.

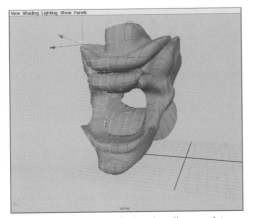

Figure 5.37 Instancing and mirroring allows updates of both sides of the face with one movement.

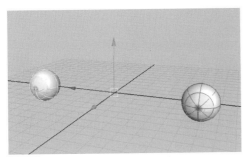

Figure 5.38 Body parts are ideal for mirroring because they have identical counterparts. The pivot point's placement in the scene determines how far apart the mirrored objects end up.

Mirroring an object produces a precise reverse copy of the object. This technique is great for creating one side of a face and then mirroring it across an axis to complete the whole face (**Figure 5.36**). Often, this command is used in conjunction with instancing, allowing continued manipulation of the one side but updating both (**Figure 5.37**). We will look at instancing directly after this task. Although using one half to complete a whole is an important use of mirroring, so is mirroring an object an equal distance away from the pivot point to create a mirrored version of the object a specified distance away. In this example we will mirror a sphere across an axis as if to create two eyes (**Figure 5.38**).

To mirror an object:

1. From the Create menu select NURBS Primitives > Sphere, or select an object to mirror.

2. Type –2 in the Translate X field in the Channel Box (**Figure 5.39**).

   This moves the object 2 units down the negative *x*-axis.

3. Press w or click the Move tool icon ⬚ in the toolbar.

4. Press Insert/Home on the keyboard to go into pivot-point edit mode.

5. Holding down x, move the pivot point to the origin (**Figure 5.40**).

   x snaps to the grid, which ensures that the pivot point is precisely at the origin.

6. Press Insert/Home on the keyboard to get out of pivot-point edit mode.

7. From the Edit menu select the box beside Duplicate.

   This opens the Duplicate Options window.

8. Select Edit > Reset Settings in the Duplicate Options window to reset the settings, then set the Scale X field to –1.

9. Select Duplicate.

   A mirrored copy is duplicated an equal distance away from the pivot point (**Figure 5.41**).

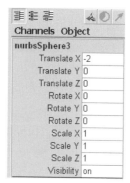

Figure 5.39 Type –2 in the Translate X field of the Channel Box to move the object 2 units in the negative *x* direction.

Figure 5.40 Move the pivot point to the origin to send the copy an equal distance away from the origin.

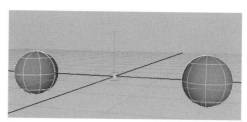

Figure 5.41 A mirrored copy is duplicated an equal distance away from the pivot point.

Figure 5.42 Oil drums are instanced to cut down on the amount of edits to be made. The objects are rotated to hide their similar attributes.

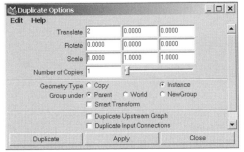

Figure 5.43 Set the Translate X field (the field on the left) to 2.

Figure 5.44 Copy simply duplicates the object, but Instance makes an additional connection to the original object.

Instancing is a great way to save time, both in modeling and in rendering. An instanced object will follow the edits of the original, making instancing ideal for any object that will have identical copies anywhere else in the scene (**Figure 5.42**). You can still scale, rotate and move the objects independently once they're instanced.

To make an instance of an object:

1. Select an object by clicking it.

2. From the Edit menu select the box next to Duplicate.

   This opens the Duplicate Options window.

3. Set the Translate X field to 2 and all the rest of the Translate and Rotate fields to zero (**Figure 5.43**).

   We add a translate here so the copy does not sit directly on top of the original.

4. For the Geometry Type, select Instance (**Figure 5.44**).

5. Select Duplicate.

   The duplicate is now an instance or "virtual copy" of the original.

6. With one of the objects selected, press [F8] to go into component-selection mode.

continues on next page

DUPLICATION OPTIONS

7. Marquee-select across the top third of the object to select one of its components (**Figure 5.45**).

8. Press ⟨w⟩, and translate the components in any direction.

Notice that the other object follows the translation of the selected surface (**Figure 5.46**).

✔ Tip

■ Once you have instanced an object, you will never be able to modify its components independently.

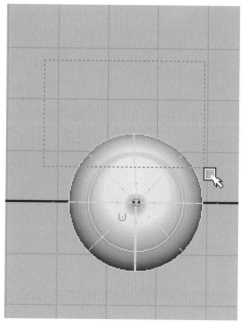

Figure 5.45 Marquee-select across the top third of the object to select CVs to manipulate.

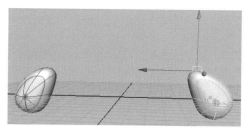

Figure 5.46 The other object follows the translation of the selected surface but reacts in the opposite motion, similarly to objects in a mirror.

DUPLICATION OPTIONS

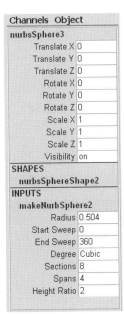

Figure 5.47 A primitive sphere's Inputs node holds the editable history of the sphere.

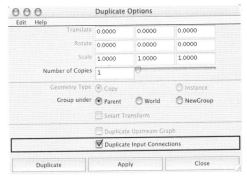

Figure 5.48 Select the Duplicate Input Connections check box in the Duplicate Options window to copy the input connections to the new object.

Figure 5.49 Enter the amount of duplicates desired in the Number of Copies field.

Often you want to keep the history attached to an object when creating a copy of it. You can do this by selecting the Duplicate Input Connections check box in the Duplicate Options window. The objects will then share the same input node, and both the original and the duplicates will be changed by it.

To duplicate an object with its input connections:

1. Select an object that has input connections attached to it—a primitive sphere, for example (**Figure 5.47**).

2. From the Edit menu select the box next to Duplicate.
   This opens the Duplicate Options window.

3. Check the box next to Duplicate Input Connections (**Figure 5.48**).
   This connects the duplicated object to the input node of the original. So if you make a change to the input node of one of them, it will change it on all duplicates.

4. Type the number of duplicates you want to produce in the Number of Copies field (**Figure 5.49**).

continues on next page

DUPLICATION OPTIONS

5. Click Duplicate.

A copy of the object is made, and its connections are attached to it (**Figure 5.50**). The new object sits directly on top of the original.

6. Select the Move tool, and move the duplicated object away from the original.

7. In the Channel Box select the End Sweep attribute name, and middle mouse button-drag in the view pane to confirm the connections made.

The End Sweep is changed on both objects interactively.

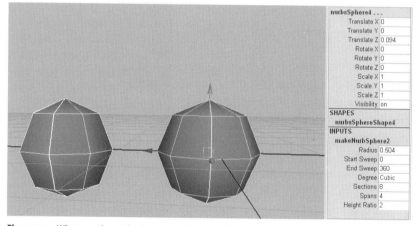

Figure 5.50 When you keep the Inputs node on duplicated objects, the opportunity to make individual changes to the surfaces remains.

DUPLICATION OPTIONS

GROUPING, PARENTING, AND ALIGNING

6

Grouping, parenting, and aligning help organize and control an object's relationship to other objects. If you are looking to move many objects around the scene at the same time, then you might want to group the objects together so they will move as one unit, requiring only one selection instead of multiple selections.

Grouping has what you might call a distant cousin, named parenting. Parenting and grouping perform a similar action on the objects that can be hard for new users to differentiate. In short, the difference is that the parented surfaces (**Figure 6.1**) have a relationship where one will follow the other (**Figure 6.2**); in a grouped relationship the objects can act independently or as one entity. We will be exploring and explaining the differences throughout this chapter.

Aligning objects and surfaces can be a difficult task if you are trying to align objects by sight only. Maya has a few tools to help align surfaces, curves, and objects with each other.

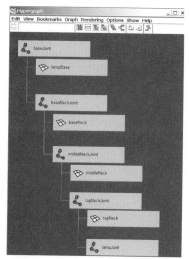

Figure 6.1 Multiple parented surfaces are shown in the Hypergraph.

Figure 6.2 When a parent joint is moved, all of the children move along with it.

GROUPING, PARENTING, AND ALIGNING

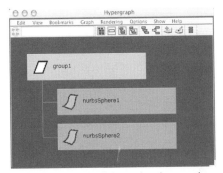

Figure 6.3 The top node is used to change values of the entire group without changing the current values of the individual objects.

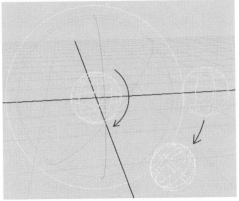

Figure 6.4 Rotating the group node rotates all of the surfaces in the group at the same time around one pivot point.

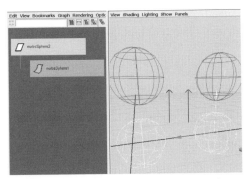

Figure 6.5 The sphere on the left is parented to the sphere on the right. So the sphere on the left moves when the sphere on the right is moved.

Grouping vs. Parenting

Grouping two or more objects together connects them with an additional node (**Figure 6.3**) to be used when you want to perform an action to both, such as moving them at the same time. Even though they are grouped, you can still select one of the objects and move or perform an action on it without affecting the other objects in the group. You can also select the group node and affect the grouped objects as if they were just one object (**Figure 6.4**).

Parented objects react slightly differently from objects that are grouped. Parented objects have a child-and-parent relationship. When the child is holding a parent's hand in real life, the child must follow the parent wherever he or she goes, at least in theory. The same is true in 3D—an object that is parented to another object has to follow the other object around (**Figure 6.5**). When you parent one object to another, no extra node is created. Maya knows which you want to be the parent and which you want to be the child by the order in which you select them.

To group two or more objects together:

1. Select two or more surfaces by dragging a box around them with the Arrow tool (**Figure 6.6**), or [Shift]-click to select multiple objects.

2. From the Edit menu select Group (**Figure 6.7**).

   The objects are grouped together with an additional node.

3. From the Window menu select Hypergraph.

   The Hypergraph opens in a new window.

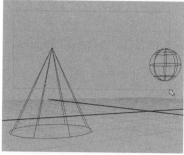

Figure 6.6 You can drag a marquee to select multiple surfaces. The marquee only needs to touch any part of the surface.

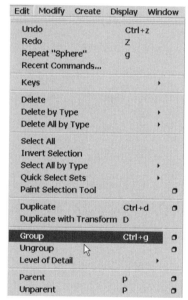

Figure 6.7 Select Edit > Group to group objects together.

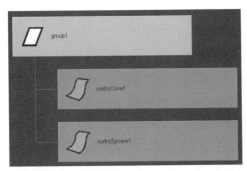

Figure 6.8 The node at the top is an extra node created when a group is made. This node can be used to control all the nodes below it.

Figure 6.9 The group node's default name is group#, with # being the number of groups created so far.

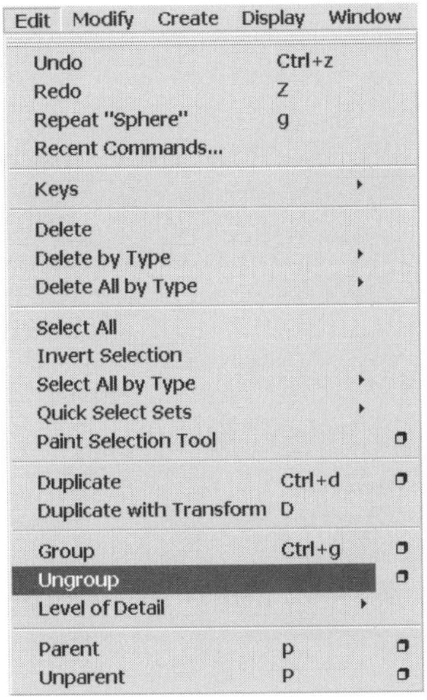

Figure 6.10 Select Edit > Ungroup to pull objects out of the group.

4. Press f to zoom the Hypergraph to the selection.

There is now one more node than the number of objects. This node is the group node, named group# (**Figure 6.8**).

✔ Tip

■ You can select the group node to move all the grouped objects at the same time, or you can select a surface's node to move it separately from the group.

To ungroup an object:

1. Select the group node in the Hypergraph (**Figure 6.9**).

2. From the Edit menu select Ungroup (**Figure 6.10**).

The geometry is no longer grouped, and the group node is deleted.

Once objects are grouped together, they can be translated, rotated, or scaled as if they were one object. One of the reasons Maya creates an extra group node is so you have an additional pivot point to use as the center point of rotating or scaling around. When an object is grouped, the pivot point of the group node is placed at the origin. The pivot point can then be moved anywhere in the scene to determine its rotation and scale center point.

To translate, rotate, or scale a group:

1. Select the group node in the Hypergraph, or click one of the grouped objects with the Pick mask set to hierarchy mode ![icon] to select the group node.

2. Select the Rotate, Scale, or Move tool in the toolbar, or use their respective hotkeys.

3. Press Insert/Home to go into pivot-point edit mode.

4. Move the pivot point to where you want the group to rotate around or scale from (**Figure 6.11**).

   It is not necessary to complete this step if you are just translating the object.

5. Press Insert/Home to get out of pivot-point edit mode.

6. Translate, rotate, or scale the group by selecting a manipulator's (**Figure 6.12**) axis and middle mouse button-dragging left or right in the pane to change the axes' value.

✔ Tip

■ You can move the pivot point to the center of the group by selecting Modify > Center Pivot (**Figure 6.13**).

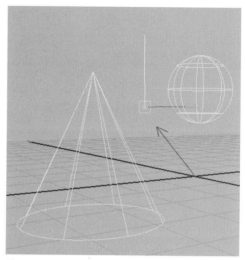

Figure 6.11 The group node's pivot point is used as the center point for the entire group.

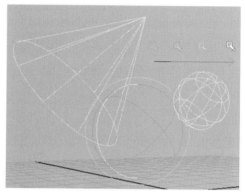

Figure 6.12 You translate, rotate, or scale a group the same way you do an individual object.

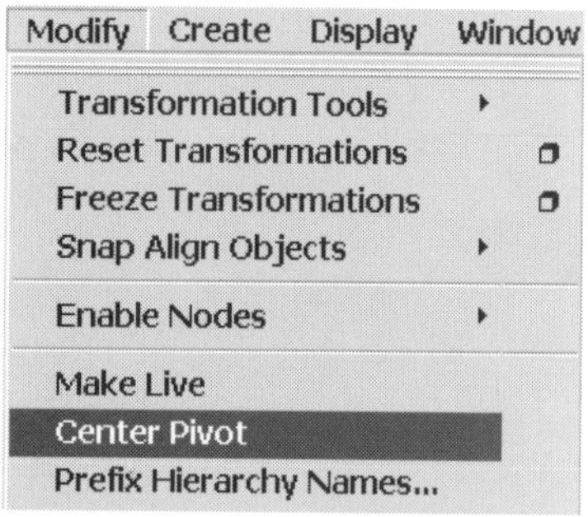

Figure 6.13 The Modify > Center Pivot command is a useful tool when you want to quickly center the pivot of a group.

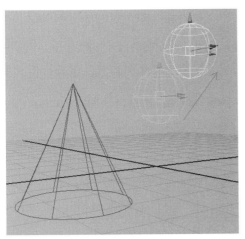

Figure 6.14 Grouped objects can still be edited individually by selecting just that object and not the group node.

To move one object within a group:

1. Select the object you want to move with the Pick mask set to object-type mode.

2. Select the Move tool icon from the toolbox, or press w.

3. Translate the object by selecting any axis of the Move tool's manipulator, and middle mouse button-dragging left or right in the pane to change its value.

   The selected object moves, but the rest of the group does not (**Figure 6.14**).

✔ Tips

■ You can use these same steps to rotate or scale an object within a group without affecting the rest of the group.

■ Once you have a member of a group selected, press ↑ to move up the hierarchy, and select the group node.

GROUPING VS. PARENTING

A solid parenting example is a biped skeleton. We will use an arm as an example here. Your arm starts at your shoulder blade and continues down, connecting your shoulder to your upper arm to your lower arm to your wrist to your palm to your fingers. There is a relationship created that forces the fingers to follow the rest of the arm. This relationship is called a parent/child relationship. In this case, the parent is the upper arm and its child is the lower arm. The lower arm is the parent of the wrist, which is the child of the lower arm and parent of the palm. Whenever the upper arm is moved, all the children under it move, creating the whole arm movement (**Figure 6.15**).

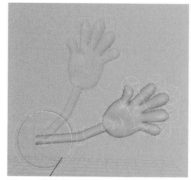

Figure 6.15 The fingers are children of the palm, and the palm is a child of the lower arm. When the lower arm is rotated, all the joints and surfaces below the parent joint follow.

The entire relationship of the parts of the skeleton is called a *hierarchy* (**Figure 6.16**). A hierarchy determines which objects control other objects. The order of the hierarchy is important to both selecting and translating.

When parenting two objects together, the order in which you select objects is very important. The second object selected becomes a parent of the first object selected. After being parented, the child will follow the parent's translations.

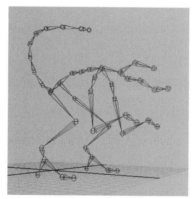

Figure 6.16 An entire hierarchy is formed through parenting one bone to another until they are all connected.

To parent two objects together:

1. Select the object you want to become the child by clicking it.

2. Select the object you want to become the parent by (Shift)-clicking it (**Figure 6.17**).

3. From the Edit menu select Parent, or press (p).

   The second selected object becomes a parent of the first object (**Figure 6.18**).

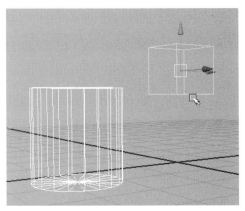

Figure 6.17 Shift-click additional objects to add them to the selection.

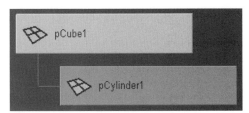

Figure 6.18 The cube is the parent of the cylinder. This is shown in the Hypergraph by a connecting line.

✔ Tips

■ Because no additional node is added when objects are parented, the pivot point of the parent is used as the center point of the topmost node in the hierarchy.

■ If more than two objects are selected, all selected objects become children of the last object selected.

■ You can parent one object to another by middle mouse button-dragging the child onto the parent in the Hypergraph and the Outliner.

To unparent objects:

1. Select each of the children you want to unparent by clicking the first and Shift-clicking additional children in the Hypergraph or with the Pick mask set to object mode.

2. From the Edit menu select Unparent to unparent the object, or press Shift-p (**Figure 6.19**).

   This pulls the object out of the hierarchy, and it now acts separately from the parented hierarchy.

✔ Tip

■ You can also middle mouse button-drag the object out of the hierarchy in the Hypergraph and the Outliner.

Edit	Modify	Create	Display	Window	
Undo			Ctrl+z		
Redo			Z		
Repeat "Poly Cube"			g		
Recent Commands...					
Keys				▶	
Delete					
Delete by Type				▶	
Delete All by Type				▶	
Select All					
Invert Selection					
Select All by Type				▶	
Quick Select Sets				▶	
Paint Selection Tool					□
Duplicate			Ctrl+d		□
Duplicate with Transform			D		
Group			Ctrl+g		□
Ungroup					□
Level of Detail				▶	
Parent			p		□
Unparent			P		□

Figure 6.19 Select Edit > Unparent to separate two or more parented surfaces.

About Aligning Objects

Curves and surfaces can be aligned with other curves and surfaces. This is useful for positioning and attaching surfaces side by side.

To align two curves by their positions:

1. Draw two curves to be used for alignment (**Figure 6.20**), or open a file that has two curves.

2. Select a curve point on the first curve you want to align by right mouse-clicking it and selecting Curve Point from the Marking Menu, then click a point on the curve (**Figure 6.21**).

3. Select a point on the second curve you want to align by right mouse–clicking the curve and selecting Curve Point from the Marking Menu, then [Shift]-click a point on the curve (**Figure 6.22**).

4. From the Edit Curves menu select the box next to Align Curves.

   The Align Curves Options dialog box opens.

5. In the Align Curves Options dialog box, set the Continuity to Position, and Modify Position to First (**Figure 6.23**).

   Position continuity aligns the first Control Vertex (CV) of the first curve to the selected point of the second curve. Modify Position set to First moves the entire first curve into alignment with the second curve.

6. Press Align to align the two curves.

   The entire curve selected first moves into alignment with the second curve.

✔ Tips

■ You can align the entire second selected curve with the first by selecting Second for Modify Position.

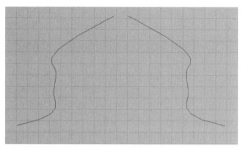
Figure 6.20 Two curves ready for alignment.

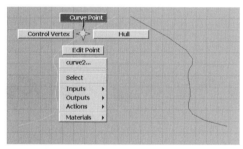
Figure 6.21 Right mouse-clicking a curve pulls up its Marking Menu that allows you to select the chosen component.

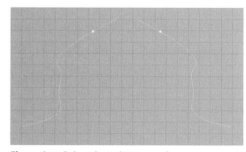
Figure 6.22 Select the points on each curve you want to align with.

■ You can have both curves move to meet at their center points by selecting Both for Modify Position.

ABOUT ALIGNING OBJECTS

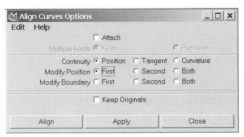

Figure 6.23 The Position setting will keep the original shape of the curves.

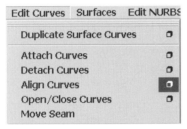

Figure 6.24 Select the box next to Align Curves in the Edit Curves menu to open the Align Curves Options dialog box.

Figure 6.25 This is the Align Curves Options window. It is currently set to Tangent, which creates a smooth connection between curves.

Tangent is a good setting when you are concerned about keeping the shape of the original curves but also want to have a smooth connection (tangent).

To align two curves by tangent continuity:

1. Draw two curves to be used for alignment, or open a file that has two curves.

2. Select a curve point on the first curve you want to align by right mouse-clicking it and selecting Curve Point from the Marking Menu, then click a point on the curve.

3. Select a curve point on the second curve you want to align by right mouse-clicking the curve and selecting Curve Point from the Marking Menu, and then (Shift)-click a point on the curve.

4. From the Edit Curves menu select the box next to Align Curves (**Figure 6.24**). The Align Curves Options dialog box opens.

5. In the Align Curves Options dialog box, set the Continuity to Tangent, and Modify Position to Second (**Figure 6.25**).

   Tangent continuity aligns the first CVs of the curves. Modify Position set to Second moves the position of the second curve to align with the first.

6. Click Align to align the two curves.

   The entire curve selected second moves over to align with the first curve.

✔ Tip

- You can have both curves move to meet at their center points by selecting Both for Modify Position.

About Aligning Objects

The curvature setting will make the smoothest connection between the two start CVs and end CVs but will alter the original surface shapes the most.

To align two curves by curvature continuity:

1. Draw two curves to be used for alignment, or open a file that has two curves.

2. Select a Curve Point on the first curve you want to align by right mouse-clicking it and selecting Curve Point from the Marking Menu (**Figure 6.26**).

3. Select a Curve Point on the second curve you want to align by right mouse-clicking the curve and selecting Curve Point from the Marking Menu, and then Shift-click a point on the curve (**Figure 6.27**).

4. From the Edit Curves menu select the box next to Align Curves.

   The Align Curves Options dialog box opens.

5. In the Align Curves Options dialog box set the Continuity to Curvature, Modify Position to Both, and Modify Tangent to Second (**Figure 6.28**).

   Curvature continuity aligns the third CVs of the curves. This will give you the smoothest connection between the two curves. Modify Position set to Both moves the positions of both curves to meet at the middle point between both curves. Modify Tangent set to Second adjusts the tangent of the second curve into alignment with the first. The second curve changes the most.

6. Press Align to align the two curves.

   Both entire curves selected are moved.

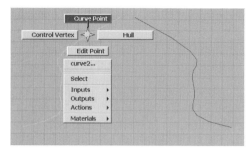

Figure 6.26 Select Curve Point from the Marking Menu to prepare the curve for point selection.

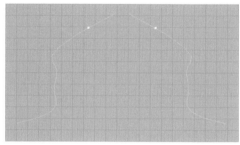

Figure 6.27 Shift-select a point on each curve to align the curves with.

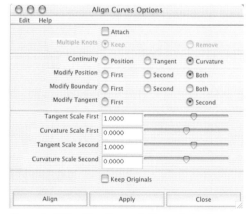

Figure 6.28 The Align Curves Options window is now set to Curvature continuity, which maintains a very smooth connection between curves.

ABOUT ALIGNING OBJECTS

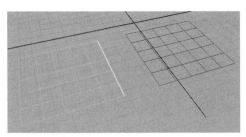

Figure 6.29 The rightmost isoparm on the left surface is selected for alignment of these two surfaces.

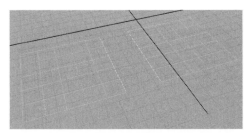

Figure 6.30 The rightmost isoparm on the left surface and the leftmost isoparm on the right surface are selected for alignment of these two surfaces.

The Align Surfaces and Align Curves options react the same. The only difference is that the alignment is done to the selected isoparm and its points instead of just to a selected point as in curve alignment. See the "Common Align Curves and Align Surfaces Options" section below for specific descriptions. For best results, use the Edit NURBS > Align Surfaces options to align two surface end isoparms or trimmed edges. These alignment options deal with the way the two surfaces connect, not their positions relative to each other. If you are aligning two surfaces, such as two spheres, with each other, most of the time you will get better results using snaps to align them (see Chapter 5). Good candidates for the Align Surfaces options are open-ended surfaces, lofted surfaces, and planar surfaces.

To align two surface edges:

1. Select an isoparm on the first surface (**Figure 6.29**).

2. Shift-select an isoparm on the other surface (**Figure 6.30**).

3. Select Edit NURBS > Align Surfaces to align the surfaces.

   The two surface's boundaries meet.

Common align curves and align surfaces options

Below is a list of common options for aligning curves and surfaces with other curves and surfaces (**Figure 6.31**).

◆ **Attach**—Combines the aligned curves or surfaces into one curve or surface after aligning.

◆ **Multiple Knots**—Knots are the edit points on each curve or surface. When two curves or surface edges are combined, the new curve or surface often has two knots close to, if not directly on top of, each other. If this option is set to Remove, the second set of knots is removed. Sometimes this changes the look of the final surface.

◆ **Position**—Aligns the first CVs of two curves or the ends of two surfaces, making them meet on top of each other. With Position continuity, the connection point of the two curves stays in its original alignment with the rest of the curve, keeping the original slope of each curve (**Figure 6.32**).

◆ **Tangent**—Aligns the second CVs of two curves or second row of CVs on two surfaces to achieve tangent continuity, causing the curves or surfaces to be placed end to end (**Figure 6.33**).

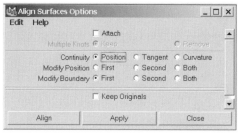

Figure 6.31 The Align Surfaces Options dialog box holds the same options as the Align Curves Options dialog box.

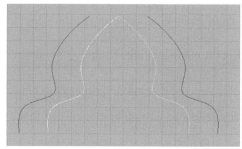

Figure 6.32 The two outside curves were aligned using positional continuity resulting in the inside curve. Note that they meet at a point, the shape of the curves is not changed.

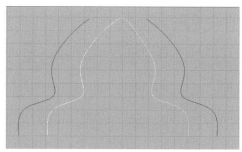

Figure 6.33 With Tangent continuity the connection point of the two curves becomes smoother. Compare this point to that in Figure 6.32.

ABOUT ALIGNING OBJECTS

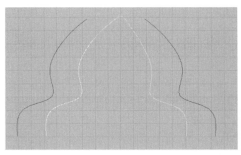

Figure 6.34 Continuity set to Curvature connects the two start CVs of the two curves to be very smooth but alters the shape of the original curves.

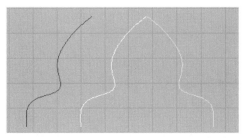

Figure 6.35 Modify Position set to First moves the first curve selected over to align with the second curve.

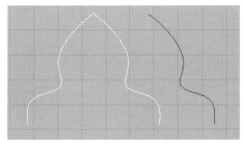

Figure 6.36 Modify Position set to Second moves the second curve selected over to align with the first curve.

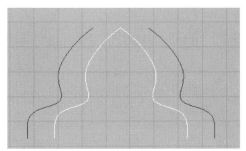

Figure 6.37 Modify Position set to Both moves both curves over to meet at the center point between them.

◆ **Curvature**—Aligns the third CVs of the curves or surfaces to achieve curvature continuity, causing the points to meet with the same arch in curvature. This aligns the surfaces with the smoothest or slowest arcs at the curve or surface connections (**Figure 6.34**).

◆ **Modify Position**—Each of the position settings moves the entire curve or surface around.

▼ **First**—Moves the entire first selected curve or surface over to the second (**Figure 6.35**).

▼ **Second**—Moves the entire second selected curve or surface over to the first (**Figure 6.36**).

▼ **Both**—Moves the entire first and second curves or surfaces, meeting at the point halfway between them (**Figure 6.37**).

ABOUT ALIGNING OBJECTS

- **Modify Boundary**—Each of the boundary settings moves selected points around.

  - ▼ **First**—Moves the first selected point of one curve over to the second (**Figure 6.38**).
  - ▼ **Second**—Moves the second selected point of one curve over to the first (**Figure 6.39**).
  - ▼ **Both**—Moves both of the selected points to a point halfway between the two curves or surfaces (**Figure 6.40**).

- **Modify Tangent**—Each of the tangent settings modifies the tangents of the curves. In general, a tangent is a line or vector that is used to determine the slope of a curve at a given point. When we are determining tangency, we are usually referring to the smoothness of the slope at which points on a curve or multiple curves meet. Modify Tangent uses the first and second points on a line to align the curves together to make the connections of the end points smooth.

  - ▼ **First**—Moves the first curve's or surface's tangent into alignment with the second curve or surface.
  - ▼ **Second**—Moves the second curve's or surface's tangent into alignment with the first curve or surface.
  - ▼ **Keep Originals**—This option allows you to keep the old curves or surfaces and produce an additional curve or surface that shows the new alignment.

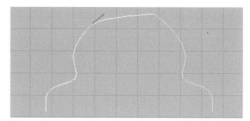

Figure 6.38 Boundary set to First makes the start CV of the first curve move over to the start CV of the second curve.

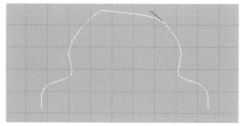

Figure 6.39 Boundary set to Second makes the start CV of the second curve move over to the start CV of the first curve.

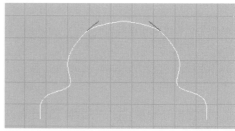

Figure 6.40 Boundary set to Both makes the start CVs of each curve meet at their centers.

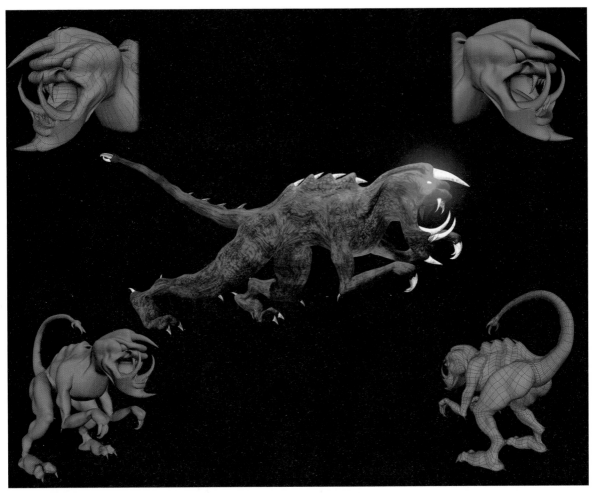

NURBS Creature   by Danny Riddell (www.riddelldesign.com, www.upaxis.com)

Alley by Danny Riddell (www.riddelldesign.com, www.upaxis.com)

Dark Warehouse by Danny Riddell (www.riddelldesign.com, www.upaxis.com)

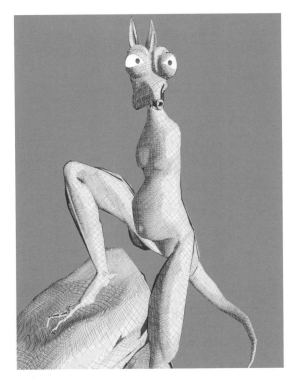

Crosshatch Creature
by Andrew S. Britt

Shark by Danny Riddell (www.riddelldesign.com, www.upaxis.com)

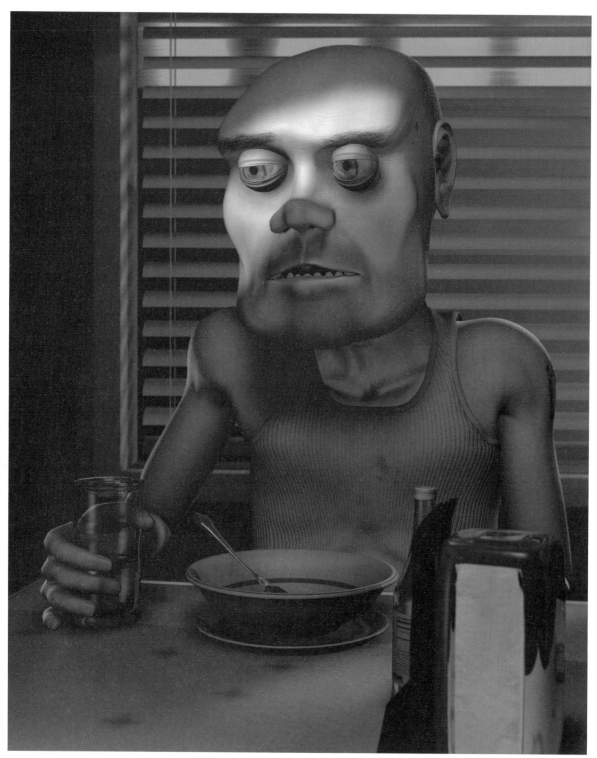

Man at Table by Howard Campbell (www.expression.edu/~hcampbell)

NURBS Curves
and Surfaces

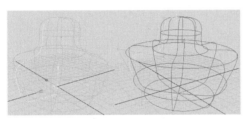

Figure 7.1 Creating NURBS curves in Maya is similar to using a Bézier tool in a graphics application.

NURBS curves and surfaces can be used to create nearly any object—a medieval knight, a detailed car, an alien, or any object you can imagine. NURBS surfaces can be highly organic, characterized by sinuous, rounded shapes. This makes them great for creating trees, faces, or streamlined vehicles.

NURBS curve creation should come quite naturally to anyone who has used other software programs with Bézier curves, like Adobe Illustrator. Although NURBS curves are different than Bézier curves, they are created and edited similarly. NURBS curves can be used to outline surfaces, which speeds object creation, and they can also be helpful editing tools after a surface has been created (**Figure 7.1**).

About NURBS Objects

NURBS object creation is one of Maya's strengths because of the precise control the user has over the final surface. There are two types of NURBS objects: *curves* and *surfaces*.

NURBS curves have three main components: *CVs (control vertices)*, *edit points*, and *hulls* (**Figure 7.2**). These components are used to create and edit curves in different ways. As you create NURBS curves, you will probably come to prefer a certain component and use that editing method more than others.

NURBS surfaces have the same components as curves but with the addition of *surface normals*, *patch centers*, and *surface origins* (**Figure 7.3**). You can edit a NURBS surface at any time by editing components of the original curve used to create the surface, or by editing the surface's components directly.

Each NURBS component can be shown and edited individually (**Figure 7.4**), or with other components (**Figure 7.5**). NURBS curves are an important part of NURBS modeling because they help you create and edit surfaces. This chapter will give you the foundation needed to control the look of NURBS curves and surfaces.

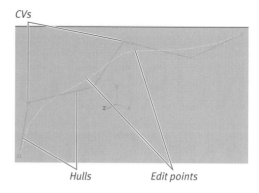

CVs

Hulls   *Edit points*

Figure 7.2 NURBS components are used to easily and quickly change the look of the curve or surface.

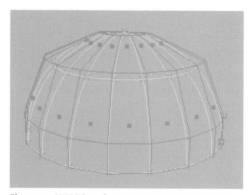

Figure 7.3 NURBS surface components are used to manipulate the look and feel of the surface.

Figure 7.4 Surface edit points can be shown by themselves to make selection and editing easier. You can select each component by clicking its icon, in this case a small *x*.

Figure 7.5 Maya allows you to show or hide as many components as you want to view at any given time; this helps you narrow down your selection while still getting a good idea of what the object's other components look like.

ABOUT NURBS OBJECTS

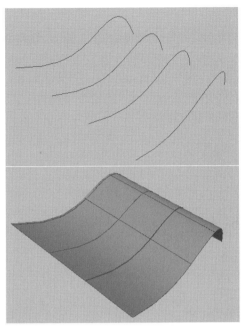

Figure 7.6 Curves used to create a framework for the surface (top), and the same curves with a surface laid over them (bottom).

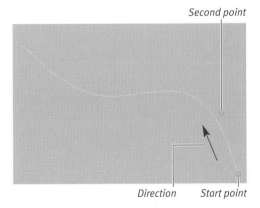

Second point

Direction   Start point

Figure 7.7 The U direction of a curve is determined by the first and second CVs created.

Creating NURBS Curves

Learning curve creation and editing can help any Maya user to take full advantage of the Maya modeling tools. NURBS curves allow excellent control over their shape and placement by providing multiple points to use for editing.

Curves are often used to create a wire representation of a surface, and then a skin can be added over the curves to make the final surface (**Figure 7.6**). You can create this final surface using a number of Maya commands, such as lofting, extruding, and revolving. We will be looking at each of these methods throughout this chapter.

Anatomy of a curve

Each NURBS curve has a direction associated with it, derived from the order in which the CVs were created. A curve's direction becomes important in determining the look of the final surface. If you are not paying attention to the direction in which a curve is created, you will often get undesirable results when you go to create the final surface. Curves created in opposite directions can twist and fold the final surface.

The direction of a curve is determined by the first and second CVs created for the curve. The first CV is called the *start point* and is represented by a small square. The second CV is represented by the letter *U*. The start point followed by the U shows the user the direction in which the curve is headed; this determines the U direction of any surface created from the curve (**Figure 7.7**).

continues on next page

Each curve has the following components (**Figure 7.8**):

Control vertices (CVs)—CVs are points that are placed slightly away from the curve and are the components most used to edit a curve's shape.

Edit points (knots)—Edit points are points directly on the curve, represented by a small *x*. Edit points are another way to edit a curve's shape.

Hulls—Hulls are straight lines connecting each CV. Showing the hulls can help clarify which row of CVs each CV is connected to. By clicking on a hull you select the entire row of CVs along the hull.

Spans—A span is the area between two edit points. Each time an edit point is added, a span is added. Spans are not directly edited like edit points but are more a result of the edit. Spans are used for creating and rebuilding curves and surfaces.

Curve point—A curve point is an arbitrary point on a curve often used as a point to detach or align a curve with. A curve point can be anywhere along a curve.

Start of curve—The start of a curve is the first CV created for the curve and is represented by a small square.

Curve direction—The direction of a curve is determined by the first and second CVs created for the curve.

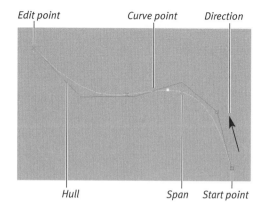

Figure 7.8 This image shows all of the NURBS curve components at once.

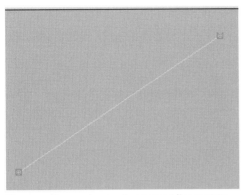

Figure 7.9 A curve degree of 1 creates a linear curve, and a linear surface if a surface is created from the curve.

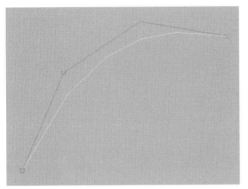

Figure 7.10 A curve degree of 3 produces a smooth curve without using an excessive number of CVs.

Figure 7.11 This is a 7 degree curve and therefore requires 8 CVs to be created.

Creating curves of various degrees

Every curve has a certain degree; the higher the degree, the smoother the curve. A curve can have a degree of 1, 2, 3, 5, or 7. A curve with a degree of 1 is a linear curve and only requires two points to define it (**Figure 7.9**). Linear curves and surfaces are characterized by straight lines and sharp corners. A curve degree of 3 will produce a smooth curve without using an excessive number of CVs to describe the curve (**Figure 7.10**). A curve with a degree of 3 is the most common and versatile curve. Because of the accuracy needed for manufacturing, car designers often use degrees higher than 5. Usually a degree of 3 is high enough for animation.

Each curve requires one additional CV to create it. For example, a curve with a degree of 3 requires four CVs before the curve is created (**Figure 7.10**), and a 7th-degree curve requires eight CVs before the curve is created (**Figure 7.11**). It is for this reason that a degree of 3 or 5 is usually most ideal.

Creating profile curves

You can create many objects by drawing an outline curve in the shape of the object's profile. This profile curve can then be revolved to complete the full surface (**Figure 7.12**). The profile curve can be altered to tweak the object's shape after the final surface is created (**Figure 7.13**).

If you are drawing a profile curve for a vase, glass, pot, or any object that has thickness to it, you should draw the profile of the inside as well as of the outside (**Figure 7.14**). If you do not draw the inside and outside profiles your object will be paper-thin—real objects have some thickness. The thickness of the glass is defined by the profile curve.

Figure 7.12 This surface was created with one revolved curve.

Figure 7.13 By tweaking a point of the curve— which is how this revolved surface was created—you can interactively sculpt the object.

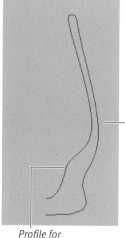

Profile for outside of vase

Figure 7.14 When drawing a profile curve, make sure you add the inside of the surface to add thickness to the final object.

Profile for inside of vase

CREATING NURBS CURVES

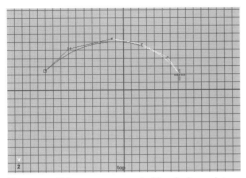

Figure 7.15 This curve was created by placing points using the CV Curve tool.

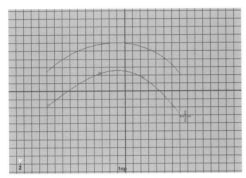

Figure 7.16 This curve was created using the EP Curve tool.

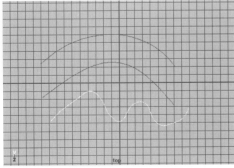

Figure 7.17 The bottom curve was created using the Pencil Curve tool.

There are three typical ways to create a curve. You can use the CV Curve tool, the EP Curve tool, or the Pencil Curve tool.

To create a curve with the CV Curve Tool:

1. From the Create menu select CV Curve Tool.

2. In the top view, click in several places.
   A CV will appear with each click, and a curve will appear on the fourth click (**Figure 7.15**).

3. Press ⌊Enter⌋ to complete the creation of the curve.
   The curve becomes highlighted because it is selected.

To create a curve with the EP Curve Tool:

1. From the Create menu select EP Curve Tool.

2. In the top view, click in several places.
   A curve is created once the second edit point is placed, and it continues to take shape with each subsequent point (**Figure 7.16**).

3. Press ⌊Enter⌋ to complete the creation of the curve.

To create a curve with the Pencil Curve Tool:

1. From the Create menu select Pencil Curve Tool.

2. Click and drag in the top view to draw a line.
   The curve is completed once you release the mouse. The Pencil Curve tool tends to be a less efficient way to create a curve because you end up with more points then necessary to describe the shape (**Figure 7.17**).

As stated earlier, each curve has a direction, called the U direction. Sometimes you will want to reverse a curve's direction because you are getting undesirable surfaces from the curves (**Figure 7.18**).

To reverse a curve's direction:

1. Select a curve in object mode.

2. From the Edit Curves menu select Reverse Curve Direction (**Figure 7.19**).

3. Press F8 to view the new curve direction in component mode (**Figure 7.20**).

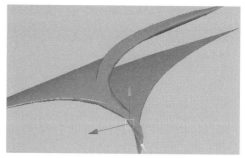

Figure 7.18 Curve direction can cause unwanted surface problems. It is best to keep all curves of the same surface facing in the same direction.

Figure 7.19 Select Edit Curves > Reverse Curve Direction to change the direction of a curve.

Figure 7.20 The curve on top shows the direction before it was reversed; the curve below shows the direction after it was reversed.

CREATING NURBS CURVES

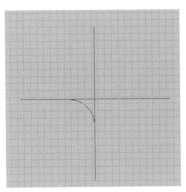

Figure 7.21 A 2D fillet is a good tool for adding smooth corners to a set of curves.

Figure 7.22 Two curves are intersecting.

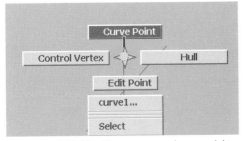

Figure 7.23 A Marking Menu appears when you right mouse button-click the curve. This is a convenient way to choose which component type you'd like to be able to select.

Circular 2D fillets

A *fillet* is a concave junction where two curves or surfaces meet. You can create 2D fillets to combine multiple curves with an arc between them. Sometimes it is easier to create two curves and fillet them together to create a corner than it is to draw out one curve with the corner in it. An example might be when you need to create a corner out of two perpendicular curves (**Figure 7.21**).

To create a circular 2D fillet:

1. Create two curves to fillet between (**Figure 7.22**).

2. Right mouse button–click the first curve, and select Curve Point from the Marking Menu (**Figure 7.23**).

continues on next page

CREATING NURBS CURVES

3. Click the first curve, and drag the point to where you want the fillet to arc (**Figure 7.24**).

4. Right mouse button–click the second curve, and select Curve Point from the Marking Menu.

5. Shift-click the second curve, and drag the point to where you want the fillet to arc (**Figure 7.25**).

6. From the Edit Curves menu select Curve Fillet.

An arc is created between the two curve points (**Figure 7.26**).

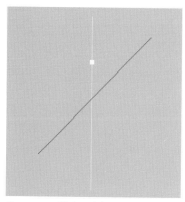

Figure 7.24 Click and drag a curve point into the place where you would like the arc to begin.

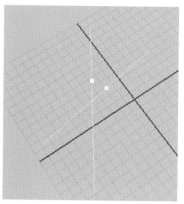

Figure 7.25 The two curve points determine the start and end points of the arc.

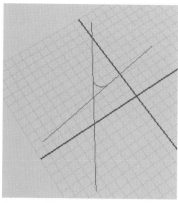

Figure 7.26 An arc is created between the two curve points selected on each curve.

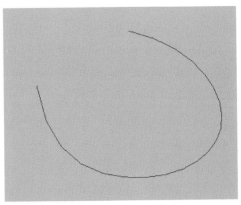

Figure 7.27 An incomplete circle is called an open curve.

Opening and closing curves

A curve that does not start and end on the same point is called an open curve (**Figure 7.27**). Many Maya commands will not function correctly on open curves, so the curves must be closed. A closed curve has the same start and end point, making it continuous (**Figure 7.28**).

To open or close a curve:

◆ From the Edit Curves menu select Open/Close Curves (**Figure 7.29**).

An open curve will become closed and a closed curve will become open.

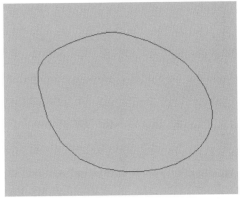

Figure 7.28 A closed curve has the same start and end point.

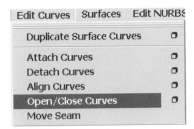

Figure 7.29 The Open/Close Curves command opens a closed curve and closes an open curve.

To detach a curve:

1. Select a curve with the Pick mask set to Component: Parm Points mode .

2. Select the edit point *x* where you would like to detach the curve (**Figure 7.30**).

3. From the Edit Curves menu select Detach Curves.

   The curve is now broken into two curves (**Figure 7.31**).

✔ Tip

- If Keep Originals is selected in the Detach Curves options dialog box, you will have three curves after detaching—the original curve and two detached curves. Deselect Keep Originals before you detach to automatically delete the original curve.

Figure 7.30 An edit point is represented by an x; when selected, it can be used as a curve's breaking point.

Figure 7.31 Two curves are created out of the detachment at the edit point.

CREATING NURBS CURVES

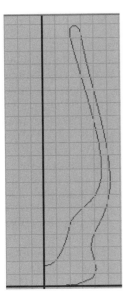

Figure 7.32 A profile curve illustrates the outline of the object used for revolving.

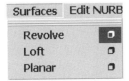

Figure 7.33 From the Surfaces menu select the box next to Revolve to open the Revolve Options window.

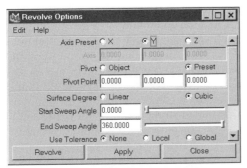

Figure 7.34 The revolve axis is very important to the look of the final surface. The axis you want to choose is the axis that goes through the middle of the final surface.

Creating Surfaces from Curves

There are several commands in Maya that let you turn curves into surfaces. They include Revolve, Loft, Planar, Extrude, Birail, and Boundary.

To revolve a curve to make a vase:

1. In the front view draw a curve for the shape of the vase's profile as in the figure (**Figure 7.32**).

2. Select the curve in object mode.

3. In the Surfaces menu select the box next to Revolve (**Figure 7.33**).
   The Revolve Options window opens.

4. Select the axis you want the object to revolve *around* (**Figure 7.34**). We will use the *y*-axis for our illustration.

continues on next page

5. Click Revolve to create the surface of the vase.

If you get unexpected results, you may have the object revolving around the wrong axis.

6. Press ③ to increase the smoothness to see the full surface (**Figure 7.35**).

✔ Tips

■ You can adjust the Start Sweep Angle and End Sweep Angle in the Revolve Options to make a revolved surface that is not a complete 360 degrees.

■ To interactively change the shape of a revolved surface by changing the angle of the axis revolution, you can use the Show Manipulator Tool.

One of the best ways to create a surface from multiple curves is to use the Loft command. The Loft command creates a surface from one selected curve to the next until each curve is covered with a surface.

To loft across multiple curves

1. Create two or more curves with which to create a surface (**Figure 7.36**).

2. Shift-select each curve in the order in which you would like the surface to loft across.

Curve selection order is important. The surface will start at the first selected curve and cover each additional curve in the order you select them.

3. With all the curves selected, choose Surfaces > Loft to create a surface over the curves (**Figure 7.37**).

✔ Tip

■ A new surface displays in rough mode and will look as if it is not fully touching the curves with which it was created. Select the surface and press ③ to view it in smooth display mode.

Figure 7.35 Increasing surface smoothness helps clarify where the actual revolved surface lies.

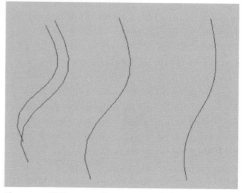

Figure 7.36 When creating curves to loft across, you must consider each curve describing the contour of the final surface.

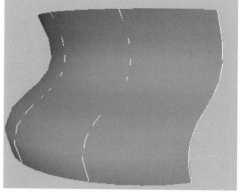

Figure 7.37 A lofted surface keeps a connection to the original curves for future editing of the surface using the original curves.

Figure 7.38 Any curve shape can be used for an extrude; if you are looking for a tube-like shape, for example, use a closed curve.

side

Figure 7.39 The second curve you create for an extrude is used for the path and length of the extruded surface.

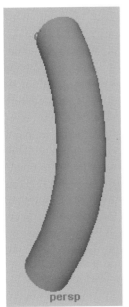

persp

Figure 7.40 A surface is created from the extrude that follows the angle of the profile curve.

The Extrude command creates a surface by sweeping one curve (the profile) along another curve (the path). The Extrude command is often used to add depth to text.

To extrude a curve:

1. Create a profile curve the shape you would like the final extrude to be. For example, if you would like to extrude a tube, you can create a circle (**Figure 7.38**).

2. Starting from the already created curve, create a CV curve the length of the final surface you want to create (**Figure 7.39**). This is referred to as the path curve.

3. Select the circle, then Shift-select the path curve.

4. From the Surfaces menu select Extrude to sweep the profile curve along the path curve.

    A new extruded surface is created (**Figure 7.40**).

✔ Tip

■ By default the new surface starts at the angle of the profile curve and mimics the angles of the curve. With this default setting the extruded surface only follows the path curve if the profile curve is perpendicular to the path curve. To ignore the angle of the profile curve and have the curve follow the path curve, select At Path in the Extrude Options window.

The Make Planar command is used to make a flat surface out of a curve. An example is the flat top of a guitar (the part with the hole in it) (**Figure 7.41**). The outline of the body of the guitar can be made with a curve, and then made planar to complete the flat surface.

To make a curve planar:

1. Create a closed curve with all the CVs on the same axis (**Figure 7.42**).

2. From the Surfaces menu select Planar. A planar surface is created from the curve (**Figure 7.43**).

✔ Tips

- The curve must be closed or self-intersecting for the Planar command to work.

- All CVs must lie exactly on the same axis for the command to work. To ensure that the CVs are all on the same axis, you can grid-snap each CV to a grid plane.

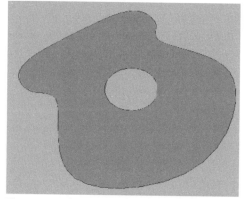

Figure 7.41 Make Planar works well for any closed, flat curve out of which you would like to make a flat surface.

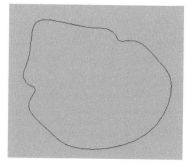

Figure 7.42 This closed curve will determine the outline of the surface. Use grid snap to be sure all of the points of the curve lie on the same plane.

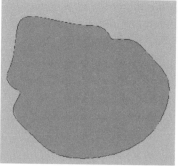

Figure 7.43 A flat surface is created, with the curve used as the border of the surface.

CREATING SURFACES FROM CURVES

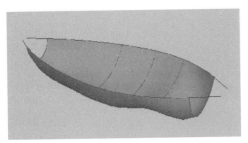

Figure 7.44 The hull of a boat can be created from a few profile curves and two rail curves.

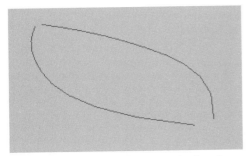

Figure 7.45 You always use two curves for the rails.

Rail curves   Profile curve

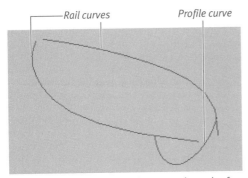

Figure 7.46 It is essential to curve-snap the ends of each profile curve to the rails or the command will not function correctly.

Figure 7.47 From the Surfaces menu select Birail > Birail 1 Tool.

The Birail tool is similar to Extrude, except that instead of having one path curve and one profile curve, it has two path curves (rails) and any number of profiles curves. The hull of a boat is a good example where two path curves can determine the outline of the hull, and profile curves can determine the depth and shape of the hull (**Figure 7.44**).

To create a birail surface:

1. Draw two curves to use for the rails of the surface (**Figure 7.45**).

2. Draw a new curve from the first curve to the second curve using curve snap (hold down C and click and drag on the rail curve) for the first and last points (**Figure 7.46**). It is essential that the curves touch each other or the operation will not work. Curve snap helps ensure that the profile curve touches both rails.

3. From the Surfaces menu select Birail > Birail 1 Tool (**Figure 7.47**).

   Use Birail 2 Tool if you have two profile curves. Use Birail 3+ if you are using three or more profile curves.

4. Click the profile curves, and then click the rail curves (**Figure 7.48**).

   The birail surface is created.

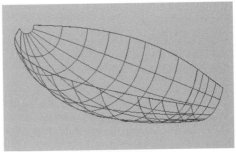

Figure 7.48 A surface is created from the three curves using Birail.

CREATING SURFACES FROM CURVES

The Boundary command requires three or four curves that intersect or meet at each other's ends. One use for a boundary surface is when you have three surfaces connecting at a corner and you want to use three of the edges to complete a rounded corner between the surfaces (**Figure 7.49**).

To create a boundary surface:

1. Draw three or four curves with intersecting ends (**Figure 7.50**). You can make sure the ends intersect by curve-snapping the first and last CVs to the other curves.

2. Select all the curves that complete the boundary (**Figure 7.51**).

3. From the Surfaces menu select Boundary. The boundary surface is created (**Figure 7.52**).

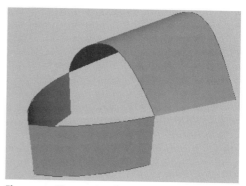

Figure 7.49 The gap that these surfaces leave between them would be a good candidate to be filled using the Boundary.

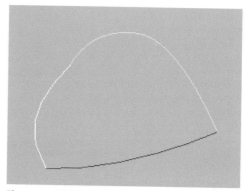

Figure 7.50 With boundary surfaces, as with birail surfaces, it is essential to curve-snap each end point.

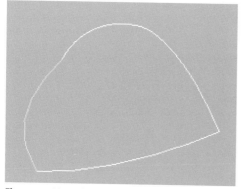

Figure 7.51 You can select curves or isoparms on which to use the Boundary command.

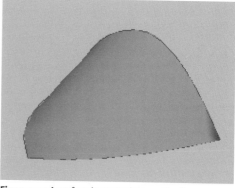

Figure 7.52 A surface is created across the three curves.

Figure 7.53 In the Text Curves Options window set the Text, Font, and Type options, and then click Create.

Figure 7.54 From the Surfaces menu select Bevel.

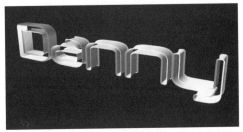

Figure 7.55 The curves that outlined the letters have been turned into beveled surfaces.

To create beveled text:

1. In the Create menu select the box next to Text. The Text Curves Options dialog box opens.

2. In the Text field type the text you want.

3. Select a font for the text.

4. Select Curves for the Type.

5. Click Create (**Figure 7.53**).

6. From the Surfaces menu select Bevel (**Figure 7.54**).

   The text bevel can be edited with the Inputs node afterwards or in the Text Curves Options dialog box before creation.

   The text now appears with a bevel (**Figure 7.55**).

✔ Tip

■ You can adjust the width and depth of the extrude in the bevel's Inputs node accessible in the Channel Box.

In order to draw a curve directly on a surface, you must make the surface live. Once a surface is live, a curve can be created and edited directly on the surface itself.

To make a surface live:

1. Select a surface to make live (**Figure 7.56**).

2. From the Modify menu select Make Live or click ⟲ to make the surface live.

   The surface wireframe turns green to indicate that it is a live surface (**Figure 7.57**).

✔ Tip

- To make a surface not live, select Make Not Live from the Modify menu.

To draw a curve on a live surface:

1. Make the surface live.

2. From the Create menu select CV Curve Tool (**Figure 7.58**).

3. Click points on the surface where you want to create the curve (**Figure 7.59**).

4. Press Enter to complete the curve.
   A curve is created on the surface.

5. From the Modify menu select Make Not Live to bring the surface back to normal mode (**Figure 7.60**).

✔ Tip

- You can move the curve along the surface in the U or V direction using the Move tool.

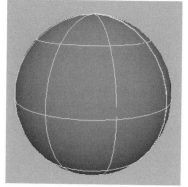

Figure 7.56 The sphere is selected to make it live so that a curve can be drawn on it. Any surface can be made live.

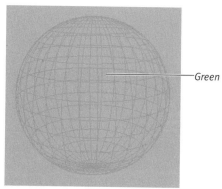

Green

Figure 7.57 The surface wireframe turns green to indicate it is a live surface.

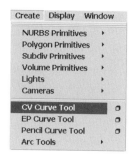

Figure 7.58 From the Create menu select CV Curve Tool.

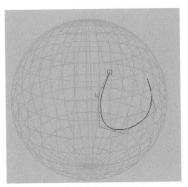

Figure 7.59 It is helpful to tumble your view around the surface to get a straight look at where you want to place each CV.

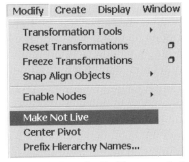

Figure 7.60 From the Modify menu select Make Not Live to return to normal mode.

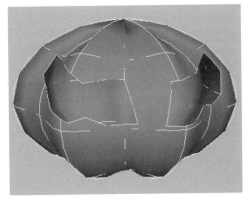

Figure 7.61 Curves on surfaces work well when you want to later trim out part of a surface, as with this pumpkin.

When you project a curve, it creates a new curve on the selected surface. Imagine projecting the image of a curve at an object from a slide projector. The shape of the object may warp the image of the curve. Likewise, when you project a curve in Maya, the resulting projected curve on an object's surface is warped to some degree.

A pumpkin's eyes are a good example: You can draw the shape of the eyes you want to cut out of a pumpkin in the front view, and project these curves onto the pumpkin shape, later to be trimmed out of the surface (**Figure 7.61**). The trim function is often used after projecting a curve onto a surface to cut out the curve shape.

continues on next page

To project a curve onto a surface:

1. Create a surface for the curve to be projected onto—a primitive sphere, for example.

2. In the front view create a curve to project onto the surface; a primitive circle will be used for this example (**Figure 7.62**).

3. Select the curve to be projected, and the surface (**Figure 7.63**).

4. With the front view active, select Edit NURBS (Windows) or Edit Surfaces (Mac) > Project Curve On Surface (**Figure 7.64**).

   The curve becomes projected on both sides of the sphere's surface (**Figure 7.65**).

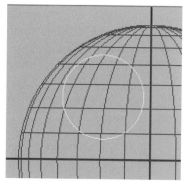

Figure 7.62 This circle will be projected onto the surface of the sphere.

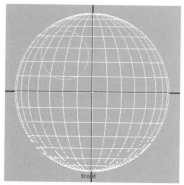

Figure 7.63 Both the curve and the surface must be selected for the projection to work.

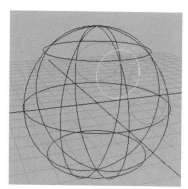

Figure 7.65 The curve is projected on both sides of the object.

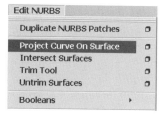

Figure 7.64 The active view becomes the angle from which the curve is projected.

POLYGONS AND SUBDIVIDED SURFACES

8

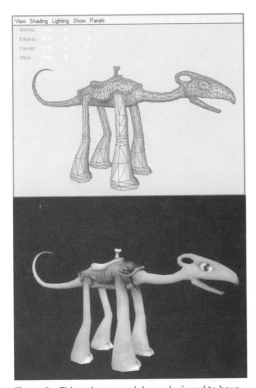

Figure 8.1 This polygon model was designed to have the lowest number of faces possible. The textures make up for the lack of detail. Modeled and textured by Toby Marvin.

Polygons are a fun, easy way to model a surface. A polygon is a surface made up of smaller, flat surfaces with three or more sides. These smaller surfaces are called *faces*. Working with polygons has more of a rigid construction feeling, and working with NURBS has a more pliable, sculptural feeling.

Games use polygons extensively because they are bound by limitations of complexity if they want to maintain fast interaction with real-time rendering. If your character has a low poly (short for polygon) count—that is, a low number of faces—it will render and interact quickly. A character in a game is usually limited to a specific number of polygons so that the game can run in real time (**Figure 8.1**).

However, polygons can also be used to make smooth, highly detailed, even organic surfaces (**Figure 8.2**). Some surfaces may be easier to build in polygons than in NURBS surfaces. A character's body could be made out of a seamless polygon surface, which would not be possible with one NURBS surface, which can only be four-sided.

Subdivision surfaces are a recent addition to Maya. They combine some of the best of NURBS and polygons, plus a few tricks of their own. If you know how to model polygons, you can model a subdivision surface as well—they use many of the same tools.

Subdivision surface modeling is a feature offered only in Maya Unlimited. It is not supported in Maya 3.5 for Mac OS X.

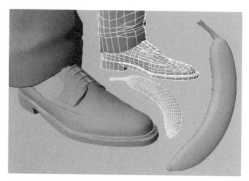

Figure 8.2 Polygons can be used to make both smooth shapes, such as a banana, and hard edges, as on this shoe. Shoe and trouser leg modeled by Adrian Niu.

Figure 8.3 The faces are displayed on this sphere. The highlighted face was selected by clicking the dot in the center of the face.

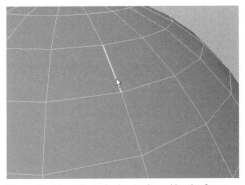

Figure 8.4 The selected edge is shared by the faces on either side of it. Any change to the position or size of this edge will affect all of the faces it touches.

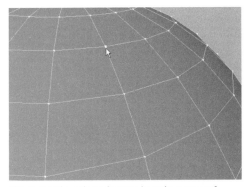

Figure 8.5 The selected vertex is at the corner of four faces.

About Modeling Polygons

The most common way to create a complex polygon model is to start with a primitive poly cube. By transforming this simple object and manipulating its existing components, you can get the basic shape for your model. From there, you can build on to the object by adding more complexity to the surface.

Polygons have four kinds of components, which are important for both modeling and texturing: *face, edge, vertex,* and *UV*.

Some of the most commonly used polygon tools are the Extrude Face tool and the Split Polygon tool. Many other tools are used to manipulate a poly surface, including Extrude Edge and Subdivide.

Polygon components

- ◆ A face is one of the many smaller surfaces that make up the polygon object as a whole. You can choose it by selecting the point in the center of each face (**Figure 8.3**).

- ◆ An edge is one border of a polygonal face (**Figure 8.4**).

- ◆ A vertex is at the corner of a face. Vertices become yellow when selected (**Figure 8.5**). If it is moved, it will change the shape of the four faces of which it is a part.

- ◆ UVs are used for texturing, not modeling; they become green when selected (see Chapter 14).

✔ Tip

- ■ Once a face, vertex, or edge is selected, you can move, rotate, or scale the component. For the fastest workflow, use the Marking Menu.

To select and transform polygon components:

1. Create any polygon primitive (see Chapter 3).

2. Right mouse–click a polygon surface.

3. Select Vertex from the Marking Menu (**Figure 8.6**).

4. Select some vertices. You can marquee-select by clicking and dragging with the left mouse button (**Figure 8.7**).

5. Press [w] or click the Move tool icon 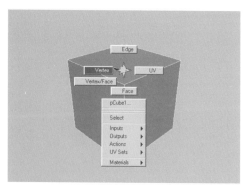 in the toolbar.

6. Move the vertices (**Figure 8.8**).

✔ Tips

■ If you are in wireframe mode, you must click a component of the surface, such as an edge, for the Marking Menu to show up. If you are in shaded mode, you can click anywhere on the surface.

■ Any of the polygon components can be selected and transformed using the method described above.

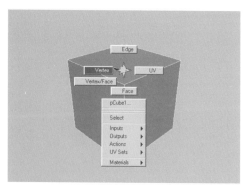

Figure 8.6 Generally, only one kind of component is displayed at a time. This Marking Menu, accessible from the right mouse button, is a convenient way to switch between the different component displays.

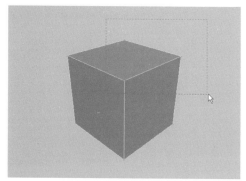

Figure 8.7 Three vertices are selected simultaneously using marquee select.

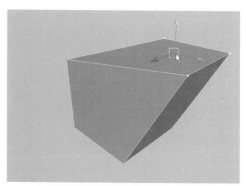

Figure 8.8 The selected vertices are moved using the Move tool. The shape of every face that shares these vertices is changed.

ABOUT MODELING POLYGONS

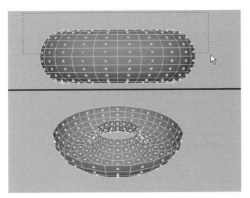

Figure 8.9 Top, the faces of a torus are being selected in the side view. It is often helpful to switch views to get a better angle on your selection. Bottom, you see the torus after the selected faces have been deleted.

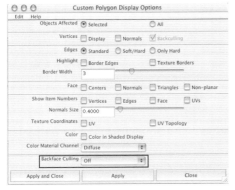

Figure 8.10 In the Custom Polygon Display Options window, you can choose whether to have the display options affect all polygon objects or just the selected one(s)—for Objects Affected, choose Selected or All.

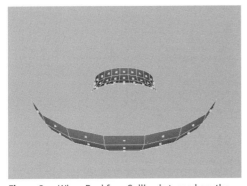

Figure 8.11 When Backface Culling is turned on, the components on the far side of the object disappear so you can't select them. This works for all kinds of polygon components.

When using polygons, you are often dealing with a large number of components. Maya has several tools to help you select components and to prevent you from selecting some by mistake. These include *Backface Culling*, which prevents you from picking points on the far side of the object, as well as tools that allow you to grow, shrink, and convert your existing selections.

To use Backface Culling:

1. From the Create menu select Polygon Primitives > Torus.

2. Right mouse–click a polygon surface, and select Face from the Marking Menu.

3. In the side view, marquee-select the top half of the torus, and then delete the faces (**Figure 8.9**).

4. From the Display menu select the box next to Custom Polygon Display.

   This opens the Custom Polygon Display Options window (**Figure 8.10**).

continues on next page

ABOUT MODELING POLYGONS

161

5. From the Backface Culling menu select On. Click Apply.

The portions of the torus on the far side of the Camera view disappear. They cannot be selected (**Figure 8.11**).

6. From the Backface Culling menu select Keep Wire. Click Apply.

You can see the wireframe of the back side, but you cannot select components from that part of the surface (**Figure 8.12**).

7. From the Backface Culling menu select Keep Hard Edges. Click Apply.

You can see the hard edges of the back side only—that is, edges along the sides of holes in the surface (**Figure 8.13**).

8. From the Backface Culling menu select Off. Click Apply.

This resets the Custom Polygon Display Options to default. Now you are able to select the back sides of polygon surfaces again.

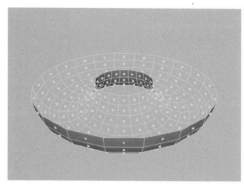

Figure 8.12 Backface Culling is set to Keep Wire. This allows you to see the shape of the object while preventing you from selecting unwanted components on the back side of the object.

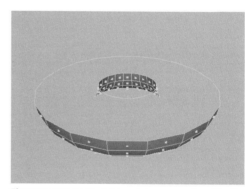

Figure 8.13 Keep Hard Edges lets you see the object's basic shape, but only the edges that border a hole in the object.

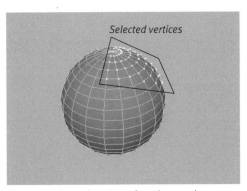

Figure 8.14 Several vertices of a polygon sphere are selected. With Backface Culling off, points on the back of the sphere were selected as well.

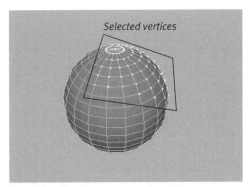

Figure 8.15 Surgically picking poly vertices one by one can be difficult. One way to save time is to use Edit Polygons > Selection > Grow Selection Region. This selects the points around the ones that are currently selected, making the selected area larger.

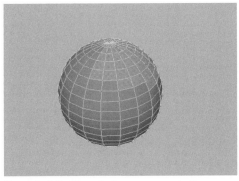

Figure 8.16 The faces that were surrounded by selected vertices are now selected, and the points are deselected.

To grow, shrink, and convert a selection:

1. From the Create menu select Polygon Primitives > Sphere.

2. Right mouse–click a polygon surface, and select Vertex from the Marking Menu.

3. Select several vertices (**Figure 8.14**).

4. From the Edit Polygons menu choose Selection > Grow Selection Region.

   The vertices surrounding the existing selection are also selected. Repeat this step to increase the size of the selected area (**Figure 8.15**).

5. From the Edit Polygons menu select Selection > Shrink Selection Region.

   The region of selected vertices becomes smaller. Repeat this step to shrink it more.

6. From the Edit Polygons menu select Selection > Convert Selection to Faces.

   The vertices are deselected, and the faces they surrounded are selected (**Figure 8.16**).

✔ Tips

- A selection of any kind of polygon component can similarly be converted to edges, vertices, or UVs.

- Some polygon-modeling tools only work on faces, such as Extrude Face. Convert Selection saves you the time of meticulously selecting the faces one by one to run this tool on the faces if you already have the region selected as vertices.

ABOUT MODELING POLYGONS

Extrude Face is a great way to begin the basic construction of your surface. It allows you to pull additional geometry from the surface. You simply select a face or several faces, extrude them, and then manipulate the new faces.

To extrude faces of a cube:

1. From the Create menu select Polygon Primitives > Cube.

2. Right mouse–click the cube, and select Face from the Marking Menu.

3. Marquee-select all of the faces (**Figure 8.17**).

4. From the Edit Polygons menu select Extrude Face.

   A manipulator appears with which you can move, rotate, and scale the new faces (**Figure 8.18**). Even though it only shows up on one face, it affects all the faces that were just extruded. It transforms them locally, which means that they move relative to their surface normal, which is a line perpendicular to the center of each individual face.

5. Move one face out from the center of the cube with the Translate manipulator.

   All newly extruded faces will move out from the center as well (**Figure 8.19**). This is very helpful for making symmetrical objects.

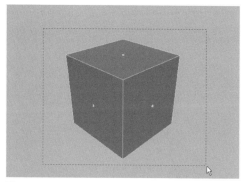

Figure 8.17 When marquee-select is used around the entire object, even the faces on the far side of the object are selected.

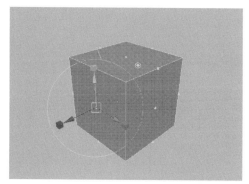

Figure 8.18 This manipulator appears when Edit Polygons > Extrude Face is selected.

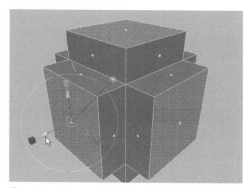

Figure 8.19 When one face is moved outward, all of the faces move outward. By scaling with this tool, all of the selected faces will scale simultaneously, relative to their center.

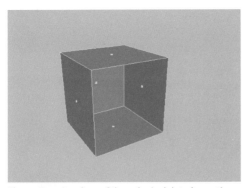

Figure 8.20 One face of the cube is deleted, creating an opening.

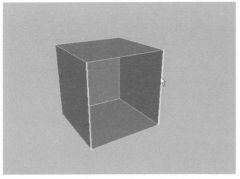

Figure 8.21 The edges on the left and right side of the opening are selected.

✔ Tips

- When you first extrude a face, points appear on the center of each edge of the face you chose to extrude (**Figure 8.18**). These points are the new faces that resulted from the extrude, but until you move or scale the selected face, these new faces are flat. Beware any time you see these points along an edge; it can cause trouble later on. To avoid this, make sure you scale or move a face after every extrude.

- After extruding, you will often want to scale the face proportionally. Simply click any one of the scale manipulators, and a proportional scale manipulator appears in the center. To rotate along a single axis, click the outside rotate manipulator, and three rotate manipulators, one for each axis, appear.

To extrude edges:

1. From the Create menu select Polygon Primitives > Cube.

2. Right mouse–click the cube, and select Face from the Marking Menu.

3. Select a face on the side of the cube and press `Delete`.

   The face disappears, and you see the inside of the cube (**Figure 8.20**). (An edge or vertex can also be deleted, but it does not make an opening, it just makes a larger face defined by the edges left behind. To try this, pick some vertices and select Delete Vertex from the Edit Polygons Menu.)

4. Right mouse–click the cube, and select Edge from the Marking Menu.

5. Select the left edge, and `Shift`-select the right edge of the hole you created (**Figure 8.21**).

continues on next page

ABOUT MODELING POLYGONS

6. From the Edit Polygons menu select Extrude Edge.

7. Move the edge out and away from the cube. Two new faces have been created, and it should look like an open box (**Figure 8.22**).

✔ Tip

■ An edge should not be shared by more than two faces. This means that you should only extrude edges that are adjacent to an opening in the polygon. It is possible to do otherwise, but it is not recommended (**Figure 8.23**).

The Split Polygon tool is used extensively in polygon modeling. It allows you to split one face into two faces along an edge that you create. You can split multiple faces simultaneously to save time.

Because of the way perspective distorts the view of an object, it can be difficult to select the center of an edge. To help you split in the right place, the Split Polygon tool snaps to the center of an edge. This means that if the spot where you want to split is close to the center of an edge, the tool jumps to the precise center.

In general, it is best to have only three- and four-sided faces, known as triangles and quads, respectively. Quads and triangles respond more predictably to other polygon modeling tools. If a face has five or more sides, you should split it into smaller faces.

To split a face:

1. From the Create menu select Polygon Primitives > Cube.

2. From the Edit Polygons menu select the box next to Split Polygon Tool.

This opens the Tool Settings window with Split Polygon Tool options.

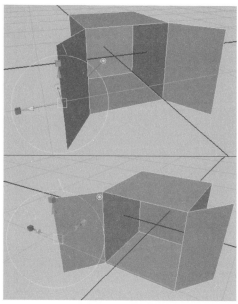

Figure 8.22 The edges have been extruded, which creates new faces. When one edge is moved, the other edge moves in the same direction for one axis, but in the opposite direction for the other axis; it depends on which side of the cube is removed. Here are two possible results.

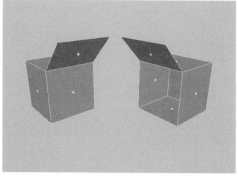

Figure 8.23 The object on the left has an edge that is shared by three faces; the object on the right does not because it has an opening in the front. It is not good construction to have an edge shared by more than two faces. One problem is that the polygon object cannot be converted into Subdivision Surfaces.

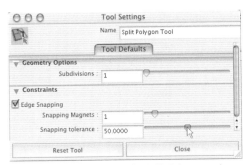

Figure 8.24 The options for the Split Polygon tool can make it easy to split a polygon in half, thirds, quarters, and so on.

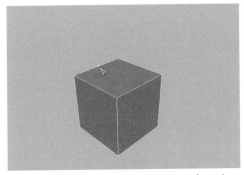

Figure 8.25 A point is placed at the center of an edge with the Split Polygon tool.

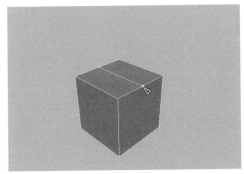

Figure 8.26 The new edge is defined by the two points placed by the Split Polygon tool. If you press [Enter] now, it completes the command. However, you could continue splitting and go all the way around the cube, by clicking a point on one edge at a time.

3. Adjust the slider next to Snapping Tolerance to about the middle of the range. Close the window (**Figure 8.24**).

4. Click and drag along a top edge to the center. The point should snap to the center of the edge. Release the mouse button (**Figure 8.25**).

5. Click and drag along the edge on the opposite side of the top of the cube to the center of that edge (**Figure 8.26**).

6. Press [Enter]. The face is now split in half.

7. Right mouse–click the cube, and select Edge from the Marking Menu.

continues on next page

ABOUT MODELING POLYGONS

8. Select the new edge you created, and move it up. The object should look like a simple house (**Figure 8.27**).

9. From the Edit Polygons menu select Split Polygon Tool.

10. Click and drag up the left side of the cube until the point snaps to the corner. Repeat for the right side (**Figure 8.28**).

11. Press [Enter].

    Now the five-sided face, which formed the front of the house, is split into a three-sided face and a four-sided face.

✔ Tips

- Make sure that your split always successfully creates an edge. If you click one edge and press [Enter] without successfully clicking another edge of the same face, it will only put a vertex on that edge. This is bad construction. To avoid this problem, just make sure to undo if the Split Polygon tool does not make a new edge.

- Sometimes snapping can make it difficult to split where you want it to. To turn off snapping, in the Split Polygon Tool options in the Tool Settings dialog box uncheck the box next to Edge Snapping.

- You are not limited to only snapping to the middle of an edge—you can snap to more than one point of an edge. If you want to snap to a point one-third of the way along an edge, you can select 2 from Snapping Magnets in the Split Polygon Tool options in the Tool Settings dialog box. This makes it so that there are two points evenly spaced along the edge that the tool will snap to.

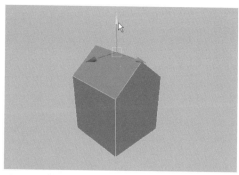

Figure 8.27 The new edge is moved up, creating a simple house shape. Note that the front of the house has five edges. More than four edges is generally considered bad construction.

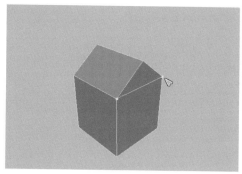

Figure 8.28 A new edge is created splitting the front face into two separate faces.

Figure 8.29 The cube is scaled to the shape of a door.

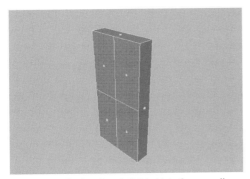

Figure 8.30 The face is subdivided into four, smaller faces. A face can be subdivided into more faces by adjusting Subdivision Levels in Edit Polygons > Subdivide > Options.

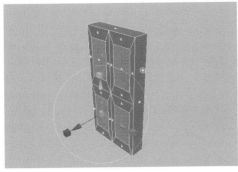

Figure 8.31 The extruded faces are scaled down relative to their centers.

The Subdivide tool splits a face into quads (four-sided faces) or triangles (three-sided faces). It is a quick way to add detail to your surface in the form of additional faces. This should not be confused with subdivision surface. In this example, we will combine Subdivide with Extrude Face to make a door.

To subdivide a polygon face:

1. From the Create menu select Polygon Primitives > Cube.

   It is a common technique to start out with a cube roughly scaled to the size of an object and use the Edit Polygon tools to model the surface.

2. Scale the cube to the shape of a door (**Figure 8.29**).

3. Right mouse–click the cube, and select Face from the Marking Menu.

4. Select the face on the front.

5. From the Edit Polygons menu select Subdivide. The face should be split into four faces (**Figure 8.30**).

6. From the Edit Polygons menu select Extrude Face.

   The manipulator and new faces show up.

7. Scale the faces down a little using the manipulator tool (**Figure 8.31**).

continues on next page

8. From the Edit Polygons menu select Extrude Face again.

The manipulator and new faces show up.

9. Scale the new faces down a little and move them in toward the middle of the object. It now looks like a door with four panels (**Figure 8.32**).

Polygons naturally have sharp edges and corners during construction. Those can be rounded out by using the Polygons > Smooth function. This function subdivides surfaces into many smaller polygons to round out corners and edges.

To smooth a polygon:

1. Select a polygon object, such as the door from the previous section.

2. From the Polygons menu, select the box next to Smooth.

The Polygon Smooth Options dialog box opens.

3. Adjust the slider next to Subdivision Levels to set it to 3 (**Figure 8.33**).

4. Click Smooth.

5. Press F8 to return to object mode.

6. Deselect the object to see the smoothed surface (**Figure 8.34**).

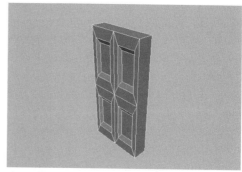

Figure 8.32 A completed four-panel door. Had the face on the opposite side of the door been selected before the Subdivide function, the exact same steps would have modeled the back side of the door simultaneously.

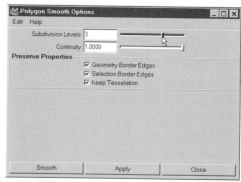

Figure 8.33 Higher Subdivision Levels in the Polygon Smooth Options dialog box make smoother objects with more faces. Continuity adjusts how closely the new shape resembles the original, versus how rounded it is. A low continuity will look more similar to the original shape, a high continuity will produce a very rounded shape.

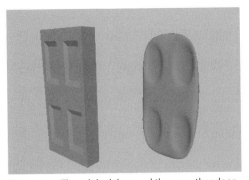

Figure 8.34 The original door and the smoother door side by side. The basic structure of a polygon object should be complete before the Smooth function is run. Smoothing produces a dense object with many faces, making it more difficult to work with.

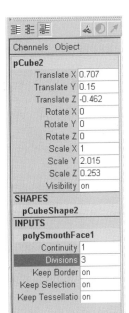

Figure 8.35
The inputs in the Channel Box allow you to change smooth options after the function is run. However, once additional tweaks are made to the surface, going back and changing the options on the polySmoothFace input will produce undesirable results.

✔ Tips

- You can set the Subdivision Levels in the Polygon Smooth Options dialog box up to 4; however, 3 is generally high enough, and any higher could give you a cumbersome surface.

- You can change the level of smoothing after the function is finished by clicking polySmoothFace1, which should be at the top of the list of inputs in your Channel Box. You will then see a field labeled Divisions that you can change from 0 (no smooth) to 4 (very smooth) (**Figure 8.35**).

- A portion of a polygon surface can be smoothed by selecting the faces of the part of the surface you want smoothed and then applying the Smooth operation (**Figure 8.36**).

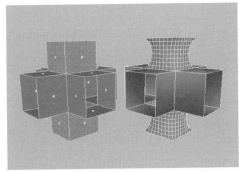

Figure 8.36 Left, faces on the top and bottom of the object are selected. Right, the result of those faces only being smoothed. Smooth works by selecting whole polygon objects or faces of the object; you cannot smooth by selecting vertices or edges.

ABOUT MODELING POLYGONS

About Subdivision Surface Modeling

Subdivision surface modeling, which combines NURBS and polygons, is a feature offered only in Maya Unlimited. It is not supported in Maya 3.5 for Mac OS X. Subdivision surfaces have two modeling modes, *standard* and *polygon*. In polygon mode, you can use all of the polygon tools on the surface. In standard mode, you mostly work with vertices, which act similarly to NURBS control vertices (CVs). But standard mode also has edges and faces, similarly to a polygon. Standard mode has the unique capability of moving between *display levels*, that is, different levels of detail. This allows you to move back and forth between low and high levels of detail on an object (**Figure 8.37**).

In polygon mode, you see the edges of a polygon shape surrounding a smooth surface, which is the subdivision surface. In this mode, all of the components are the same as with any other polygon (**Figure 8.38**).

In standard mode, there is a different set of components. They can be manipulated at different display levels. Note that subdivision surfaces, like NURBS surfaces, have smoothness levels of rough, medium, and fine that can be activated by the ①, ②, and ③ keys, respectively. However, these should not be confused with display levels, which actually make the surface more complex.

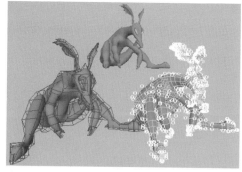

Figure 8.37 This odd creature is called a Huffer. It was designed by Roy Miles and modeled by Andrew Britt using subdivision surfaces. Left, polygon mode; right, standard mode with vertices visible; top, standard mode with no components visible.

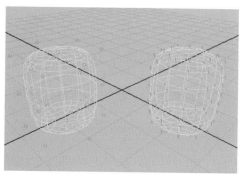

Figure 8.38 These are two copies of a subdivision cylinder. The one on the left is at display level 0, while the one on the right is at display level 1.

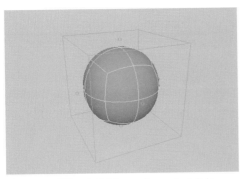

Figure 8.39 This subdivision surface sphere is in display level 0 and has its faces displayed.

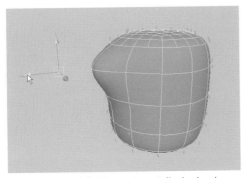

Figure 8.40 A subdivision vertex, at display level 1, has been moved. The surface responds much as a NURBS surface responds to moving a control vertex.

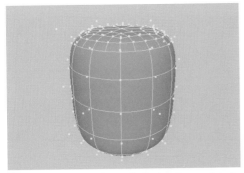

Figure 8.41 UVs don't have display levels associated with them, therefore they show up as points, not as numbers.

Subdivision surface components

Subdivision Surfaces have four different kinds of components while in standard mode. They are face, vertex, UV and edge.

◆ A face generally appears offset from the subdivision surface. It has three or more sides; however, the most efficient subdivision surfaces have four sides. The number in the center tells which display level it is in (**Figure 8.39**).

◆ A vertex generally appears offset from the surface. It is represented by the number of the display level it is in. When moved, it controls the area of surface nearest to it (**Figure 8.40**).

◆ UVs are points that turn green when selected. They are used for texturing, not modeling. See Chapter 14 (**Figure 8.41**).

◆ An edge is one border of a face (**Figure 8.42**).

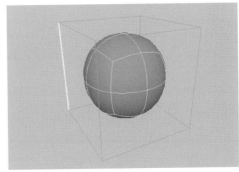

Figure 8.42 An edge of the sphere is selected in standard mode.

To select a subdivision surface component:

1. From the Create menu, select Subdiv Primitives > Sphere.

2. Press ③ to go into the fine level of sub-division surface display smoothness (**Figure 8.43**).

   The surface should appear smoother in the view. Changing these settings has no influence on the construction of the model, only in how it is displayed.

3. Right mouse–click the sphere, and select Face from the Marking Menu (**Figure 8.44**).

   The faces should now appear surrounding the sphere.

4. Select and move the face (**Figure 8.45**).

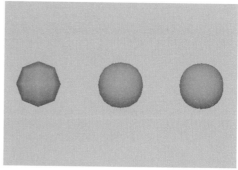

Figure 8.43 From left to right, Rough, Medium and Fine Subdiv Smoothness.

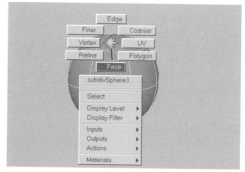

Figure 8.44 The Marking Menu for subdivision surfaces is accessible by right mouse button–clicking the sphere's surface. Much of what is needed to work with subdivision surfaces is right here.

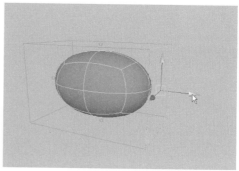

Figure 8.45 A face is moved and the sphere is elongated.

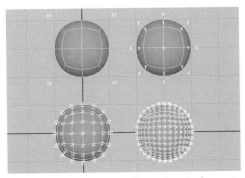

Figure 8.46 A subdivision surface sphere is shown at display levels 0 (from top left), 1, 2, and 3. By default, the sphere only has levels 0 and 1. It needs to be refined to access higher levels.

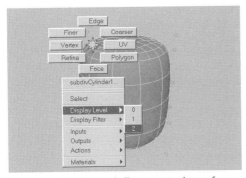

Figure 8.47 Display Level allows you to choose from any of the existing levels.

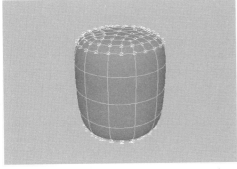

Figure 8.48 The level 2 vertices only show up on the default cylinder where detail is needed. If you need the 2s to be evenly distributed, go to display level 1 and refine.

Sculpting subdivision surfaces

Subdivision surfaces allow you the freedom to move back and forth between different levels of detail. There are a few terms you should understand to be able to manipulate this functionality.

Display level—Subdivision surface objects have different display levels; that is, different levels of refinement. This means that you can work with many points close together on the surface that affect only a small area, or with fewer points farther apart on a surface that affect a large area. You can move back and forth between these levels (**Figure 8.46**).

Refine—This function gives the selected area of the surface a higher level of detail. If it is at level 1, Refine will make the area of selected points have level 2 points.

Finer and Coarser—These functions allow you to move quickly to a higher level of detail (Finer) or a lower level of detail (Coarser).

To change display levels on a subdivision surface:

1. From the Create menu, select Subdiv Primitives > Cylinder.

2. Press ③ on the keyboard to go into the fine level of subdivision surface smoothness.

3. Right mouse–click the cylinder, and select Vertex from the Marking Menu.

4. Right mouse–click the cylinder, and select Display Level > 2 from the Marking Menu (**Figure 8.47**).

   Many more points appear labeled as 2 (**Figure 8.48**).

continues on next page

ABOUT SUBDIVISION SURFACE MODELING

5. Right mouse–click the cylinder, and select Coarser from the Marking Menu (**Figure 8.49**).

The display level goes down to 1 (**Figure 8.50**).

6. Right mouse–click the cylinder, and select Finer from the Marking Menu.

The display level goes back up to 2.

To add detail to a subdivision surface:

1. From the Create menu, select Subdiv Primitives > Cube.

2. Press ③ to go into the Fine level of subdivision surface smoothness.

3. Right mouse–click the cube, and select Vertex from the Marking Menu.

4. Select a vertex (**Figure 8.51**).

5. Right mouse–click the cube, and select Refine from the Marking Menu.

The 0s are replaced by 1s in the area around the original point, and there are more of them (**Figure 8.52**).

6. Right mouse–click the cube, and select Refine from the Marking Menu again.

The 1s are replaced by even more 2s.

7. Select and move a point (**Figure 8.53**).

8. Right mouse–click the cube, and select Display Level > 0 from the Marking Menu.

9. Select and move a point (**Figure 8.54**).

The changes to the level 2 point remain when you are working with level 0 points. You can move back and forth between the display levels.

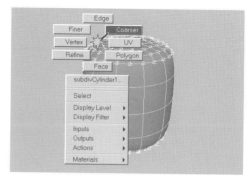

Figure 8.49 Coarser and Finer are another way to change the display level.

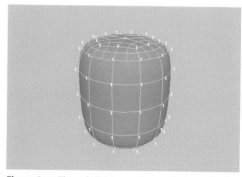

Figure 8.50 The subdivision surface cylinder at display level 1.

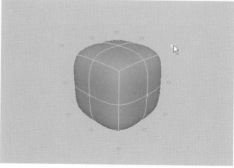

Figure 8.51 A vertex is selected to determine the area that will be refined.

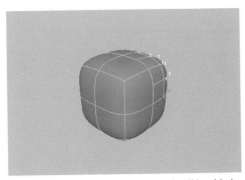

Figure 8.52 With the Refine function, detail is added only around the selected component.

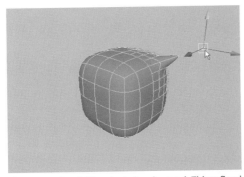

Figure 8.53 A point is selected and moved. This refined area allows for tweaks to small portions of the surface.

Figure 8.54 Tweaks to large portions of the surface can be made by returning the display level to 0.

✔ Tips

- The Refine function also works with edges and faces.

- You can refine up to a display level of 13. However, it is not recommended to go above 3 because the speed of interactivity decreases dramatically as the levels get higher.

- You cannot delete a subdivision surface component. However, if you transform any component at a display level of 1 or higher and then try to delete it, it will return to its original position.

Subdivision surfaces polygon mode

While standard mode is good for adding fine details, polygon mode is essential for creating the basic structure of the surface. One common tactic is to model a polygon to get the rough form and then convert it to subdivision surfaces. This is helpful because you can work quickly, and the polygon primitive cube has a simpler construction than the subdivision primitive cube.

It is a good practice to finish all the manipulation you plan to do in polygon mode before you begin refining the surface in standard mode. It is possible to lose changes made to the surface if you frequently switch back and forth between modes.

To model a turtle out of subdivision surfaces using polygon mode:

1. From the Create menu select Subdiv Primitives > Sphere.

2. Press ③ to go into the Fine level of subdivision surface smoothness.

3. Scale the sphere down along the *y*-axis to make it flatter (**Figure 8.55**).

4. Right mouse–click the sphere, and select Polygon from the Marking Menu.
   A rectangular polygon shell should appear around the sphere.

5. Right mouse–click the sphere, and select Face from the Marking Menu. Select the face on the front side of the polygon (**Figure 8.56**).

6. From the Edit Polygons menu select Extrude Face. Scale down the face (**Figure 8.57**).

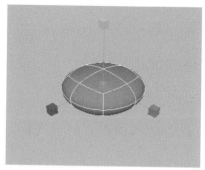

Figure 8.55 The sphere is scaled flatter to resemble a turtle shell.

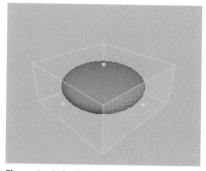

Figure 8.56 The front face is selected.

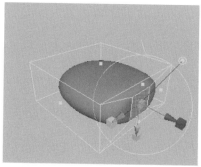

Figure 8.57 The face is scaled down. To get the Proportional scale manipulator in the center, click any of the other scale manipulators.

ABOUT SUBDIVISION SURFACE MODELING

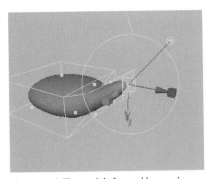

Figure 8.58 The neck is formed by moving the face out and up.

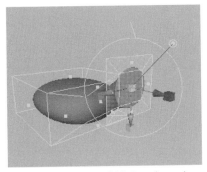

Figure 8.59 The scale of this face determines the size of the back of the turtle's head.

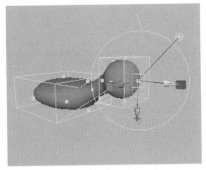

Figure 8.60 Move this face forward to give the head some length.

7. From the Edit Polygons menu select Extrude Face again. Move the face forward and up (**Figure 8.58**).

This will be the neck of the turtle.

8. From the Edit Polygons menu select Extrude Face again. Proportionally scale the face up (**Figure 8.59**).

9. From the Edit Polygons menu select Extrude Face again. Move the face forward (**Figure 8.60**).

This will be the head of the turtle.

continues on next page

10. Select the face on the bottom of the sphere.

11. From the Edit Polygons menu select Subdivide (**Figure 8.61**).

12. From the Edit Polygons menu select Extrude Face. Proportionally scale the faces to be smaller (**Figure 8.62**).

13. From the Edit Polygons menu select Extrude Face again. Move the faces down (**Figure 8.63**).

You've made a turtle!

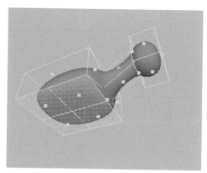

Figure 8.61 Looking at the object from below, the bottom has been subdivided.

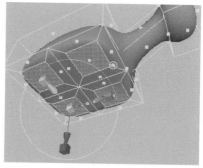

Figure 8.62 The bases of the legs are scaled down simultaneously.

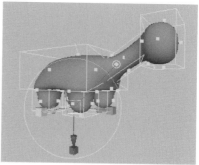

Figure 8.63 Move these faces down to determine the length of the legs. A simple turtle shape is completed.

ABOUT SUBDIVISION SURFACE MODELING

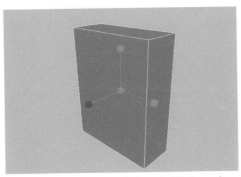

Figure 8.64 The polygon cube is scaled flatter and narrower.

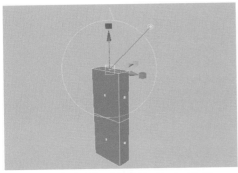

Figure 8.65 The height of the object is doubled by extruding the top face.

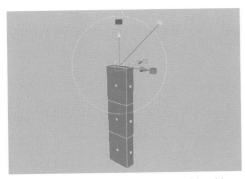

Figure 8.66 The three faces on the front of the object should be about equal.

To model a SubD telephone receiver, starting with a polygon:

1. From the Create menu select Polygon Primitives > Cube.

2. Scale the cube down in the *z* direction so that it is flatter. Scale it down in the *x* direction so that it is narrower (**Figure 8.64**).

3. Right mouse–click the cube, and select Face from the Marking Menu.

4. Select the top face of the cube.

5. From the Edit Polygons menu select Extrude Face. Move the face up to double the height (**Figure 8.65**).

6. From the Edit Polygons menu select Extrude Face again. Move the top face up so that you have three equal faces on the front of the object (**Figure 8.66**).

7. Select the top and bottom faces of the front of the object.

8. From the Edit Polygons menu select Extrude Face. Move the faces along the *z* axis (**Figure 8.67**).

continues on next page

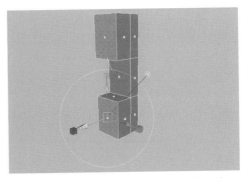

Figure 8.67 Move out the extruded faces to form the receiver and mouthpiece of the telephone.

ABOUT SUBDIVISION SURFACE MODELING

9. Switch the Pick mask mode to object mode by pressing F8 (**Figure 8.68**). The object should be selected.

10. From the Modify menu select Convert > Polygons to Subdiv (**Figure 8.69**).

   You've made a simple telephone receiver (**Figure 8.70**).

✔ Tips

- Subdivision surfaces can be turned back into polygons by using Modify > Convert > Subdiv to Polygon.

- You can also convert a NURBS surface to subdivision by selecting NURBS to Subdiv from the Modify > Convert menu. Whether you are converting from NURBS or polygons, you should always start out with a simple surface. An already dense surface converted to subdivisions will prove very difficult to work with.

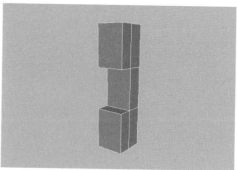

Figure 8.68 The telephone before conversion to subdivision surfaces. The mode has been switched from Pick mask to object.

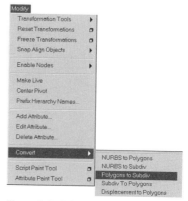

Figure 8.69 Select Modify > Convert > Polygons to Subdiv.

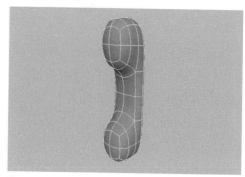

Figure 8.70 The subdivision telephone has all smooth, rounded surfaces.

ABOUT SUBDIVISION SURFACE MODELING

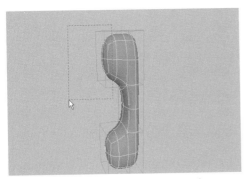

Figure 8.71 With the camera lined up correctly, Marquee-select makes it easy to select several edges at once.

Figure 8.72 Note that in addition to creasing from this menu, edges can be uncreased by selecting Uncrease Edge/Vertex.

Subdivision surfaces tend to be smooth all around. To get flatter areas and sharp edges, Maya has provided the Crease tools.

To add a partial crease:

1. Create the telephone receiver from the previous page.

   Be sure you are in standard mode. From the Subdiv Surfaces menu select Standard Mode. The following steps will not work in polygon mode.

2. Right mouse–click the surface, and select Edge from the Marking Menu.

3. Select the eight edges that form a cube around the top part of the telephone (**Figure 8.71**).

4. From the Subdiv Surfaces menu select Partial Crease Edge/Vertex (**Figure 8.72**).

5. Repeat steps 3 and 4 for the mouthpiece of the telephone.

   The mouthpiece and receiver now have a flatter, more squared look (**Figure 8.73**).

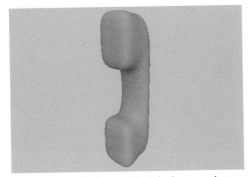

Figure 8.73 This is the resulting telephone receiver after using partial crease on the top and mouthpiece.

To add a full crease to vertices:

1. From the Create menu select Subdiv Primitives > Cylinder.

2. Scale the surface along the *y*-axis so that it is about three times the original length.

3. Right mouse–click the surface of the cylinder, and select Vertex from the Marking Menu.

4. Select the point in the middle of the top and move it up.

5. From the Subdiv Surfaces menu select Full Crease Edge/Vertex.

   The top point becomes sharp (**Figure 8.74**).

6. Marquee-select the bottom row of points, and scale them in.

7. With those points still selected, right mouse–click the surface, and select Refine from the Marking Menu.

8. Select four evenly spaced points on the bottom of the surface (**Figure 8.75**).

9. From the Subdiv Surfaces menu select Full Crease Edge/Vertex.

10. Move the points down, and scale them out.

    You have created a simple rocket ship (**Figure 8.76**).

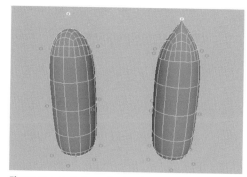

Figure 8.74 Left, the point has been moved up. Right, the surface has a point on top from the Full Crease function.

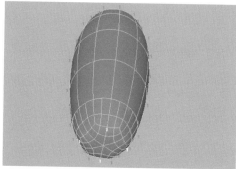

Figure 8.75 Carefully select four evenly spaced points from the bottom of the surface. It helps to tumble around the camera to be sure the right ones are selected.

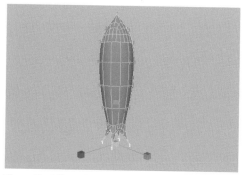

Figure 8.76 The points are moved down, and proportionally scaling them moves them out from the center. They now form the legs of a simple rocket ship.

Figure 8.77 This is the completed rocket ship from the previous section.

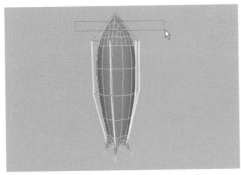

Figure 8.78 By Shift-selecting the vertical edges one bunch at a time, you can avoid selecting the horizontal edges.

Figure 8.79 The edges of the rocket ship are sharp, giving it a more interesting shape.

To add a full crease to edges:

1. Create the rocket from the previous section (**Figure 8.77**).

2. Right mouse–click the surface, and select Edge from the Marking Menu.

3. Right mouse–click the surface, and select Display Level > 0.

4. Right mouse–click the surface, and select Edge from the marking menu that appears.

5. Select all of the vertical edges.

   To avoid selecting horizontal edges, marquee-select the vertical edges at the bottom, then Shift-select those at the middle, and finally Shift-select those at the top (**Figure 8.78**).

6. From the Subdiv Surfaces menu select Full Crease Edge/Vertex.

7. Your rocket now has sharp edges (**Figure 8.79**).

✔ Tip

- You can remove a crease by selecting the edge that the crease is on and choosing Uncrease Edge/Vertex from the Subdiv Surfaces menu.

SKELETONS AND IK

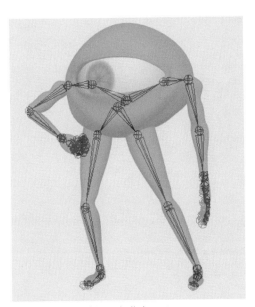

Figure 9.1 Inside this eyeball character you can see the skeleton, which is used to pose and animate her.

Once you model a character, you need to put a skeleton in it to be able to animate it. The skeleton is built as a hierarchy of joints with bones connecting them.

In general, the best template you can use for placing joints is nature. Use pictures of skeletons, whether of humans or animals (**Figure 9.1**). A shoulder joint should go at the shoulder; an elbow joint should go at the elbow. However, you don't need to be too literal. For example, although the human foot has 26 bones, you can animate a shoe with three bones. Wherever you want something to bend, that's where you need a joint.

Joints are hierarchical, so the joints above on the hierarchy will move those below. The first joint you place will be at the top of the hierarchy, and it is often referred to as the *root joint*—that is, the joint that moves the whole skeleton. The knee, ankle, and foot joints are below the hip joint, so when the hip joint is rotated, the rest of the leg moves with it. Animating in this fashion is called *forward kinematics* (FK) (**Figure 9.2**).

Inverse kinematics, usually referred to as IK, is a way of animating from the bottom of the hierarchy up. So you could move the foot around, and the knee and hip would rotate accordingly (**Figure 9.3**).

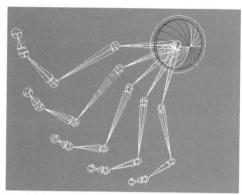

Figure 9.2 Illustrating the principle of forward kinematics, when the hip joint is rotated, all of the joints below rotate with it.

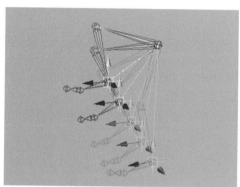

Figure 9.3 The foot is moved using an IK handle. Some animators avoid IK because it tends to move limbs in straight lines rather than natural arcs.

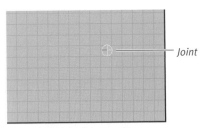

Joint

Figure 9.4 A joint is created in an orthographic view by selecting Skeleton > Joint Tool.

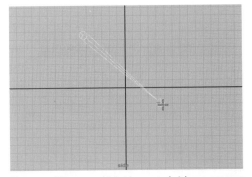

Figure 9.5 The second joint is created. A bone appears between them, showing that they are parented together. The thicker side of the bone shows which joint is the parent, and the thinner side of the bone shows which bone is the child.

About Joints

When you create joints, the bones appear automatically. The order in which you create joints is important because the first one will be at the top of the hierarchy, the second joint will be parented to the first, the third will be parented to the second, and so on down the line.

A joint is like a pivot point in a hierarchy. You can't take a joint's pivot point away; the joint will always stay with its pivot point. Its position in the hierarchy determines which joints will rotate with it; the joints below it in the hierarchy will rotate with it, the joints above it will not. Don't confuse this hierarchy with joints that are above and below physically. One joint can be above another in the Y direction but below it in the hierarchy.

To create joints:

1. From the Skeleton menu select Joint Tool.

2. In the Side view, click where you want the joint.

   A joint appears. You should generally use an orthographic view when you create joints (**Figure 9.4**).

3. Click where you want the next joint.

   A bone appears between the two joints (**Figure 9.5**).

4. Click and drag to place the third joint. Once the mouse button is released, the joint is placed.

   continues on next page

5. Press [Enter].

The skeleton is completed, and you are no longer in the Joint tool. The top joint of the hierarchy is selected, which causes the whole skeleton to be highlighted.

✔ Tips

■ It is often a good idea to build a skeleton with grid snap turned on. A convenient way to do this is to hold down [x] when you place joints.

■ You can make the joints appear bigger or smaller by selecting Display > Joint Size and choosing from the list.

■ To delete a joint, select the joint, and then press [Delete]. The joint will be deleted, along with any joints below it in the hierarchy.

Often you want to branch off from a joint in the hierarchy. For example, both arms branch off from the chest joint.

To branch off from an existing skeleton:

1. Create the skeleton from the previous page.

2. Click the Joint tool icon 🦴 .

3. Click the joint you want to branch off from.

   This will select the joint, not create a new one.

4. Click where you want the new joint

   A new joint appears with the bone branched off from the original skeleton (**Figure 9.6**).

5. From the Window menu select Hypergraph to see the resulting hierarchy.

   Note that two joints are at the same level in the hierarchy, both parented under the same joint (**Figure 9.7**).

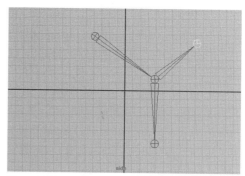

Figure 9.6 A new joint is branched off from the existing joints.

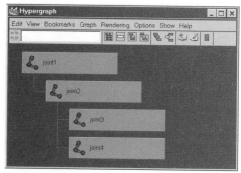

Figure 9.7 Joint3 and joint4 are both children of joint2. That means that if joint2 is rotated, joint3 and joint4 will rotate with it.

✔ Tip

■ Sometimes, when you try to branch off from an existing joint, it creates a new joint instead of selecting the one you want to branch off from. This happens when joints are turned off in the Pick mask.

   To fix this, make sure that joints are selected in the Pick mask, then select the joint you want to branch off from, then select the Joint tool and continue with step 3 above.

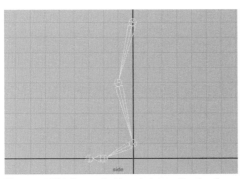

Figure 9.8 This is a typical leg skeleton. Starting from the top, the joints are named hip, knee, ankle, ball, and toe. If the character is wearing shoes, you do not need bones for each toe; one bone is sufficient to rotate the front of the shoe.

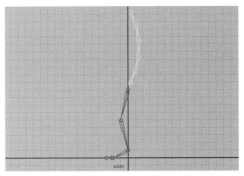

Figure 9.9 A spine joint is created from the bottom up. This makes the bottom joint the parent of the rest of the spine. The rest of the joints are below in the hierarchy even though they are above it in space.

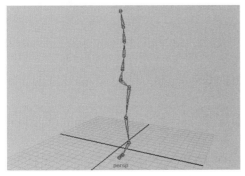

Figure 9.10 The leg has been parented to the spine. Now the bottom joint of the skeleton is the root joint for the whole character. When this joint is moved, the whole character moves.

Bones can be thought of as a visual representation of which joint is parented to which. When you parent one joint to another, a bone appears. If you unparent a joint, the bone disappears. Sometimes it is easier to create separate hierarchies and then put them together into a single skeleton by parenting them.

To parent joints:

1. Create the skeleton of a leg and foot out of five joints in the Side view (**Figure 9.8**).
   Press Enter to complete the creation.

2. As a separate hierarchy, create spine joints in the Side view, starting from the bottom and working your way up (**Figure 9.9**).

3. In the Front view, move the leg to the side.

4. Select the top joint of the leg. Shift-select the bottom joint of the spine. Press p.

5. A bone appears between the leg and the spine. It is now one hierarchy (**Figure 9.10**).

✔ Tip

■ You can similarly unparent joints. Select the joint you want to unparent and press Shift p. The joint becomes unparented, and the bone disappears.

To save time, once you create a leg or arm, you can mirror the joint, which makes a duplicate leg or arm on the other side of the body.

To mirror joints:

1. Create the leg from the previous sections.

2. Select the hip joint (**Figure 9.11**).

3. From the Skeleton menu, select the box next to Mirror Joint.

   This opens the Mirror Joint Options dialog box.

4. For Mirror Across, select YZ (**Figure 9.12**).

5. Click Mirror. A new leg appears on the other side (**Figure 9.13**).

✔ Tips

■ If the leg was built in the Side view, the YZ plane should be the correct one to mirror across. To figure out which you should use, look at the view axis in the corner of the panel and imagine two of the axes forming a plane that you want to mirror across. If the new leg does not appear in the correct location, undo the mirror joint and try a different plane to mirror across in the Mirror Joint Options dialog box.

■ Do not mirror a joint that falls on the center line of the body or you will get two joints on top of each other.

Figure 9.11 The hip joint is selected so that the leg can be mirrored over to the other side.

Figure 9.12 The YZ option is chosen so that the leg will mirror across the YZ plane.

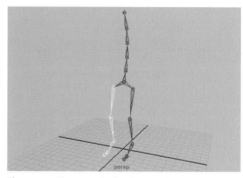

Figure 9.13 The opposite leg is created using the Mirror Joint Options dialog box from the Skeleton menu.

ABOUT JOINTS

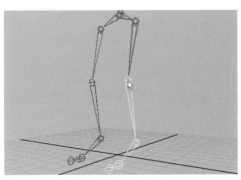

Figure 9.14 The knee joint of the leg is selected so that it can be moved.

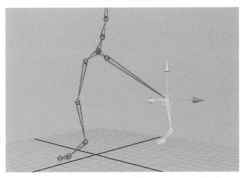

Figure 9.15 The knee is moved back, moving the foot bones with it. Note that the bone between the hip and the knee becomes longer.

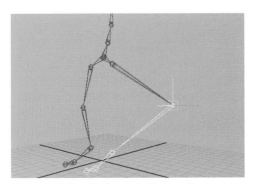

Figure 9.16 When the knee joint is moved in pivot move mode, the foot, which is below in the hierarchy, stays put.

You can move a joint after it is created to position it, and all the joints below in the hierarchy will move with it. You can also move a joint independent of its position in the hierarchy by using pivot move mode.

To move a joint:

1. Create a skeleton like the one from the previous sections.

2. Select the knee joint (**Figure 9.14**).

3. Press ⓦ.

4. Move the knee backward.
   The rest of the leg moves with it (**Figure 9.15**).

5. Press ⓩ to undo the last move.

6. Press [Insert]/[Home] on the keyboard.
   You are now in pivot move mode.

7. Move the knee forward.
   The rest of the leg does not move with it (**Figure 9.16**).

8. Press ⓩ to undo the last move. Press [Insert]/[Home] again to get out of pivot move mode.

To insert a joint:

1. Create a skeleton of several joints (**Figure 9.17**).

2. From the Skeleton menu select Insert Joint Tool.

3. Click on a joint and drag out the new joint.

   The new joint will be inserted between the joint you clicked on and the joint that was below it in the hierarchy. It is easiest to do this in an orthographic view (**Figure 9.18**).

4. Press (Enter) to finish, and exit the tool.

✔ Tip

■ You cannot insert a joint from one that branches in two or more directions; it will just make another branch. You can solve this problem by creating a new joint, parenting it to the joint you want to be above it in the hierarchy, and parenting the joint you want to be below in the hierarchy to the new joint.

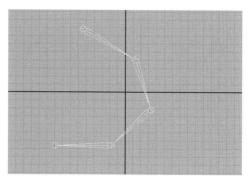

Figure 9.17 A skeleton of several joints is created in an orthographic view.

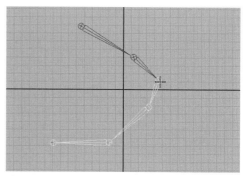

Figure 9.18 A new joint is created between two existing joints. It is between the joints physically as well as in the hierarchy.

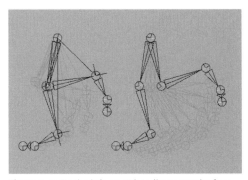

Figure 9.19 On the left, an IK handle moves the foot. On the right, both the hip and ankle are rotated to move the foot.

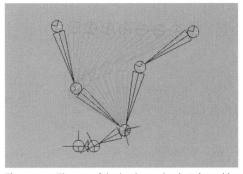

Figure 9.20 The top of the leg is moving but the ankle is staying put because it has an IK handle, which is keyframed. Note that this foot also has an IK handle going from the ankle to the ball and from the ball to the toe. These IK handles keep the rest of the foot in place.

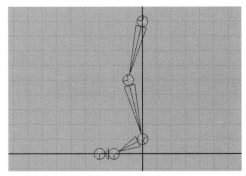

Figure 9.21 This is a typical leg skeleton. Sometimes a heel joint is added, but it is used merely as a placeholder since the ankle joint bends but the foot does not bend at the heel.

About IK Handles and Solvers

Inverse kinematics (IK) makes animation easier in many situations. For example, to put a foot in a certain position using forward Kinematics (FK), you would need to rotate the hip and the knee. By using an IK handle on the ankle, you can simply move the ankle into position, and the hip and knee will rotate accordingly (**Figure 9.19**).

An IK handle can also make a foot or hand stick in one spot. When your character is walking and you want one foot to stay planted on the ground, IK handles make it much easier to keep the foot in place (**Figure 9.20**). Once it is keyframed, the foot will do its best to stay where it is. The same goes for arms and hands. If your character is climbing a ladder or leaning against a wall, an IK handle will help keep it in place.

To add an IK handle:

1. Create a leg out of five joints (**Figure 9.21**).

2. From the Skeleton menu select IK Handle Tool.

3. Click the hip joint.

4. Click the ankle joint.
   An IK handle is created.

continues on next page

5. Move the IK handle around (**Figure 9.22**).

6. Select Twist in the Channel Box.

7. Middle mouse button–drag from left to right in the Perspective view.

The leg rotates around the IK chain. The twist attribute only works on a Rotate Plane (RP) type of IK handle (**Figure 9.23**).

By default, a Rotate Plane solver is created when you make an IK handle. If you move the IK handle up too high, the leg flips around, and the knee points in the opposite direction (**Figure 9.24**). You can solve this problem by adjusting the pole vector attributes, which are in the Channel Box for the IK handle.

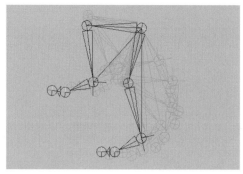

Figure 9.22 The IK handle is moved around, allowing for easy placement of the foot.

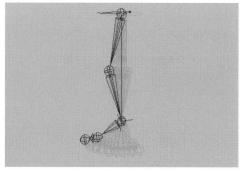

Figure 9.23 The leg rotates around by using the twist attribute.

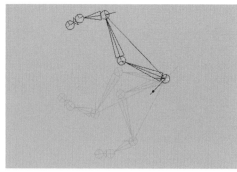

Figure 9.24 When lifted too high, a leg can flip over if you are using an RP IK handle.

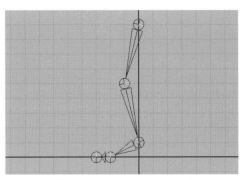

Figure 9.25 This is the basic skeleton for a leg.

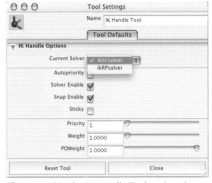

Figure 9.26 In the IK Handle Tool options in the Tool Settings window, ikSCsolver is chosen. This type of IK handle will not cause the flipping problem that an RP handle can cause.

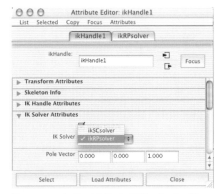

Figure 9.27 In the Attribute Editor for the IK handle, you can change the type of solver after it is created.

You can also create a Single Chain solver, which doesn't permit the Twist, but it also doesn't have the flipping problem. When using a Single Chain solver, you can rotate the limb by rotating the IK handle. Rotate Plane is considered more predictable because it is not affected by the rotation of the IK handle.

To create a Single Chain IK handle:

1. Create a leg out of five joints (**Figure 9.25**).

2. From the Skeleton menu select the box next to IK Handle Tool.

   This opens the options window.

3. Select ikSCsolver from the pop-up menu next to Current Solver (**Figure 9.26**).

4. Click the hip joint.

5. Click the ankle joint. An IK handle is created with a Single Chain solver.

6. Rotate the IK handle.

   The limb rotates around.

✔ Tip

- You can also change the type of solver after the IK handle is created. To do this, select the IK handle and open the Attribute Editor. If you click IK Solver Attributes, you will be able to choose the solver type from the pop-up menu (**Figure 9.27**).

About Spline IK

Spline IK provides a way of controlling many joints using a curve instead of having to rotate them directly. It is especially useful when there are many joints in a continuous chain, as in a spine or a tail. You can quickly move the skeleton into a shape you want without having to rotate each individual joint (**Figure 9.28**).

To create a Spline IK:

1. Create a spine skeleton, starting from the bottom and working your way up (**Figure 9.29**).

2. From the Skeleton menu select Spline IK (Windows) or IK Spline Handle Tool (Mac).

3. Click the top joint of the skeleton.

4. Click the joint second from the bottom of the skeleton.

    Two things are created, the Spline IK handle and a curve. By default, the curve is automatically parented to the joints.

5. Select Twist in the Channel Box.

6. Middle mouse button–drag from left to right.

    The bones rotate around.

7. From the Hypergraph select the curve that was just created (**Figure 9.30**).

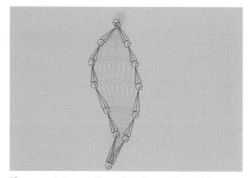

Figure 9.28 By creating a IK spline on these joints, this animation of a spine skeleton can be done by moving just one point. Keyframing the rotation of each joint to achieve the same effect would be much more difficult.

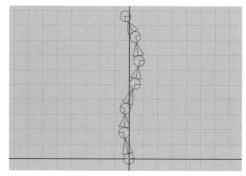

Figure 9.29 The human spine has a natural curve. When creating a spine for the character, it is helpful to match the shape of its back.

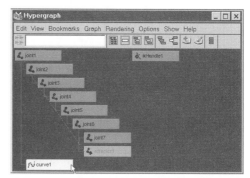

Figure 9.30 It is easier to select the curve in the Hypergraph.

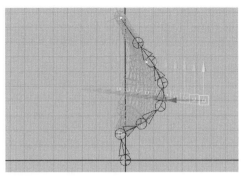

Figure 9.31 When the CV is moved, the spine bends to form the shape of the control curve.

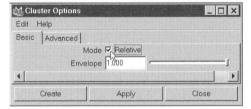

Figure 9.32 In the Cluster Options dialog box, Relative is checked.

8. In the Pick mask, select component mode. You can now see the CVs of the curve.

9. Select and move a CV (**Figure 9.31**).

The joints rotate in response and stick to the shape of the control curve.

✔ Tip

■ In general, you do not want to use the root joint of the skeleton as part of your Spline IK chain. If you do, when you are moving the CVs around, the whole skeleton will rotate. To avoid this, choose one joint above the root joint of the skeleton as the base of your Spline IK.

When you are using Spline IK to animate, you move and keyframe CVs. However, CVs don't have their own node, they are components, so they don't show up in the Hypergraph or Outliner. It can be helpful to make a cluster for each CV of the curve so that there is a node that you can keep track of when animating.

To create clusters for a Spline IK's CVs:

1. Create a Spline IK as in the previous section.

Be sure that the root joint of the skeleton is not part of the IK chain.

2. Select one of the CVs of the control curve.

3. From the Deform menu select the box next to Create Cluster. The Cluster Options dialog box opens.

4. Check the box next to Relative (**Figure 9.32**).

Checking this will make the cluster move relative to the curve. It prevents a "double transform." In this case, if Relative were not checked, when the root joint was moved, the cluster would move twice as much.

continues on next page

5. Click Create.

The cluster is created and is represented as a C (**Figure 9.33**).

6. [Shift]-select the root joint of the skeleton.

7. Press [p]. The cluster is now parented to the root joint so it will move with the whole skeleton.

8. Repeat steps 2 through 7 for all the CVs of the control curve except the bottom one.

There are now clusters for each of the CVs. These can be easily selected and animated (**Figure 9.34**).

✔ Tip

■ When you are making clusters out of the CVs of the curve for an IK spline, do not make a cluster for the bottom CV of the curve. Moving this CV will stretch out the bone, which is usually undesirable.

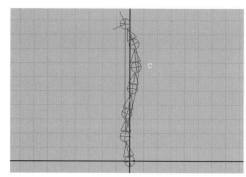

Figure 9.33 A C for the cluster appears where the CV is. The cluster controls the CV.

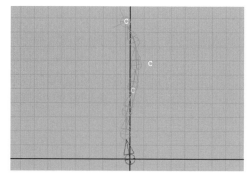

Figure 9.34 A cluster has been created for each joint except the bottom joint. When the cluster is moved, the CV will be moved, thus allowing you to shape the spine.

PARENTING AND BINDING TO A SKELETON

10

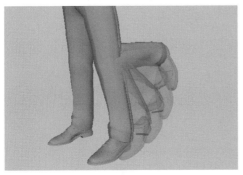

Figure 10.1 For the leg to bend at the knee, it needs to be bound to a skeleton.

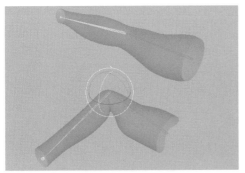

Figure 10.2 When the elbow joint is rotated, only the forearm rotates with it.

Once you have created a skeleton, you need to either parent or bind the surfaces to the joints in order for the surfaces to move with the skeleton. Anything that doesn't need to bend, like a hat, glasses, or eyeballs, can be parented to the joints. But something that does need to bend, like an arm, leg, or torso, needs to be bound to the skeleton (**Figure 10.1**).

Parenting to joints works much like parenting to anything else. The bone is the parent, the surface is the child, so the surface rotates and moves with the bone.

Binding is different. When a surface is bound to a skeleton, only a portion of that surface will move with a bone. For example, an arm has a shoulder joint and an elbow joint. Only the forearm should move when the elbow is rotated; the shoulder and biceps should stay put (**Figure 10.2**). When you bind the arm, you make the forearm part of the arm attached to the elbow joint, and the shoulder and biceps part of the arm attach to the shoulder joint.

At the heart of binding are *clusters*. A cluster is like a set of points that have weight. Weight is the amount of influence a cluster has over each individual point included in the set. Understanding clusters and weight is an important step along the way to understanding binding.

There are two kinds of binding—*rigid bind* and *smooth bind*. Rigid bind works well for things like arms, legs, and fingers—things that bend clearly at a joint and are rigid in between. Smooth bind works well for things like torsos, tails, and snakes—things that bend gradually along a surface (**Figure 10.3**). Either can be used for any kind of surface, and in some cases it just comes down to personal preference.

The surface of a simple character, such as a robot, might be able to be parented to a skeleton rather than bound to it. If all the parts are made out of metal and don't bend, it does not need to be bound. This is a good way to create your first character. It is easy to set up and quick to animate.

To parent surfaces to joints:

1. Create the surfaces of a character (**Figure 10.4**).

2. Create a skeleton (**Figure 10.5**). (See Chapter 9.)

3. Select a surface.

4. (Shift)-select the joint to which it will be parented.

5. Press (p).

   Now when you select and rotate that joint, the surface will rotate with it.

6. Repeat steps 3 through 6 for all the other surfaces.

   Now when any joint is rotated, the parented surface moves with it (**Figure 10.6**).

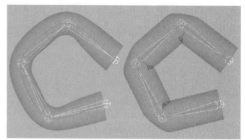

Figure 10.3 The two objects have identical geometry and the same joints, which are rotated equally. However, the one on the left is smooth bound, and the one on the right is rigid bound. The surface on the left bends more smoothly; and the one on the right bends more abruptly and is straighter between joints.

Figure 10.4 This character is built from simple shapes. Since he is a robot made of steel, he does not bend. Therefore, he is a good candidate to have his surfaces parented to joints rather than bound to them.

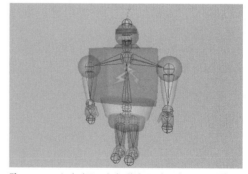

Figure 10.5 A skeleton is built into the character. The root joint, which is at the top of the hierarchy, is at the waist.

Figure 10.6 Once all the surfaces have been parented to the appropriate joints, you can pose or animate the character.

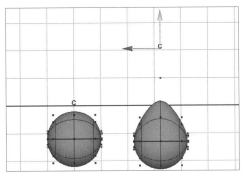

Figure 10.7 A cluster is made with one CV whose weight is set to 0.5. The point moves only half the distance of the cluster (right).

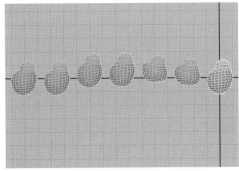

Figure 10.8 The points that make up the belly are included in a cluster. That cluster is parented to the belly and animated to make it bouncy.

About Clusters and Weights

A cluster is a way of controlling a set of points as a group. The points could be NURBS control vertices (CVs), polygon vertices, or lattice points.

The points that are members of a cluster have weight. As mentioned earlier, weight is the amount of influence the cluster has over the points in it. Weight is generally set between 0 and 1. A point with a weight of 0 will not move with the cluster at all. A point with a weight of 1 will move exactly as much as the cluster moves. Anything in between will make the point move a fraction of how much the cluster moves.

For example, suppose a CV in a cluster has a weight of 0.5. If the cluster is moved up two grid units in the y direction, the CV will move only one unit (**Figure 10.7**). You simply multiply the weight by the distance the cluster moves and you will get the distance the point moves.

Clusters are a convenient way to animate portions of a surface. For example, if you wanted to animate the movement of a character's fat belly, you could make a cluster out of the points that form his belly and then animate that cluster (**Figure 10.8**).

Understanding clusters is also the key to understanding binding. What binding does, in the background, is create clusters of portions of your surface, then parents those clusters to the joints. Once the surface has been bound, you can adjust the weight of the points to get the surface to deform the way you want it. When you understand parenting, clusters, and weight, binding no longer seems mysterious.

continues on next page

To create a cluster:

1. From the Create menu select NURBS Primitives > Plane.

2. Select makeNurbPlane1 from the INPUTS section of the Channel Box (**Figure 10.9**).

3. Increase Patches U and Patches V to 30. The plane becomes denser (**Figure 10.10**).

4. Press F8 to go into component mode.

5. Select some points in the center of the plane (**Figure 10.11**).

6. From the Deform menu select Create Cluster.

   A C appears in the middle of where the points were selected.

7. Press w to go into move mode and then move the cluster.

   The CVs move with it (**Figure 10.12**).

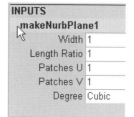

Figure 10.9
When you click on makeNurbPlane1 in the Channel Box, it will expand these options.

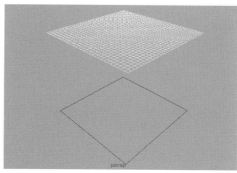

Figure 10.10 At the bottom is the plane before the patches were increased. At the top is the plane after the patches were increased.

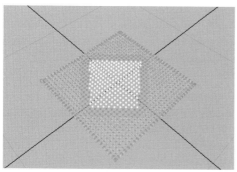

Figure 10.11 The plane is dense, so it has many points. The CVs in the center have been selected so that they can be made into a cluster.

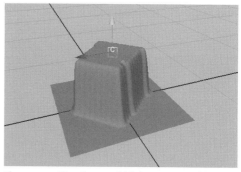

Figure 10.12 The cluster, which is represented by a C, has been moved up. The CVs, which are members of the cluster, move with it, forming a plateau.

ABOUT CLUSTERS AND WEIGHTS

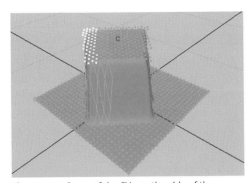

Figure 10.13 Some of the CVs on the side of the cluster have been selected so that their weight can be changed.

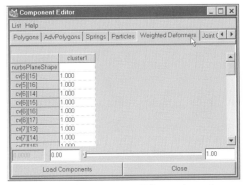

Figure 10.14 In the Component Editor, a cluster is referred to as a Weighted Deformer. The weights of the selected points show up when this tab is selected.

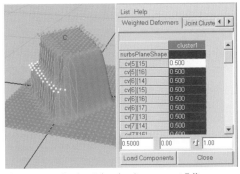

Figure 10.15 On the right, the Component Editor shows that the weights of the selected points have been reduced to 0.5. On the left, the selected points are only moved up half the distance of the cluster because of their lower weight.

To weight the points of a cluster using the Component Editor:

1. Create a cluster as in the previous section.

2. Select some of the CVs that are included in the cluster (**Figure 10.13**).

3. From the Window menu select General Editors > Component Editor.
   The Component Editor Window appears.

4. Select the Weighted Deformers Tab in the Component Editor (**Figure 10.14**).

5. Click on the topmost numeric field and drag down to highlight all of the weights.

6. Type .5 in the field, and press (Enter).
   All the weights in that column become 0.5 (**Figure 10.15**).

7. For Windows, click the cluster1 button that is above the column of weight numbers. (Ctrl)/(Control)-click the top field in the column of weights.

8. When you use the slider at the bottom of the Component Editor, the CVs move, and the weights change interactively.

ABOUT CLUSTERS AND WEIGHTS

About the Attribute Paint tool

Another way of adjusting the weights of a cluster is by using the Attribute Paint tool. It is especially helpful when working with dense surfaces, and it has several options to interactively change the weighting on points (**Figure 10.16**).

There are four settings for Paint Operations:

Replace—When Paint Operation is set to Replace, the current weight of the points that are painted will change to whatever number is set in the Value field.

Add—When Paint Operation is set to Add, the Value will be added to the weight of the points that are painted. This is useful for increasing the weights of points by small increments.

Scale—When Paint Operation is set to Scale, the current weight of a point will be multiplied by the Value when it is painted. If you have a value of 0.9, you can incrementally decrease the weight of a point.

Smooth—This averages the weights of the adjacent points to make the area smoother.

The Flood button can speed up work considerably. Rather than having to paint on an effect, you can have the settings of the Attribute Paint tool affect all the points simultaneously by pressing Flood. This is useful for such situations as setting all the points to the same weight or smoothing all the points.

To edit cluster weights using the Attribute Paint tool:

1. Create a cluster, and move it up as in the previous sections.

2. Select the surface.

3. Right mouse button–click the surface. In the Marking Menu that appears, select Paint > cluster-cluster1 > weights (**Figure 10.17**).

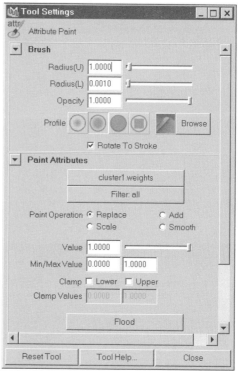

Figure 10.16 The Attribute Paint Tool can be used for interactively changing the weights of points. The options shown here control how the weight is changed.

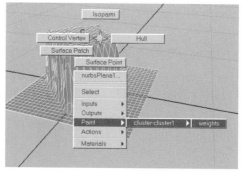

Figure 10.17 Using the Marking Menu, which pops up when you right mouse button–click the surface, is the most convenient way to access the Attribute Paint tool.

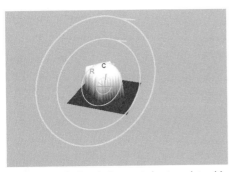

Figure 10.18 The brush size started out much too big for this small surface. Here we see the progression as the brush size gets smaller.

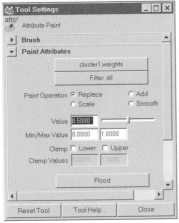

Figure 10.19 Using Replace with a value of 0.5 will bring about the same result as if you typed it in as the weight in the Component Editor.

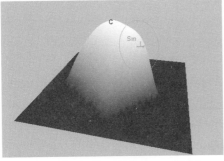

Figure 10.20 Flood will apply the current Paint Operation setting to all the members of the cluster. In this case it is set to Smooth so that all the points are smoothed simultaneously when you click Flood which is quicker than having to paint the surface.

This activates the Attribute Paint tool. Color feedback should show up as long as you are in shaded mode. The area of the surface that has CVs in the cluster turns white; the rest appears black.

4. Hold down b and drag the mouse from right to left to shrink the brush size (**Figure 10.18**).

5. Double-click the Attribute Paint tool in the toolbox. The Tool Settings window for the Attribute Paint tool appears.

6. Change the Value to 0.5.
   The Paint Operation should already be set on Replace (**Figure 10.19**).

7. Click and drag on the surface.
   The part that is painted moves down because the weight of the points has been changed to 0.5.

8. Change the Paint Operation to Smooth.

9. Click Flood several times.
   The lump becomes smooth (**Figure 10.20**).

About Binding

When you bind skin, you are making the surfaces move with the bones. At first the process may seem mysterious, but it is for the most part a combination of what you already know.

We've learned that when you parent a surface to a joint, it rotates with that joint. We also know that a cluster is a set of points that have weight. Binding skin is like a combination of these two things. It creates a cluster that is made up of the points nearest to a bone, and then parents that cluster to the bone. After this is done, you can adjust the weight to make the points rotate more or less with a specific joint (**Figure 10.21**).

As mentioned earlier, there are two kinds of binding—rigid and smooth. When you use rigid bind, each point can only be a member of one joint. When you use smooth bind, each point is a member of more than one joint. Its weight is spread out among two or more joints, but the total weight always adds up to 1 (**Figure 10.22**).

To bind skin using rigid bind:

1. From the Create menu select NURBS Primitives > Cylinder.

2. Increase the Scale Y to 8 (**Figure 10.23**).

3. In the Channel Box select makeNurbCylinder1.

4. Increase the Spans to 8 (**Figure 10.24**). Bound surfaces require extra detail, particularly in the areas where they bend.

5. Create three joints in the surface (**Figure 10.25**). (See Chapter 10 for more on joints.)

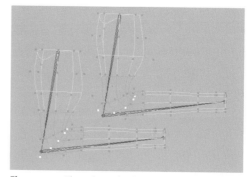

Figure 10.21 The selected points of the arm on the top have a weight of 1. They rotate as much as the elbow rotates. The same points on the bottom arm rotate only half as much as the elbow joint rotates because their weight is set to 0.5.

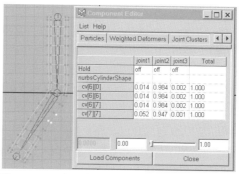

Figure 10.22 The cylinder on the left has been smooth bound. The weights of the selected points show up in the Component Editor. Their weight is spread among the three joints; however, they are primarily influenced by joint2.

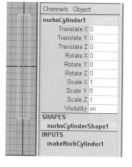

Figure 10.23 On the left is the cylinder with a y scale of 8; on the right is the channel box, which is a convenient place to change the scale to a precise number.

INPUTS
makeNurbCylinder1

Radius	1
Start Sweep	0
End Sweep	360
Degree	Cubic
Sections	8
Spans	8
Height Ratio	2

Figure 10.24 On the left is a cylinder with 8 spans; on the right is the Channel Box with attributes for this cylinder.

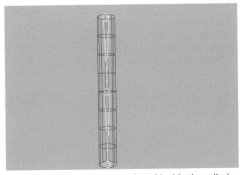

Figure 10.25 Three joints are placed inside the cylinder, which produces two bones.

Figure 10.26 The Rigid Bind Skin Options window is set to Bind to Complete Skeleton and Color Joints. Complete Skeleton means that the skin will be bound to every joint in the hierarchy, as opposed to just the selected ones. Color Joints means that the joints and the points that become members of those joints will be color-coded the same, once the skin is bound.

6. Select the joints, and (Shift)-select the surface.

7. From the Skin menu select the box next to Bind Skin > Rigid Bind.
   The Rigid Bind Skin Options window opens.

8. Select Complete Skeleton in the "Bind to" menu, and check Color Joints next to Coloring (**Figure 10.26**).

9. Click the Bind Skin button.

10. Select the middle joint and rotate it.
    The lower half of the surface moves with the bone (**Figure 10.27**).

✔ Tips

■ Any kind of surface can be bound to a skeleton—NURBS, polygon, or subdivision. You can also bind a lattice, or just a selection of points.

■ You can bind a whole character with multiple surfaces at once. To do this, select the root joint of the skeleton and all of the surfaces involved, then bind the skin.

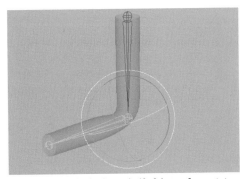

Figure 10.27 Only the lower half of the surface rotates with the middle joint.

A point is a member of a specific joint when you use rigid bind. Sometimes it is a member of the wrong joint. The Edit Membership tool allows you to change which joint the point is a member of.

To edit the membership of a point

1. Create the bound cylinder from the previous section.

2. Select the middle joint.

3. From the Deform menu select Edit Membership Tool.

   The cursor changes.

4. Click the middle joint.

   The points that are members of that joint are selected.

5. Shift-select the middle row of points (**Figure 10.28**).

   This adds points to the membership of the middle joint, and they, too, are selected. If you do not hold down Shift, it will not work.

6. Select and rotate the middle joint.

   The points that were just added now rotate with the joint (**Figure 11.29**).

✔ Tips

- If you Ctrl/Control-select points, they will be removed from the membership of a joint when you are in the Edit Membership tool. However, if they are not added to a joint, the points will be left behind when the character moves.

- The Edit Membership tool can be used for any deformer, such as a lattice or a blend shape.

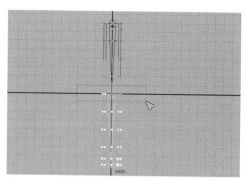

Figure 10.28 The Edit Membership tool allows you to change which joint the points are members of. Here some of the points that were not members of the middle joint are being added to that joint.

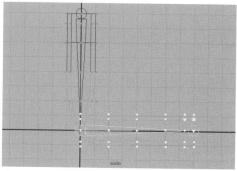

Figure 10.29 When a joint is rotated, all the points that are members of that joint rotate with it. Therefore, the points we just added rotate along with the joint as well.

ABOUT BINDING

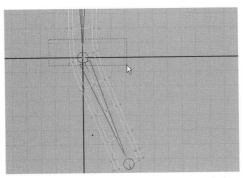

Figure 10.30 Some of the CVs of the surface are being selected so that their weight can be changed. Be sure to be in component mode when you try to select CVs.

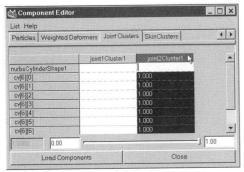

Figure 10.31 In the Component Editor, the entire column of numbers is highlighted when the button above the column is selected. This allows you to conveniently change all their weights at once.

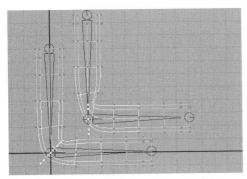

Figure 10.32 The selected points of the cylinder on top have not yet been changed—they still have a weight of 1. On the bottom cylinder, the selected points have a weight of 0.5.

To edit the weights of rigid bound points:

1. Continue with the bound cylinder from the previous section.

2. Select the row of points at the middle joint (**Figure 10.30**).

3. From the Window menu select General Editors > Component Editor.

4. Click the Joint Clusters tab.

5. Click on the topmost numeric field and drag down to highlight all of the weights. In this case it is labeled joint2Cluster1. The column is highlighted (**Figure 10.31**).

6. Type .5 in the field.

   All the weights for the selected points become 0.5. The points now rotate half the distance of the joint, creating a smoother shape around the joint (**Figure 10.32**).

Sometimes the area where a surface bends seems too rounded and you want it to be more angular, as with an elbow. A flexor is an easy way to adjust the rounding and creasing that occurs on a surface near a joint.

To create a flexor:

1. Create a rigid bound cylinder like the one in the previous sections.

2. Make sure that the joint to which you want to add the flexor is straight—that is, its rotations are zero.

3. Select the middle joint.

4. From the Skin menu select Edit Rigid Skin > Create Flexor.

5. Click Create.

    A lattice is created around the joint (**Figure 10.33**).

6. Rotate the joint about 90 degrees (**Figure 10.34**).

    When the joint is rotated, the flexor reshapes the surface automatically to prevent creasing.

7. Select the lattice that appeared when the flexor was created.

8. Click Rounding in the Channel Box.

9. Middle mouse button–drag from left to right in the panel until the bent area of the surface is more angular and elbow-shaped (**Figure 10.35**).

✔ Tip

- If you check Position the Flexor in the Create Flexor Options window, it will group the lattice and lattice base together. This allows you to reshape the lattice by moving and scaling the group without having it affect the shape of the surface.

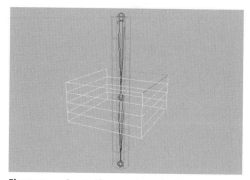

Figure 10.33 Create Flexor makes a lattice appear around the selected joint. It has special attributes that other lattices do not have. Be sure to add a flexor only when the joint is straight; otherwise you will get undesirable results.

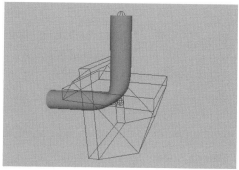

Figure 10.34 A flexor has been put on the middle joint. As the joint is rotated, the flexor improves the shape of the surface where it is bent.

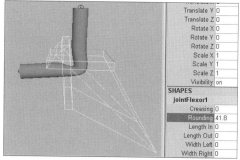

Figure 10.35 By adjusting the Rounding attribute, you can make the bent portion more angular. This is commonly used on things like elbows, knees, and finger joints. When the joint is rotated to straight again, the surface goes back to its original shape.

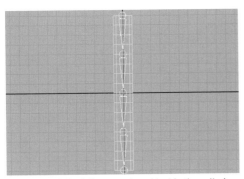

Figure 10.36 Five joints are placed inside the cylinder. Smooth bind lends itself to parts of characters that have many joints and need to bend smoothly.

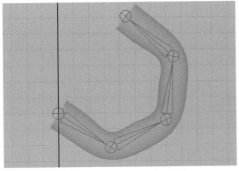

Figure 10.37 This is a smooth bound cylinder.

To bind skin using smooth bind:

1. From the Create Menu select NURBS Primitives > Cylinder.

2. Increase the Scale Y to 8.

3. In the Channel Box select makeNurbCylinder1.

4. Increase the Spans to 16.

    Bound surfaces require extra detail, particularly in the area where they bend.

5. Create five joints in the cylinder (**Figure 10.36**).

6. Select the surface, and Shift-select the root joint.

7. From the Skin menu select Bind Skin > Smooth Bind.

8. Select the top joints, and then Shift-select the rest of the joints one by one. Rotate all the joints simultaneously.

    The surface moves with the joints and bends smoothly (**Figure 10.37**).

To paint skin weights on a smooth bound surface:

1. Create a polygon shape from a cube by scaling it using Extrude Face, and then from the Polygon menu select Smooth (**Figure 10.38**). (See Chapter 8 for more on polygons.) The shape roughly represents an arm extending from a torso.

2. Create four joints in the surface (**Figure 10.39**).

3. Select the root joint, and (Shift)-select the surface.

4. From the Skin menu select Bind Skin > Smooth Bind.

5. Select and rotate the second joint.

   It bends too much of the torso portion of the surface (**Figure 10.40**).

6. Select the surface.

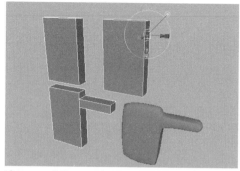

Figure 10.38 Here are four stages in creating the surface. First create a polygon cube and scale it. Extrude the side face and scale, and move it to the start point of the arm. Extrude again and pull the arm out. Finally, smooth the surface with divisions set to 3 and continuity set to 0.35.

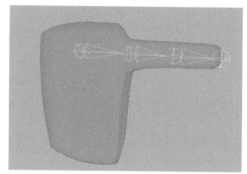

Figure 10.39 Starting from the center of the chest, four joints are placed inside the surface.

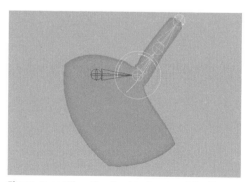

Figure 10.40 When the shoulder is rotated, it affects too much of the torso. Had there been more joints placed in the torso, this would not have been as much of a problem because the points would stick to the joints they were near. It is common practice to put rib joints in a character for this purpose.

ABOUT BINDING

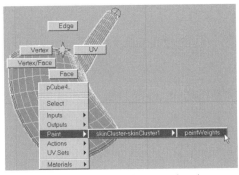

Figure 10.41 The right mouse button makes the Marking Menu appear for easy access to the Paint Skin Weights tool.

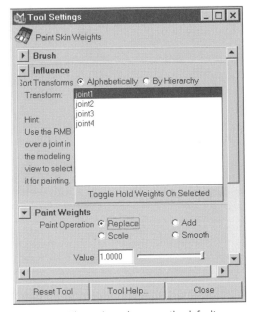

Figure 10.42 The options shown are the default settings for the Paint Skin Weights tool, and they happen to be what we need in this instance.

7. Right mouse button–click the surface, and select Paint > skinCluster-skinCluster1 > paintWeights (Windows) or skinWeights (Mac) (**Figure 10.41**).

   The Paint Skin Weights Tool is activated.

8. Double-click the Paint Skin Weights tool button in the toolbox ⚔.

   This opens the Tool Settings window for Paint Skin Weights. Under Influence, joint1 should be selected; Replace should be the Paint Operation; and the Value should be 1.0000 (**Figure 10.42**).

9. Adjust the brush size by holding down ⓑ and middle mouse button–dragging from right to left.

   continues on next page

10. Paint all over the surface of the torso (**Figure 10.43**).

It moves back to its original shape and turns white. This is because all of the weight is being put on joint1 and taken away from joint2.

11. Change the Paint Operation to Smooth.

12. Click Flood several times.

The area where the surface bends is smoothed (**Figure 10.44**).

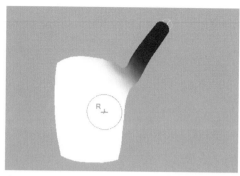

Figure 10.43 When the surface is painted, the points get a weight of 1 with the first joint, so they do not move with the shoulder joint. Be sure to get all around the surface with the brush.

Figure 10.44 Flooding with Smooth creates a smoother connection at the shoulder.

ANIMATION

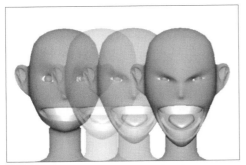

Figure 11.1 The monkey's face goes from happy to angry. The shape of his face is being animated. This monkey was created by Toby Marvin.

Maya was built for animation. It's not just motion that can be animated in Maya; almost anything you encounter can be animated, such as a color, an object's shape, or the intensity of a light (**Figure 11.1**)

Most animation is done by setting keyframes. The term *keyframe* stems from traditional hand-drawn animation. A lead animator would do *key* poses of a character—drawings at the beginning and end of an action—and an assistant would then draw the in-between frames, making the final result a smooth motion. When using Maya, you are the lead animator and the program is your assistant. To animate, you set keyframes—that is, you tell an object or attribute where to be at certain points in time—and the program in-betweens it for you.

Animations are very easy to tweak. The timing or distance covered by existing keyframes can be changed. Keyframes can be added or removed. The acceleration between keyframes can be adjusted by tweaking the animation curve that is made between them.

Animation Controls

The Time and Range sliders are Maya's primary controls for creating and fine-tuning your animation (**Figure 11.2**).

Time Slider—The Time Slider determines your position in time. It is the area at the bottom of the screen that includes the playback buttons and timeline. You can click any frame to go to that point in time, or click and drag to preview a region of animation. It is also used to select, move, and scale keyframes (**Figure 11.3**).

Current Time Indicator—This shows the present position in time (**Figure 11.4**).

Current Time—This also shows the current position in time, and you can type a number in this field to change the current time (**Figure 11.5**).

Start Time/End Time—This is the range of time for the whole animation. These numbers establish the length of time within which the Range Slider can move (**Figure 11.6**).

Range Slider— The Range Slider controls the portion of time you are looking at. It has character sets, Auto Keyframe toggle, and Animation preferences adjacent to it. The Range Slider allows you to quickly adjust what portion of the animation shows up in the timeline. You can use the buttons on the end to change the Playback Start and End times, or you can drag the range forward or backward as a whole. This is very helpful when you only want to work on small portions of an animation. The smaller the range, the easier it is to pick individual frames (**Figure 11.7**).

ANIMATION CONTROLS

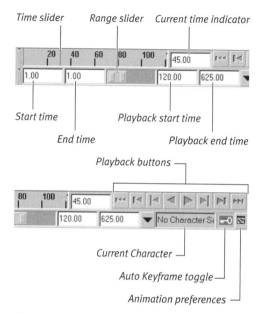

Time slider   Range slider   Current time indicator

Start time   Playback start time

End time   Playback end time

Playback buttons

Current Character

Auto Keyframe toggle

Animation preferences

Figure 11.2 The Timeline and Range Slider allow you to play back animation, control your position in time, and choose the portion of the animation you are looking at.

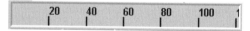

Figure 11.3 Click any point in the timeline to go to that time.

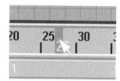

Figure 11.4 The Current Time Indicator shows what frame you are on. If you want to cut, copy, or delete a frame in the timeline, the Current Time Indicator must be over that frame.

Figure 11.5 The Current Time field also tells you where you are in time. You can type in any time, even if it is not included in the playback range, and go to that time.

Figure 11.6 The number fields on the far left and far right are the Start and End times. These should generally be set to the start and end of your entire animation. They can be changed at any time.

Figure 11.7 The Range Slider is a convenient way to change the portion of the animation that is currently in the timeline.

Figure 11.8 The Playback Start and End times are the fields on the left and right. You can type in the times that will change the beginning and end of your timeline.

Figure 11.9 From left to right, the playback buttons are: Go to start of playback range, step back one frame, step back one key, play backward, play forward, step forward one key, step forward one frame, go to end of playback range.

Figure 11.10 The Auto Keyframe function is on when the button looks like this.

Figure 11.11 This is the Animation Preferences button.

Figure 11.12 You can create and choose character sets here.

Playback Start Time/Playback End Time— Controls the range of animation that will play back, much like the Range Slider (**Figure 11.8**).

Playback buttons—These are like the buttons on a CD player. The rewind and fast-forward buttons change the current time to the start or end of the playback range. You can step forward one frame at a time, or move to the next or previous keyframe. There is a playback button to go forward or backward; it toggles to a stop button during playback (**Figure 11.9**).

Auto Keyframe toggle—This turns Auto Keyframing on and off. If it is on, any attribute that is already keyframed will be automatically keyframed again when you change its value (**Figure 11.10**).

Animation Preferences button— This opens up a window to set animation preferences. It is also a convenient way to access all general preferences in Maya (**Figure 11.11**).

Current Character—This sets which character in a scene you are currently working on. It is helpful, when working with more than one character, to be able to access individual characters' attributes (**Figure 11.12**).

About Setting Keyframes

Keyframes are at the heart of animation in Maya. Setting a keyframe means that you want a certain attribute to have a specific value at a point in time. For example, a ball could have a translate X of -2 at frame 1, and a translate X of 2 at frame 10. Between those frames it would gradually move across the screen (**Figure 11.13**).

There are many ways to set keyframes and adjust them once they are set. When you set a keyframe, a couple of things happen. The channels that were keyframed are highlighted orange in the Channel Box. Also, you will see key ticks in the timeline. Key ticks appear as thin red lines showing you where each keyframe is (**Figure 11.14**). Keyframes also show up in the Graph Editor and the Dope Sheet, discussed later in this chapter.

There are many ways to set a keyframe. The following section covers most of them.

To set a keyframe:

1. From the Create menu, select NURBS Primitives > Sphere.

2. Press Shift w.

    This keyframes only the translates. Shift e keyframes the rotates, and Shift r keyframes the scales. These correspond to the hotkeys for the move, rotate, and scale tools.

3. In the Channel Box, select Rotate X, and Shift-select Rotate Y and Z (**Figure 11.15**).

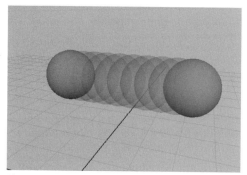

Figure 11.13 As you play back the animation, the sphere moves across the panel.

Figure 11.14 That thin line near the 10 is a key tick. It shows up red and lets you know there is a keyframe for the selected object at that time.

Channels	Object	
nurbsSphere1		
Translate X		0
Translate Y		0
Translate Z		0
Rotate X		0
Rotate Y		0
Rotate Z		0
Scale X		1
Scale Y		1
Scale Z		1
Visibility		on

Figure 11.15 Rotate X, Y, and Z are selected in the Channel Box so that they can be keyframed. You can easily select multiple attributes in the Channel Box by clicking and dragging the names.

Figure 11.16 When you right mouse button–click in the Channel Box, you can keyframe the selected attributes.

Figure 11.17 The current time is changed to 20 by typing it in the field. When you have a particularly long playback range, typing in a frame number can be easier than clicking it in the timeline.

4. Right mouse button–click in the Channel Box , and select Key Selected from the marking menu that appears. (**Figure 11.16**).

   Any channels that are selected, in this case the rotates, are keyframed.

5. Go to frame 10 by clicking that number in the timeline.

6. Move and rotate the sphere.

7. Press $\boxed{s}$.

   All attributes in the Channel Box are keyframed.

8. Turn on Auto Keyframe ⊡.

   The button will look pressed down and become highlighted.

9. Type 20 into the Current Time field to change the time in the timeline, and press $\boxed{Enter}$ (**Figure 11.17**).

10. Move the sphere.

    A new keyframe appears because when Auto Keyframe is turned on, it sets a keyframe any time an attribute is changed.

✔ Tip

- You can only set keyframes on an object when that object is selected. Likewise, you can only see the key ticks in the timeline when the keyframed object is selected.

While much of the advanced editing of keyframes can be done in the Graph Editor and Dope Sheet windows (discussed later in this chapter), you have access to the most frequently used editing tools right in the timeline.

To edit keyframes in the timeline:

1. From the Create menu, select NURBS Primitives > Sphere.

2. Change the playback start time to 1 and the playback end time to 30.

3. Set keyframes on the sphere every five frames, starting with the first frame. Move the sphere, and then change the current time after each time you set a keyframe. If Auto Keyframe is still on, you can press (Shift)(w) in the first frame, and all the other frames will automatically be keyed (**Figure 11.18**).

4. Click a frame in the timeline where there is a key tick. Right mouse button–click the timeline, and select Delete from the pop-up menu (**Figure 11.19**).
   The keyframe is removed.

5. Hold down (Shift), and click and drag over the range of two key ticks in the timeline.
   A red area should appear with two small arrows near the middle and two small arrows at the edges (**Figure 11.20**).

6. Click and drag from left to right on the two small arrows in the center of the selected area.
   The keyframes move together. You can do this with an individual keyframe as well.

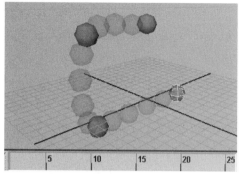

Figure 11.18 This is an example of some simple motion you can put on the object. The sphere is selected and keyframed by pressing (Shift)(w). With Auto Keyframe turned on, it will automatically keyframe the sphere every time you move it.

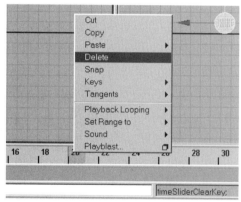

Figure 11.19 Right mouse button–clicking the timeline gives you access to a variety of convenient commands.

Figure 11.20 The highlighted section of the timeline is selected. The outside arrows allow you to scale the time, and the inside arrows allow you to move several keyframes at once.

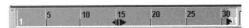

Figure 11.21 Double-clicking the timeline is a convenient way to select all of the keyframes in the playback range.

7. Double-click the timeline.

   All of the keyframes in the playback range are selected. However, the arrows used for scaling end up just outside the playback range, so you must change the playback end time to access them.

8. Change the Playback End Time to 31.

   An arrow appears at the end (**Figure 11.21**).

9. Click and drag the arrow to the left.

   The animation is scaled down, which makes it faster. Note that the key ticks do not fall on whole-number frames anymore.

10. Right mouse button–click in the time-line, and select Snap from the marking menu that appears.

    The keyframes are moved to the nearest whole-number frame.

Setting Animation Preferences

A few animation preferences are essential to set. They affect the way your animation is played back, and how you see and work with the timeline.

When a scene gets very complicated, with many animated surfaces, Maya may not be able to play back every frame of the animation at full speed. This leaves you with two choices: You can either play back at full speed or play every frame. In some cases you'll want to see the detail in the motion, other times you'll want to see the overall pace. For a simple scene, however, you can have your cake and eat it, too—that is, you can play back at full speed and see every frame of animation.

Maya is used to make animations for films, television, games, and the Internet. Films run at 24 frames per second (fps), television runs at 30 fps, and animation on the Internet often runs at 15 fps. It is important to set this option before you start animating: otherwise, the pace of the animation might be wrong when the animation is brought into its final form.

To set animation playback speed:

1. Click the Animation Preferences button ▤, which is near the lower-right corner of the interface.

   The Preferences window opens (**Figure 11.22**).

2. Select Real-time (Windows) or Normal (24 FPS) Mac) in the pop-up menu next to Playback Speed.

3. Select Settings from the Categories column.

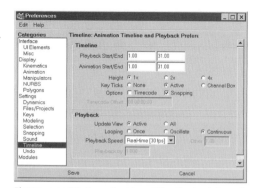

Figure 11.22 It is important to set the Playback Speed before you start animating. A wrong playback speed can cause audio to go out of sync with the animation when you render it out.

SETTING ANIMATION PREFERENCES

Figure 11.23 Real-time (30 fps) is a pretty standard setting for going to video.

4. Select your frame rate from the pop-up menu next to Time (**Figure 11.23**).

NTSC (30 fps) is a standard frame rate for video.

5. Click Save.

These settings will be recalled the next time you open Maya.

✔ Tip

■ Clicking the Animation Preferences button is a convenient way to access many of the preferences for the program. Once the window is open, try selecting different categories.

Key ticks are the red lines that appear on the timeline when you set a keyframe. You can set the key ticks to appear only for the selected channels, which is helpful if you want to make changes to some attributes and not others in the timeline.

To change key ticks options:

1. Keyframe an object.

2. Click the Animation Preferences button ⌧, which is near the lower-right corner of the interface.

3. In the Preferences window, for Key Ticks select Channel Box.

Any key ticks that were currently in the timeline disappear.

continues on next page

SETTING ANIMATION PREFERENCES

4. Select any keyframed channels in the Channel Box.

   The key ticks for those channels appear.

5. Open up the Preferences window again, and change the Key Ticks setting back to Active. Click Save.

✔ Tip

- If the key ticks options are set to Channel Box, only the attributes selected in the Channel Box will be affected when you edit them. For example, suppose you keyframe both an object's scale and rotate. You can move the keyframes of the scale alone by selecting those attributes in the Channel Box and moving the key ticks. The rotate keyframes will be left behind.

You can import sound by dragging a WAV or AIFF file onto the timeline, and the sound waves will be displayed. You can see the sound waves better if you increase the timeline's height.

To set preferences for timeline height:

1. Click on the Animation Preferences button, which is near the lower-right corner of the interface.

2. Click 2x and 4x next to Height (**Figure 11.24**).

   The timeline gets taller (**Figure 11.25**).

3. Click 1x to return it to normal. Click Save to keep these preferences.

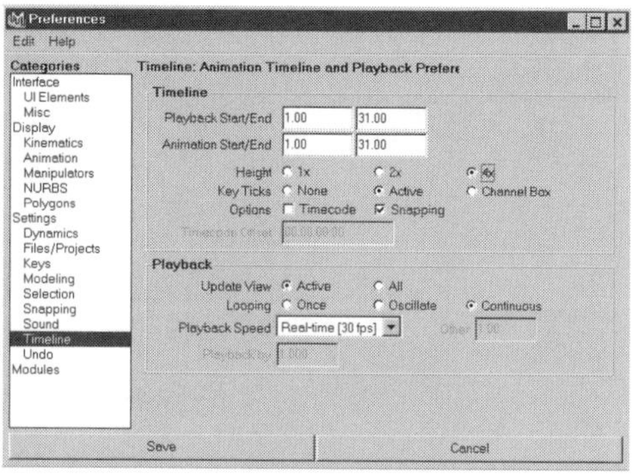

Figure 11.24 You can change the height of the timeline in the animation Preferences window.

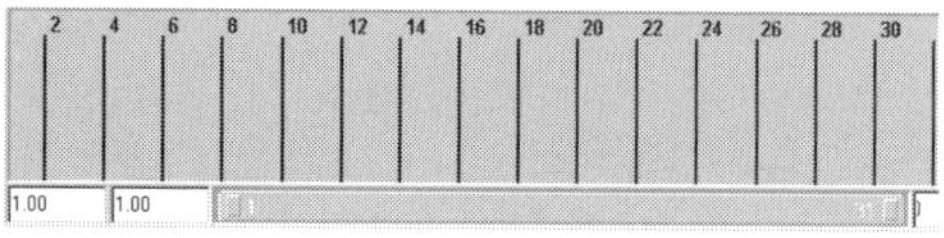

Figure 11.25 This is a timeline at the height of 4x. Unless you are using it to see audio better, the extra height just takes up valuable real estate.

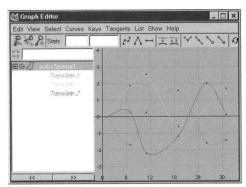

Figure 11.26 The Graph Editor is used to fine-tune your animation once you get the basic timing down.

Figure 11.27 From left to right, these are: spline, linear, and flat tangent types.

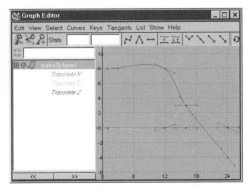

Figure 11.28 These keyframes are set to spline tangent type. Note how even though they are at the same value at frames 1 and 12, there is still a curve between those points. This causes drifting, which is sometimes a problem, particularly when you want an object to stay still.

About the Graph Editor

The Graph Editor is a window that shows a graphic representation of your animation. It has points that represent the time and position in which a keyframe was set, and curves between the keyframes, which show the acceleration (**Figure 11.26**).

By changing the distance between keyframes, you can change an object's speed. But you must adjust the curve that represents its motion between keyframes to change its acceleration.

Tangent types in the Graph Editor allow you to quickly change the shapes of the curves (**Figure 11.27**). By default, the keyframes you set will be spline tangents. You can also manually adjust the shapes of the tangents. The Graph Editor is helpful for editing, copying, and looping animation.

Tangent types

There are six tangent types, and they can all be set by selecting a keyframe or an animation curve and choosing from the Tangent menu in the Graph Editor. You can also change which tangent type is automatically assigned to keyframes before they are set, in the Keys section of the Preferences window.

Spline—This is the default tangent type. Keyframes that have a spline tangent type have a smooth curve between and through them. When animating a fish through water you might use spline (**Figure 11.28**).

continues on next page

Linear—This tangent type simply draws a straight line from one keyframe to the next. It creates jerky movement with sudden changes, which might be good for something mechanical (**Figure 11.29**).

Clamped—This acts just like a spline tangent with one very useful exception: If two keyframes are set at the same value at different points in time, it acts like a linear tangent. It prevents the problem that spline sometimes creates, which is that an object you want to be still will drift slightly (**Figure 11.30**).

Stepped—This tangent type keeps a value the same until it gets to the next keyframe, when it jumps into that position. It makes the curve look like a step, hence the name. One use for this is doing camera cuts. If you want a camera to hold in one position, then cut to another position, keyframe using stepped tangent (**Figure 11.31**).

Flat—The tangent itself becomes horizontal when using this tangent type. The kind of motion it creates is typically "slow-in slow-out." This means that it gradually accelerates between keyframes, goes quickly in the middle of the curve, then gradually decelerates as it moves to the next keyframe (**Figure 11.32**).

Fixed—With a fixed tangent type, the tangent doesn't change when you edit the keyframe.

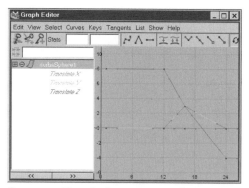

Figure 11.29 These keyframes are set to linear tangent type.

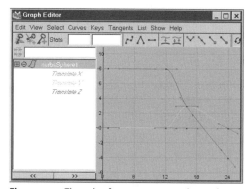

Figure 11.30 These keyframes are set to clamped tangent type. It is similar to the spline tangent except that the drifting problem between frames 1 and 12 has been removed.

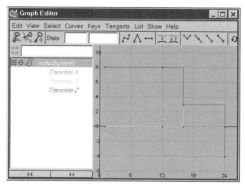

Figure 11.31 The keyframes are set to stepped tangent type.

ABOUT THE GRAPH EDITOR

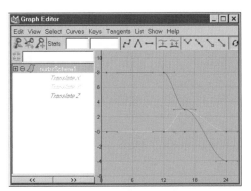

Figure 11.32 The keyframes are set to flat tangent type.

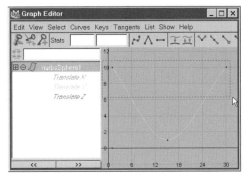

Figure 11.33 The keyframes at the top of the curve are being selected. This is when the ball is at its highest, and it needs to slow down on the way in and out of these points. This is a perfect use for the flat tangent type.

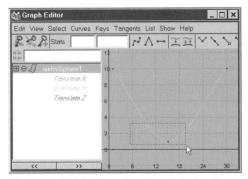

Figure 11.34 This keyframe is at the point when the ball hits the ground. As it is now, the ball doesn't seem to bounce; it just kisses the ground.

A bouncing-ball animation is a good way to learn some of the functions of the Graph Editor.

To change tangent types:

1. From the Create menu select NURBS Primitives > Sphere.

2. Move the sphere up 10 grid units.

    An easy way to do this is to type 10 in the field next to Translate Y in the Channel Box.

3. Make sure that you are at frame 1 in the timeline and that Auto Keyframe is turned on. The key icon 🔳 should appear red and pressed down.

4. Press (Shift)(w) to keyframe only the translates.

5. Go to frame 15. Move the Translate Y of the sphere down to 1.

    The ball will be keyframed once it is moved, because Auto Keyframe is on.

6. Go to frame 30. Move the Translate Y of the sphere back up to 10.

    Rewind and play back the animation. The motion of the ball does not look like a convincing bounce.

7. From the Window menu select Animation Editors > Graph Editor.

    The Graph Editor window opens. The curve for the sphere's animation should show up as long as it is still selected.

8. Marquee-select the two keyframes at the top of the graph (**Figure 11.33**).

9. Click the Flat Tangents button ➖, which is in the Graph Editor window.

10. Select the keyframe at the bottom of the curve (**Figure 11.34**).

    It can be helpful to Marquee-select even if you are only selecting one keyframe.

continues on next page

ABOUT THE GRAPH EDITOR

11. Click the Break Tangents button ⌄. This allows you to move the tangents on either side individually.

12. Select the tangent on the left of the keyframe, then (Shift)-select the tangent on the right.

13. Click the Move Nearest Picked Key Tool button, which is at the top-left corner of the Graph Editor ⌨.

14. Middle mouse button–click and drag on the tangents, and move them up one at a time. They should form a V shape (**Figure 11.35**).

Play back the animation. It should look more like a real bouncing ball.

Perhaps you want your ball to bounce again. One easy way to do this is to copy and paste keyframes in the timeline.

To copy and paste in the timeline:

1. Animate the bouncing ball as described in the previous section.

2. Make sure that the Playback End Time is set to at least 60.

You can do this by typing 60 in the Playback End Time field.

3. Hold down (Shift) and click and drag in the timeline from 1 to at least 31 (**Figure 11.36**).

4. Right mouse button–click the timeline, and select Copy from the pop-up menu (**Figure 11.37**).

5. Click frame 30.

The frame you are on when you paste is the time when the range of keyframes you paste in will begin.

6. Right mouse button–click the timeline, and select Paste > Paste.

7. Rewind and play back the animation.

The ball now bounces twice, and there are new key ticks on the timeline.

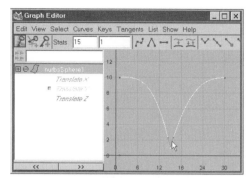

Figure 11.35 Now that the tangents have been adjusted, the ball will appear to be really bouncing.

Figure 11.36 (Shift)-click and drag the keyframes you want to copy from. If you just go to frame 30 in your selection, it will not include the keyframe at 30, so you must go one frame beyond it.

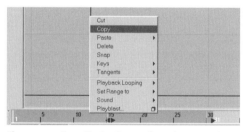

Figure 11.37 Copy the keyframes from the convenient pop-up menu.

ABOUT THE GRAPH EDITOR

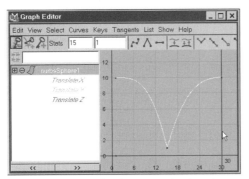

Figure 11.38 Be sure that the current time is at the point where you want to begin the paste. Otherwise, when you paste, the keyframes will end up wherever the current time indicator happens to be and overwrite whatever frames were there.

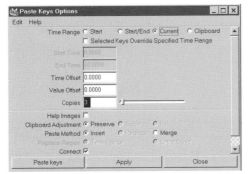

Figure 11.39 Using the Paste Keys options you can conveniently make several copies at once.

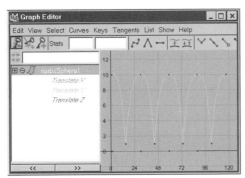

Figure 11.40 This is the result of the paste. The ball bounces four times instead of one.

Sometimes you want an animation to repeat several times. You can use the Graph Editor to do multiple pastes at once.

To copy and paste in the Graph Editor:

1. Animate a bouncing ball.

2. Make sure that the timeline goes to at least 120.

   You can do this by typing 120 in the Playback End Time field.

3. From the Window menu select Animation Editors > Graph Editor.

   The curve for the sphere's animation should show up. If it does not, select the sphere.

4. From the Edit menu in the Graph Editor select Copy.

5. Hold down k and click and drag in the Graph Editor window until the red line, which is the time indicator, is at the end of the curve (**Figure 11.38**).

6. From the Edit menu in the Graph Editor select the box next to Paste.

   This opens the Paste Keys Options window.

7. In the field next to Copies, type 3 (**Figure 11.39**).

8. While the mouse is over the Graph Editor, press f.

   The entire animation curve is framed. There are now three additional bounces (**Figure 11.40**).

9. Rewind and play back the animation.

   The ball bounces four times.

If you want to make your animation faster or slower, you can scale the time in the Graph Editor. A longer time for the same distance means slower movement, and vice versa.

You can also scale value. Perhaps all of your bounces are too high, or all of your arm swings don't go far enough. Scaling the value is just as easy as scaling an object's size.

To scale in the Graph Editor:

1. Create a bouncing ball with four bounces as in the previous section.

2. From the Window menu select Animation Editors > Graph Editor.

3. From the column on the left, select Translate Y. This isolates the Y translate curve.

4. Marquee-select the whole curve.

5. Press r to go into scale mode.

6. Move the mouse over the first keyframe on the left side of the curve (**Figure 11.41**).

   Wherever the mouse is when you begin to scale is the pivot point of the scale.

7. Middle mouse button–drag to the left.

8. Move the mouse over one of the low points of the bounces (**Figure 11.42**).

9. Middle mouse button–drag down.
   The bounces get shorter (**Figure 11.43**).

✔ Tip

■ You can also scale just a portion of a curve by selecting only those keyframes you want to scale. You can likewise scale multiple animated objects at the same time, which is often desirable so that their actions remain synchronized.

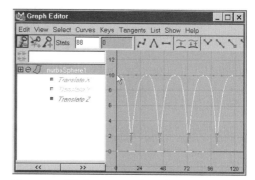

Figure 11.41 It is important to have the mouse at the correct position when you start to scale keyframes in the Graph Editor. Wherever you begin to scale is where the pivot point of the scale will be.

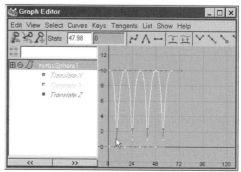

Figure 11.42 Here the time has been scaled down so the ball bounces faster. The mouse has been carefully placed at the bottom of the bounce, so that position will be the pivot point of the scale.

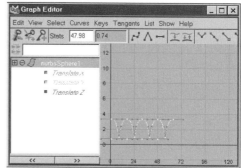

Figure 11.43 Now the value has been scaled down— that is, the bounces don't go as high as they did. Since the pivot point was at the bottom of the curve, the position at which it bounces hasn't changed, so the ball will still appear to be bouncing on the ground and not above or below it.

ABOUT THE GRAPH EDITOR

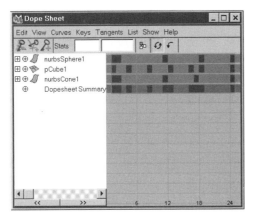

Figure 11.44 The Dope Sheet is especially helpful when working on the timing of a large number of objects.

About the Dope Sheet

The Dope Sheet is another window used for editing keyframes. You can move, scale, cut, copy, paste, and delete in it, much as you can in the timeline and the Graph Editor. It has the advantage of being a simple, clear way to move the keyframes of multiple objects in time. For this reason it is most helpful when adjusting the timing of many objects at once (**Figure 11.44**).

Path Animation

Animating the flight of an airplane could be difficult by just setting keyframes. Sometimes you'll want to establish the path first and then simply send the object along that path. Maya can even make the object automatically bank around turns and point in the direction of the path.

To animate along a path:

1. Create a curve in the Top view (**Figure 11.45**). (See Chapter 7 for more on creating curves.)

2. From the Create menu select NURBS Primitives > Cone.

3. Select the cone, then [Shift]-select the curve.

4. From the Animate menu select Motion Paths > Attach to Motion Path (Windows) or Paths > Attach to Paths (Mac).

   The cone jumps to the beginning of the curve, and when the animation is played back, it moves along the curve.

5. With the cone still selected, click motionPath1 in the Channel Box.

6. Enter –90 in the Side Twist field so that the cone points down the path (**Figure 11.46**).

   When the animation is played back now, you can see how the rotation of the cone follows the path (**Figure 11.47**).

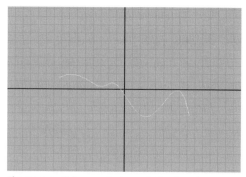

Figure 11.45 This curve is drawn in the Top view.

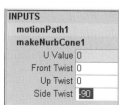

Figure 11.46 The different twists are needed to orient the cone the way you want it. You cannot simply rotate the cone because its rotate attributes are controlled by the path animation.

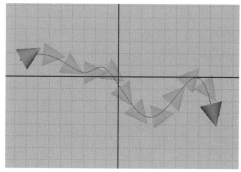

Figure 11.47 This is the resulting path animation.

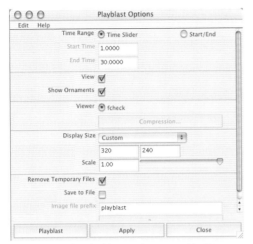

Figure 11.48 The Playblast options are set in this window. If you don't click Save to file and you close your movie player after you watch your animation, you will have to repeat the Playblast procedure on the animation again.

Previewing Your Animation

When you want to preview an animation, you can play it back in the timeline. However, a complex scene won't play smoothly at full speed. Also, you'll often want to output your animations. For this Maya provides Playblast, which does screen snapshots of your animation and turns it into an AVI or a series of numbered images.

To make a Playblast:

1. Create an animation.

2. From the Windows menu, select the box next to Playblast to open the Playblast Options window (**Figure 11.48**).

3. Choose the Time Range you want to make a movie file of.

    Time Slider will use your current Playback Start and End times. Start/End will allow you to type in your own times.

4. Adjust the resolution for the movie.
    If the Display Size is set to From Window, it will use whichever view panel is currently active as the basis for the size. If you change it to Custom, you can type in whatever resolution you want.

5. Check Save to File if you want Playblast to automatically save your series of numbered frames after you create it.

    If Save to file is checked, you can click Browse to choose where you want the files to be saved. On Windows you can make a Movieplayer file instead of a series of numbered frames.

6. Click the Playblast button.

7. You will see your animation play back one frame at a time. A moment later the FCheck window, with which you can watch your animation, will pop up.

CREATING LIGHTS

Figure 12.1 Adding an area of focus strengthens the scene.

Figure 12.2 An object can be accented through the correct use of light.

Light and shadow are essential to the three-dimensional, realistic quality of a scene. Lighting is a crucial element to setting the mood and feeling of a scene. Too much light can flatten out a scene, leaving the viewer unengaged and uninterested in the imagery. Just the right amount of light intensity and thoughtful placement can draw the eye around the scene. You can use lights to focus a viewer's attention on a particular place in your scene (**Figure 12.1**) or on an object you don't want the viewer to miss (**Figure 12.2**). Light can be used to draw spectators into the scene as if they were participants, or to leave them feeling like onlookers, outside the action.

Artists for centuries have used lighting to invoke emotion in their paintings through the use of chiaroscuro, the play of light and dark, which draws the viewer into the painting. Leonardo da Vinci; Gerrit Van Honthorst; and the master of painting with light, Caravaggio, all experimented with light in their paintings. More recently, we've seen many filmmakers use similar techniques in their movies; *Blade Runner, The Godfather,* and *Poltergeist* are all great examples. As the movies unfold, the action is supported with lighting through various colors, intensity, and placement.

Controlling light can often be tricky and time consuming. In this chapter we'll look at some of the attributes and techniques used to control lights in a Maya scene.

Setting the Scene's Mood

One of the first things to consider in lighting your scene is the time of day. A good exercise that shows how much difference lighting can make is to create and light the same scene in three or four different lighting scenarios. You can set up one scene to have a scary and luminous quality (**Figure 12.3**), and then relight the scene for a bright summer day (**Figure 12.4**). You will very quickly see how essential the lighting is to a well-produced scene.

Below is a short list of the qualities of light at different times of day, from an artistic point of view:

Dawn—Most of the sky is filled with a light glow, soft and diffused, leaving objects in the room dimly lit. Highlights and reflections become visible first, then everything else slowly comes into view. Dawn has a very subtle light, requiring some time for the human eye to adjust.

Sunrise—Light pours into the room as a new day begins. Long shadows and light patterns are projected on the wall through the window, splashing light around the room. As the sunrise progresses, the day's shadows become more transparent and shorter, leading into the sharp midday sun.

Sunset—Orange, red, and pink sunset colors fill the clouds and the sky, bringing a feeling of tranquility and closure to the day. Mountains and trees are silhouetted against the sun at the horizon, and long shadows lay along the ground.

Evening—Peaceful silvery blue light fills the room, illuminating it softly. The room is lit with candles and ceiling lights that quickly falls off into the darkness. The only light coming in from outside is the moon glowing through the haze around it, creating ominous bluish highlights throughout the scene.

Figure 12.3 Light can be used to create specific moods, ominous and scary for example.

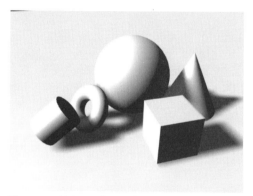

Figure 12.4 Light can be used to brighten an entire scene.

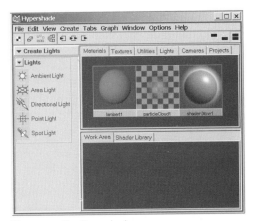

Figure 12.5 The Hypershade.

About the Hypershade

The Hypershade is a window where you can create, delete, view, and enhance lights as well as materials, textures, and utilities (**Figure 12.5**). There are several ways to open the Hypershade: You can open it in a panel by selecting Panel > Panels > Hypershade; clicking the Hypershade/Persp button right below the toolbar at the left of the layout (Windows only); or selecting Window > Rendering Editors > Hypershade (Windows) or Window > Hypershade (Mac).

When you first open the Hypershade, you see a panel on the left-hand side called the Create Bar (Windows) or Visor (Mac) (**Figure 12.6**). The Create Bar houses all the different types of nodes. You can create a new node by clicking the middle mouse button–dragging the icon into the work area to the right of it.

continues on next page

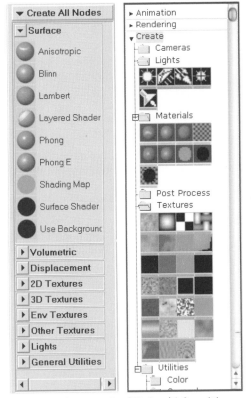

Figure 12.6 The Create Bar (Windows) left, and the Visor (Mac) right.

ABOUT THE HYPERSHADE

You can isolate the node types you want to create by clicking Create Textures at the top of the Create Bar and selecting the specific node type you want to create from the menu. For example, you can select Create Lights to have the Create Bar show only the light types (Windows) (**Figure 12.7**). The Visor (Mac) lets you view node types of expanding and collapsing menus.

The rest of the Hypershade provides tabs (Windows) or drop-down menus (Mac) for viewing already-created node types: Materials, Textures, Utilities, Lights, Cameras, and Projects. Any created node will be visible under its respective tab or drop-down menu. For instance, if you create a directional light and a point light in your scene, you can view them both by clicking the Lights tab in the Hypershade (**Figure 12.8**).

On Windows, under the pane containing the node-type tabs is a pane with the Work Area and Shader Library tabs. (To access the Work Area on the Mac, go to the drop-down menu and select Work Area. The Shader Library tab is not available on the Mac.) In the Work Area panel you can connect attributes together, view all the connections, and isolate a light or texture for fine-tuning. The Shader Library tab holds all of the premade, ready-to-use shaders, including shaders for buildings, food, glass, and other common objects. These shaders can often be a good starting point for new shaders you want to create.

In this chapter we will be exploring the lighting section of the Hypershade, Create Bar, and Visor.

Figure 12.7
The Create Bar with Create Lights selected.

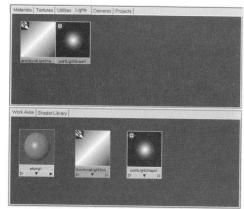

Figure 12.8 The Lights panel shows the two lights created and the work area below them.

ABOUT THE HYPERSHADE

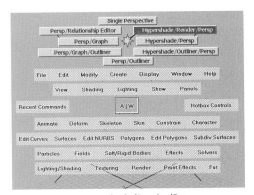

Figure 12.9 The Hypershade/Render/Persp Marking Menu.

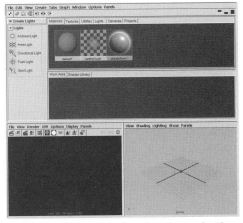

Figure 12.10 The Hypershade on top, the Render View pane on the bottom left, and the Perspective pane on the bottom right.

Setting Up for a Render

In Maya there are many ways to create the same final result. In this section we'll go over some different setups for streamlining your workflow.

Three essential windows are used to create a final render: the Hypershade, the Render View, and a camera view (front, top, side, perspective, or a camera you created). One way to streamline the render's setup is to use Hypershade/Render/Persp in the Marking Menu in the North region of the Hotbox (**Figure 12.9**). This will set the layout window to three panes. The top will become a Hypershade, the bottom-left pane will become a Render View, and the bottom-right pane will become a Perspective view (**Figure 12.10**). This is a good way to set up a scene for a render because you can tap the [Spacebar] to enlarge any of the panes, temporarily hiding the other two panes.

continues on next page

SETTING UP FOR A RENDER

Another way to set up a render is to open each window separately as needed. To open the Hypershade or Render View in its own window, select the window you want in the Window > Rendering Editors menu (**Figure 12.11**). This will open a new window with the view inside it (**Figure 12.12**).

Since most of the light attributes can be edited in the Attribute Editor, it can be helpful to temporarily change the Channel Box at the right of the Maya window to an Attribute Editor (**Figure 12.13**). You do this by clicking in the east region of the Hotbox and selecting Attributes > Attribute Editor in the upper-right corner of the Maya window. This option is nice if you have a lot of screen real estate available, but it can be cumbersome if you have limited screen space.

The Render View holds many of the tools needed to produce an effective render. We will be touching on the Render View throughout this chapter, but there is a more thorough discussion of it in Chapter 14, Cameras and Rendering.

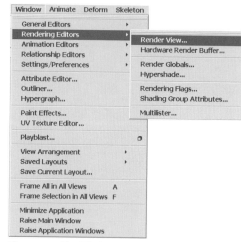

Figure 12.11 The Window > Rendering Editors menu.

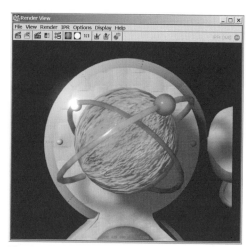

Figure 12.12 The Render View in its own pop-up window.

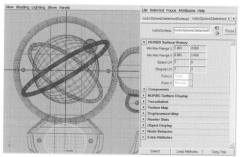

Figure 12.13 The Attribute Editor is docked beside the front view, replacing the Channel Box.

SETTING UP FOR A RENDER

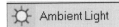

Figure 12.14 The Ambient Light icon.

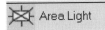

Figure 12.15 The Area Light icon.

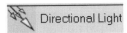

Figure 12.16 The Directional Light icon.

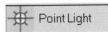

Figure 12.17 The Point Light icon.

Figure 12.18 The Spot Light icon.

About Lights

There are five light types in Maya: *ambient, area, directional, point,* and *spot.* You can combine these light types to produce nearly any lighting scenario. A Maya scene may use one or all of the above types, depending on the mood and art direction of the scene.

Here is a description of the different light types and some of their common uses:

Ambient—Produces a uniform, global ambience throughout the scene. This light type should be kept to a minimum or not used at all in a scene, because the more it is used, the more the scene will appear flat, lacking contrast (**Figure 12.14**).

Examples: light that allows you to see in a room or closet without having an actual light on; light that is not coming from an obvious source.

Area—Two-dimensional, rectangular light source that emits light out of the entire rectangle in the direction of its normal (see Chapter 8, Polygons and Subdivided Surfaces) (**Figure 12.15**).

Examples: illuminated ceiling panels, rectangular light reflections on walls.

Directional—Parallel light rays that wash light across the scene in a specific direction (**Figure 12.16**).

Examples: sunlight and moonlight.

Point—Radiates light out from its center in all directions. The farther an object is from this light, the less it is illuminated (**Figure 12.17**).

Examples: light bulbs, LEDs, torches.

Spot—Lights an area within a cone shape. The light comes from the center point and travels in a specified direction (**Figure 12.18**).

Examples: flashlights, street lamps, headlights, spotlights.

Light types have some common attributes (**Figure 12.19**).

Type—Sets the kind of light: ambient, area, directional, point, or spot. This attribute can be changed at any time to change the light from its current style to a different style, for example, point to spot.

Color—Sets the foundation color of the light. Image maps may be added to vary the color of the light.

Intensity—Sets the brightness and darkness of the light. For best results, start low and work your way up (**Figure 12.20**).

Figure 12.19 Common light attributes: type, color, intensity, and decay rate.

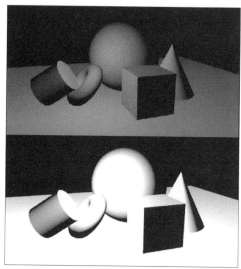

Figure 12.20 The top scene is lit with a light at low intensity, the bottom scene is lit with the same light at a high intensity setting.

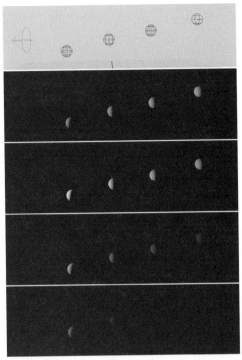

Figure 12.21 Decay rates top to bottom: wireframe, no decay, linear, quadratic, and cubic.

Decay Rate—Controls how quickly the light's intensity decreases over distance. When you change this setting, you will also have to raise or lower the intensity of the light to make up for the decay-rate change. This is not an attribute of the ambient or directional lights (**Figure 12.21**).

No Decay—Light will have the same intensity no matter the distance

Linear Decay—The light's intensity diminishes with distance less abruptly than Quadratic and Cubic decay

Quadratic Decay—The lights intensity diminishes most abruptly, substantially more abruptly than Linear and Cubic decay. This setting is closest to real-world light decay.

Cubic Decay—The light's intensity diminishes at a rate between Linear and Quadratic's decay rate.

ABOUT LIGHTS

Ambient light

Ambient light is the light that fills in every-where. It is present even when you turn the lights out; it's the light your eyes see once they adjust to the darkness. Using ambient light is a quick way to see how things render without having to set up a bunch of lights, but in general you should use ambient light sparingly because it can very quickly flatten out a scene.

First, create a practice scene.

To create a practice scene:

1. Choose File > New Scene to create a new scene to work on.

2. Create five or six primitives in the scene, and move them randomly around with the bottom of each sitting on the grid (**Figure 12.22**).

3. From the Create menu select NURBS Primitive > Plane to create a plane at the origin.

4. Scale the plane larger than the objects in your scene (**Figure 12.23**).

5. Save the practice scene as a file called practice.mb.

To create an ambient light:

1. Open the practice.mb file.

2. Choose Create > Lights, and in the sub-menu select the box next to Ambient Light (**Figure 12.24**).

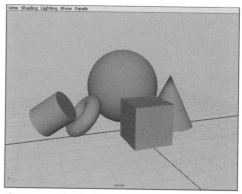

Figure 12.22 Create five or six primitives in the scene, and place them randomly.

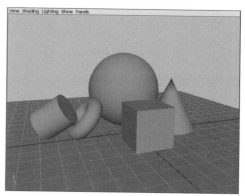

Figure 12.23 The plane is scaled larger than the objects in the scene.

Figure 12.24 Select the box next to Ambient Light in the menu.

ABOUT LIGHTS

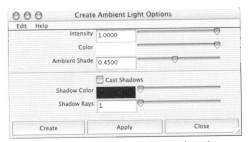

Figure 12.25 Click on the swatch beside the color attribute.

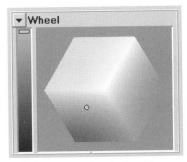

Figure 12.26 Select a color from the Color Wheel, which in Maya looks more like a color block.

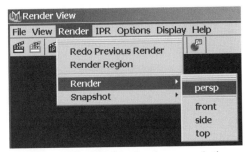

Figure 12.27 Select Render > Render > persp in the Render View to render the scene.

3. In the Options dialog box that opens, click the swatch beside the color attribute (**Figure 12.25**).

   The color wheel opens when you click on the swatch.

4. Click in the color wheel to select a color for the light (**Figure 12.26**).

5. Click Apply to lock in the color.

6. Click Create to make the ambient light.

   The ambient light is placed at the origin of the scene.

7. In the Hotbox's North region's Marking Menu, select Hypershade/Render/persp to split your window layout into these three panes.

8. In the Render View pane, select Render > Render > persp to render the Perspective view (**Figure 12.27**).

ABOUT LIGHTS

The ambient shade attribute affects the direction of the light source. If the ambient shade scale setting is 0, light comes from all directions (**Figure 12.28**). If the setting is 1, light comes from the source itself, acting similarly to a point light (**Figure 12.29**). You must be careful when adjusting this attribute because the lower the number, the flatter the image will appear.

To change an ambient light's ambient shade attribute:

1. With an ambient light selected, open the Attribute Editor by selecting Window > Attribute Editor, or pressing `Ctrl a`/`Control a`.

2. Set the ambient shade attribute to 0 (**Figure 12.30**).

   The 0 value sends light evenly over the entire scene.

3. In the Render View pane, select Render > Render > persp to render the Perspective view.

   Because the ambient shade attribute is set to 0, the objects in the scene blend together, creating a very flat image, as in Figure 12.28.

4. With the light still selected, go to the Attribute Editor and change the ambient shade attribute to .7.

   The .7 value makes the ambient light act similarly to a point light, so that its intensity fades slightly as the distance from the light source increases. Therefore, changing the ambient shade attribute changes the effect of the light.

5. Click the Redo Previous Render icon, in the Render View.

   Because the ambient shade value is higher, the scene has the appearance of more depth, similar to Figure 12.29.

6. In the Attribute Editor set the intensity to .25 (**Figure 12.31**).

Figure 12.28 The ambient shade attribute is set to 0, flattening the scene.

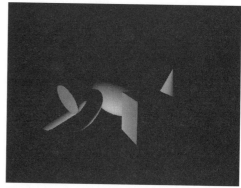

Figure 12.29 The ambient shade attribute is set to 1, so the light is similar to a point light.

Figure 12.30 Set the ambient shade attribute to 0.

Figure 12.31 Set the intensity to .25.

Figure 12.32
Select Area Light in the
Create Lights section
of the Create Bar.

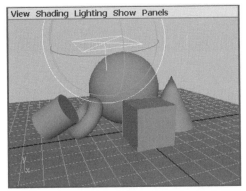

Figure 12.33 Point the surface normal at the area you
want to light.

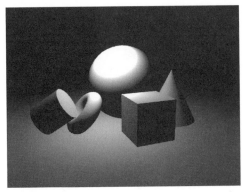

Figure 12.34 Select Render > Render > persp to render
the Perspective view.

We use .25 here to bring down the intensity of the ambient light and keep the flattening of the scene to a minimum.

7. Click the Redo Previous Render icon in the Render View.

   The scene will be very dark.

Area lights

Area lights are best used for situations that call for rectangular lighting situations. Using area lights all over a scene can slow rendering.

To create an area light:

1. Open the practice.mb file.

2. In the Hypershade select Area Light in the Create Lights section of the Create Bar (Windows) or Visor (Mac) (**Figure 12.32**).

3. Scale the light to the size you want the area light to be.

4. Move and rotate the light around the scene until the surface normal points at the object or area you want to light (**Figure 12.33**).

5. Select the light, and open the Attribute Editor.

6. Click the swatch beside the Color attribute.

7. Click in the color wheel to select a color for the light.

8. Click Accept to lock in the color.

9. Move the Intensity slider in the Attribute Editor to set the light's brightness.

10. Close the Attribute Editor.

11. From the Hotbox's North region's Marking Menu select Hypershade/Render/persp to split your panel layout into these three panes.

12. In the Render pane select Render > Render > persp to render the Perspective view (**Figure 12.34**).

ABOUT LIGHTS

Directional lights

Directional lights work great for representing lights such as sunlight or moonlight.

To create a directional light:

1. Open the practice file.

2. From the Create Menu select Lights > Directional Light.

    A directional light is created at the origin of the scene. The default direction points down the *z*-axis in the negative direction (**Figure 12.35**). The perpendicular light rays follow a horizontal direction by default (**Figure 12.36**).

3. Select the directional light by clicking it. Rotate the light around the axes until the arrows point in the direction you want the light to follow (**Figure 12.37**).

4. With the light still selected, choose a new intensity setting for the light in the Channel Box.

5. From the Window menu select Rendering Editors > Render View (**Figure 12.38**). The Render View opens in a new window.

6. In the Render window select Render > Render > persp to render the Perspective view.

✔ Tip

■ Translating a directional light has no effect on how it lights the scene but can be a good way to later find or select it.

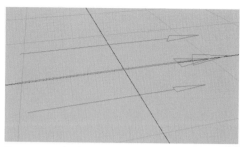

Figure 12.35 The default position of the directional light.

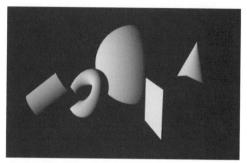

Figure 12.36 The perpendicular light rays of the directional light follow a horizontal direction by default.

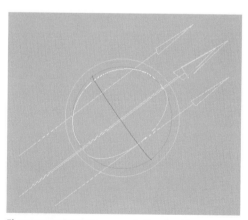

Figure 12.37 Point the arrows in the direction you want the light to follow.

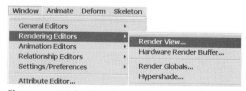

Figure 12.38 Select Rendering Editors > Render View to open the Render View in a new window.

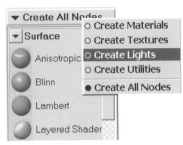

Figure 12.39 Select Create Lights from the pop-up menu in the Hypershade.

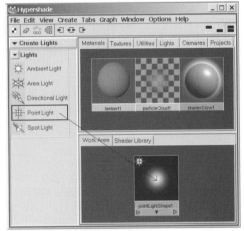

Figure 12.40 MMB-drag the Point Light icon to the Hypershade's Work Area panel.

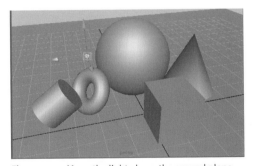

Figure 12.41 Move the light above the ground plane.

Point lights

Point lights are great for lamps and torches. They are also great for adding a little light to a dark corner or taking light away from an overlit area.

To create a point light:

1. Open the practice.mb file.

2. From the Create Bar (Windows) or Visor (Mac) select Create Lights from the pop-up menu (**Figure 12.39**).

3. Using the middle mouse button, drag the Point Light icon from the Create Lights menu to the Work Area panel inside the Hypershade (**Figure 12.40**).

4. Double-click the Point Light icon in the Work Area to open the Attribute Editor.

5. Set the color and intensity attributes, then close the Attribute Editor.

6. Click the light to select it, and move it above the ground plane to keep it from being obstructed by the plane (**Figure 12.41**).

continues on next page

ABOUT LIGHTS

7. From the Hotbox's north region's Marking Menu select Hypershade/Render/persp to split your panel layout into these three panes.

8. In the Render pane select Render > Render > persp to render the Perspective view.

   The Perspective view is rendered (**Figure 12.42**).

Spotlights

Spotlights are great for areas where you want to focus light. They can be used as stage or theater spotlights, headlights or any cone-shaped light source.

To create a spotlight:

1. Open the practice.mb file.

2. Click the Spotlight icon ![icon] in shelf 1 to create a spotlight at the origin of the scene.

3. Set the Object Pick mask to select lights only and swipe across the Spotlight icon at the origin to select it (**Figure 12.43**).

   If the Object Pick mask is selected correctly, only the light will be selected.

4. Select the Show Manipulator Tool by pressing ⊤ or selecting its icon ![icon] in the toolbar.

5. Pull up the *y*-axis translation manipulator on the spotlight to raise it above the ground (**Figure 12.44**).

   Notice when you are in the Show Manipulator tool that the end of the spotlight stays in its original position, forcing the light to point at it.

6. Select the center square of the end manipulator, and move it to the position where you would like the light to point (**Figure 12.45**).

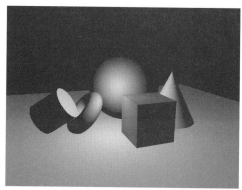

Figure 12.42 The final rendering in the Perspective view.

Figure 12.43 Set the Object Pick mask to select lights only.

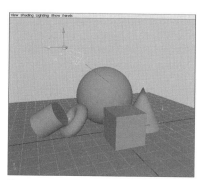

Figure 12.44 Pull up the *y*-axis translation manipulator on the spotlight to raise it above ground.

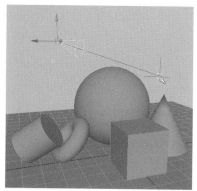

Figure 12.45 Move the end manipulator into a new position.

ABOUT LIGHTS

Figure 12.46 Select Render > Render > persp to render the Perspective view.

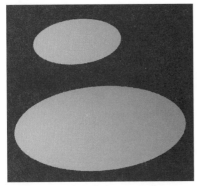

Figure 12.47 The default cone angle on top; the same light position but with a larger cone angle on the bottom.

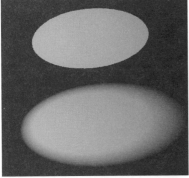

Figure 12.48 Adjusting the penumbra angle blurs the edge of the spotlight. The top light has a 0 setting, the bottom has a 7 setting.

7. From the Hotbox's north region's Marking Menu select Hypershade/Render/Persp to split your panel layout into these three panes.

8. In the Render pane select Render > Render > persp to render the Perspective view (**Figure 12.46**).

A spotlight has changeable attributes that are specifically for the spotlight. Below are the definitions of some of its attributes.

Spotlight attributes

Cone Angle—The larger the number that is input, the wider the cone, illuminating more area. The smaller the number, the smaller the diameter of the cone will become, illuminating less area (**Figure 12.47**).

Penumbra Angle—Adjusting the penumbra angle softens the edge of the spotlight by blurring it. A negative number blurs inside the edge of the cone, a positive number blurs outside the edge of the cone (**Figure 12.48**).

Dropoff—Adjusts the intensity of the light from its center out to its edge. Raising this attribute value gives a soft gradation from the center to the edge (**Figure 12.49**).

Figure 12.49 Dropoff adjusts the intensity of the light from its center out to its edge. The light at the top has a default setting of 0, the light at the bottom has a setting of 8.

Many light attributes can have an image added to them to affect the light in additional ways. An example of this is adding an image into the color attribute of a light. This projects the image through the light, similarly to having light come through a stained-glass window and project a pattern onto the floor (**Figure 12.50**). This technique can also help you create non-round light shapes.

To add an image map to a spotlight's color attribute:

1. Click a spotlight to select it.

2. With the light selected, select Window > Attribute Editor (**Figure 12.51**).

3. In the Attribute Editor select the map icon next to the Color slider  to open the Create Render Node panel.

4. In the Create Render Node panel, select File from the 2D Textures section (**Figure 12.52**).

5. In the File Attributes select the File icon next to the Image Name attribute.

6. In the Open dialog box, browse to the folder that has the image you want to use, then select it and click Open.

7. From the Hotbox's north region's Marking Menu, select Hypershade/Render/persp to split your panel layout into these three panes.

8. In the Render View pane select Render > Render > persp to render the Perspective view.

   The final image is rendered (**Figure 12.53**).

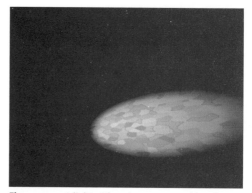

Figure 12.50 A light with an image mapped into it.

Figure 12.51 Select Window > Attribute Editor.

Figure 12.52 Select File from the 2D Textures section of the Create Render Node panel.

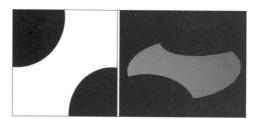

Figure 12.53 The image used is on the left, and the final render of light with the image mapped into it is on the right.

ABOUT LIGHTS

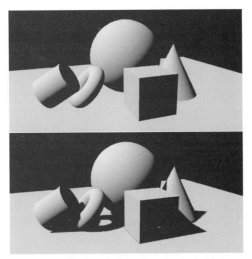

Figure 12.54 Shadows help to visually plant objects on the ground.

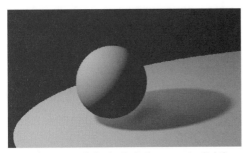

Figure 12.55 A real shadow's darkest area is slightly away from the object's edge, near the base of the shadow.

About Shadows

Shadows are an important part of a scene because they can help to visually plant objects on the ground as well as help us tell how far apart objects are from each other in the scene (**Figure 12.54**). Shadows add realism that is often unachievable in scenes without them.

A real-world shadow is the complementary color of the light source: The sun is yellow, therefore the shadows cast by the sun are purple. This is a theory you should keep in mind for both realistic and artistic shadows. There are essentially no black shadows in the real world, only very dark representations of a particular color. If you apply this theory to your 3D work, you will produce deeper, richer imagery.

A real shadow is darkest closer to an object, fading and blurring as it gets farther away. Many times, created shadows appear to be too bold and unrealistic, so understanding this simple theory can help bring your scene to life. The core, or darkest area, of a shadow is slightly away from the object's edge, near the base of the shadow (**Figure 12.55**).

Creating shadows

Shadows are turned off on all lights by default and must be turned on in the light as well as on the object to be seen in a render. An individual object will not cast a shadow if it is turned off on the object, no matter if the light has cast shadows turned on or not. This gives the Maya user incredible control over each individual shadow.

Figure 12.56 Depth map shadow.

There are two types of shadows in Maya: depth map (**Figure 12.56**) and raytraced (**Figure 12.57**). Both can produce realistic shadows, but raytracing often produces a more realistic shadow with less effort and tweaking. Raytraced shadows can take much longer to render than depth map shadows, so it becomes somewhat of a tradeoff. There is a constant battle to have good-looking shadows while keeping rendering time to a minimum within each scene.

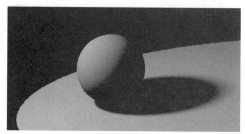

Figure 12.57 Raytraced shadow.

Depth map shadows attempt to simulate real-world shadows without adding major amounts of rendering time. A depth map is an image file that contains a depth channel (a grayscale representation of how far things are away from the camera, the lights, and each other) rendered from a light's point of view. Maya uses the depth map to determine which surfaces have light hitting them and which surfaces are in shadow. Think of the depth map as a predrawn shadow brought into the scene right before it is rendered. This image becomes a replacement for a real shadow in the scene, saving Maya valuable time it would take to calculate the real shadow. These depth map image files can be reused, saving even more rendering time.

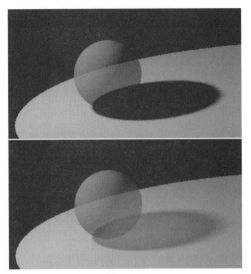

Figure 12.58 Depth map shadows do not show the object's transparency within the shadow (top), but do in a raytraced shadow (bottom).

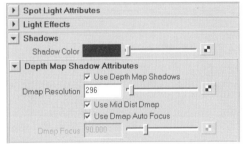

Figure 12.59 Turn on Use Depth Map Shadows.

Figure 12.60 Click the swatch next to the Shadow Color attribute to open the Color Chooser.

In most scenarios, raytraced shadows can produce great-looking, realistic images. Raytracing shadows can produce results that are not available to depth map shadows. An example of this is transparent shadows cast from a partially transparent object (**Figure 12.58**). Raytraced shadows have some restrictions as well. Raytraced shadows will not show up if rendered with Interactive Photorealistic Rendering (IPR) (see Chapter 13, Shaders and Materials), only through a rendered image. This is an additional speed cost because you can use IPR to see depth map shadows, making depth map shadow adjustment much faster.

Depth map shadows are available in all light types except ambient. Depth map shadows can produce relatively realistic shadows without greatly affecting rendering time.

To create a depth map shadow:

1. Select the light from which you want to produce a shadow.

2. Open the Attribute Editor.

3. Click the arrow next to the Shadows heading to expand the shadow options.

4. Select the box next to Use Depth Map Shadows under the Depth Map Shadow Attributes heading (**Figure 12.59**).

5. In the Shadows section above Depth Map Shadow Attributes click the swatch next to the Shadow Color attribute to open the Color Chooser (**Figure 12.60**).

continues on next page

6. In the Color Chooser, click in the color wheel to select a shadow color.

7. Click Accept to lock in the color.

8. Select the surface you want to cast shadows.

9. In the Render Stats section of the surface's Attribute Editor, make sure that Casts Shadows is on (it is on by default) (**Figure 12.61**).

10. From the Hotbox's north region's Marking Menu select Hypershade/Render/Persp to split your panel layout into these three panes.

11. Test-render the scene by selecting Render > Render > persp in the Render View pane.

The render shows a depth map shadow (**Figure 12.62**).

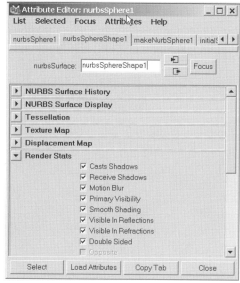

Figure 12.61 Turn on Casts Shadows in the Render Stats section of the Attribute Editor.

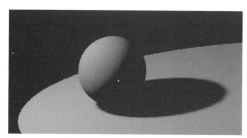

Figure 12.62 The final render with a depth map shadow.

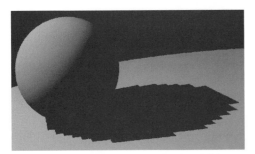

Figure 12.63 Shadow edges appear pixilated if the resolution is too low.

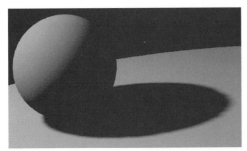

Figure 12.64 Dmap filter size controls the softness of the shadows' edges.

Common depth map shadow attributes

Dmap Resolution—The resolution of the depth map shadow file. Shadow edges appear pixilated if the resolution is too low (**Figure 12.63**). Set this as low as you can and still get acceptable results because it is very render intensive.

Dmap Filter Size—Works in unison with Dmap resolution to control the softness of the shadow's edges (**Figure 12.64**). Try to keep this at 3 or less to avoid adding excessive render time.

Dmap Bias—Moves the map closer to or away from the light. This is only necessary to use in the following two circumstances:

If a shadow appears to be detached from the shadow-casting surface, gradually decrease the Dmap bias value until the shadow looks correct.

If dark spots or streaks appear on illuminated surfaces, gradually increase the Dmap bias value until the spots or streaks disappear.

Raytraced shadows can create highly realistic shadows but can also add expensive rendering time.

In order to produce raytraced shadows, you must check three things:

◆ Use Raytraced Shadows must be selected in the light's Attribute Editor.

◆ Casts Shadows must be selected in the Render Stats section of the Attribute Editor of each object you want to cast a shadow.

◆ Raytracing must be checked in the Raytracing Quality section in the Render Globals. (See Chapter 14, Cameras and Rendering.)

To create a raytraced shadow:

1. Select the light from which you want to produce a shadow.

2. In the Raytrace Shadow Attributes section of the light's Attribute Editor, select Use Ray Trace Shadows (**Figure 12.65**).

3. Above the Raytrace Shadows Attributes, open the Shadows section and click the swatch beside the shadow color attribute to open the Color Chooser.

4. Click in the color wheel to select a shadow color.

5. Click Accept to lock in the color.

6. Select the surface you want to cast shadows.

7. In the Render Stats section of the surface's Attribute Editor, select Casts Shadows.

8. Select Window > Rendering Editors > Render Globals (Windows) or Window > Render Globals (Mac), or click the Render Globals icon in the Render View 🎛 to open the Render Globals panel (**Figure 12.66**).

9. Select Raytracing in the Raytracing Quality section of the Render Globals panel (**Figure 12.67**).

10. Test-render the scene by selecting Render > Render > persp in the Render View window.

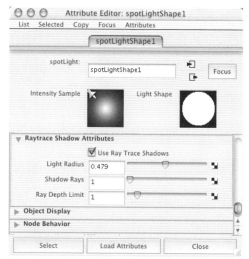

Figure 12.65 Select Use Ray Trace Shadows in the light's Attribute Editor.

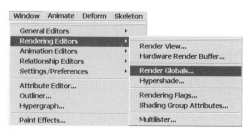

Figure 12.66 Select Window > Rendering Editors > Render Globals to open the Render Globals panel.

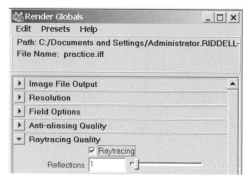

Figure 12.67 Select Raytracing in the Render Globals panel.

ABOUT SHADOWS

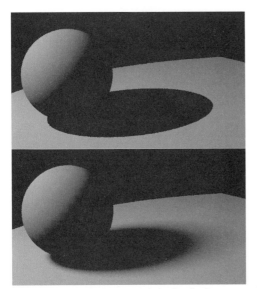

Figure 12.68 A default raytraced shadow (top), a shadow with the light radius attribute turned up (bottom).

Common raytraced shadow attributes

Light Radius—Sets the softness of the shadow's edge relative to the size of the light. For example, smaller light values have crisper shadows, and greater light values have softer shadows (**Figure 12.68**).

Shadow Rays—Sets the amount of grain visible along soft shadow edges (**Figure 12.69**). Increasing this attribute increases rendering time, so keep it as low as possible.

Ray Depth Limit—If a light bounces off multiple mirrors before it hits your object, the ray depth limit number determines whether that light will still cast a shadow.

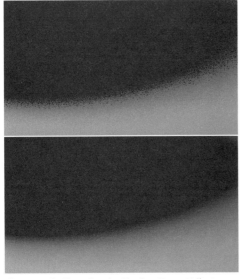

Figure 12.69 Changing the Shadow Rays attribute can cut down on grainy shadows.

SHADERS AND MATERIALS

Figure 13.1 The objects at left and the objects at right have the exact same geometry. The different shaders that have been assigned to them make them look as if they are made of different substances.

Objects in Maya start out in a drab gray color. By assigning a *shader* to a surface, you're giving the surface color or a texture map, which is an image that is mapped onto the surface.

Achieving realistic-looking surfaces goes beyond the color. You can make the default gray color on a surface look like chrome if it is shiny and reflective, or it can look like a rock if it is bumpy and matte (**Figure 13.1**).

Whether a surface is shiny or matte is determined by how it reflects light. A *material* in Maya is a part of a shader that controls an object's shininess, color, and many other attributes. There are several types of materials in Maya that deal with this reflection differently. The specular highlight is the part of the surface that appears brightest from reflecting the light. By working with the specular highlight, you can achieve the look of different substances (**Figure 13.2**).

A light bulb is not really shiny or reflective, and coloring it yellow is not going to make it look realistic. However, you can add incandescence to the shader, which makes it appear to have its own source of light. Putting glow on an object will put a kind of halo around it. By combining these two you can get a realistic light bulb (**Figure 13.3**).

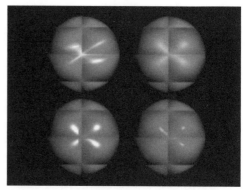

Figure 13.2 Much of what distinguishes different substances is how they reflect light. Light is reflected differently depending on what material you assign to a surface.

Figure 13.3 This light bulb is created when its material is given some incandescence and glow.

SHADERS AND MATERIALS

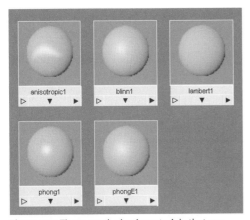

Figure 13.4 These are the basic materials that are available in the Hypershade.

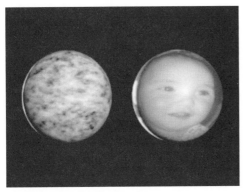

Figure 13.5 The sphere on the left has a fractal texture, which is a procedural texture. The sphere on the right has an image texture.

About the Hypershade

The Hypershade is the window in which you will do much of your work with shaders. In it you will find materials, textures, lights, and utilities.

A *material* is a node that contains most of the controls that determine the look of the object. The kind of material you use also affects the look of the object and what controls are available to it (**Figure 13.4**).

A *texture* is an image, often mapped to the color of an object. But you can also map it to the bump. A bump map makes a surface appear bumpy rather than smooth. The value of the image determines the height of the bumps. A texture can also determine what areas of a surface are transparent or shiny, or lighten the color of parts of the surface.

There are basically two categories of textures: *image* and *procedural.* An image could simply be a photograph you scanned in. A procedural texture is also an image, but is calculated based on a mathematical formula. A fractal is one example of a procedural texture (**Figure 13.5**).

Utilities are another kind of node you can find in the Hypershade. Different Maya utilities can adjust shaders in different ways. Some common ones include a bump2d utility, which allows for the creation of a bump map, and the 2d placement utility, which allows for the positioning of a texture on a surface.

Using the Hypershade

The Hypershade is split into three areas: the Create Bar, the Hypershade tabs, and the work-area tabs.

Note that the Create Bar, Hypershade tabs, work area tabs, and Shader Library are not available on the Mac version of Maya.

◆ In the Create Bar, click the "Choose which type of node to create" button. It reveals a menu from which you can choose from these selections: Create Materials, Create Textures, Create Lights, Create Utilities, and Create All Nodes. When you make a selection, the buttons beneath change to reveal the types of nodes you chose. For example, if you select Create Lights, a button for each different type of light appears (**Figure 13.6**).

◆ The Hypershade tabs allow you to see all of your materials, textures, utilities, lights, or cameras. If you create any of these nodes, they will show up under the appropriate tab. For example, if you create a material like Blinn by clicking it in the Create Bar, it will show up under the Materials tab (**Figure 13.7**).

◆ The work area is a place to work on your materials and textures. When you make a new node from the Create Bar, it also shows up here. You can middle mouse button–drag nodes from the Hypershade tabs down to the work area. Once they are there, you can make connections. An example of this is assigning a texture to the color of a material. If you middle mouse button–drag a texture onto a material and choose color from the marking menu that appears, the color of the texture will be connected to the color of the material (**Figure 13.8**).

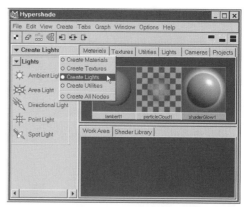

Figure 13.6 The Create Bar, which is on the left side of the Hypershade, allows you to easily create a variety of different nodes.

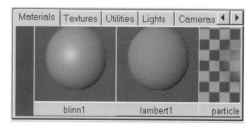

Figure 13.7 The Hypershade tabs allow you to access all of the different nodes, separated by category.

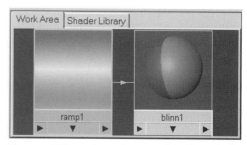

Figure 13.8 The work area is a part of the Hypershade where you can drag other nodes for the purpose of making connections. Here a ramp texture is connected to the color of a Blinn material.

ABOUT THE HYPERSHADE

◆ ▣ The Toggle the Create Bar On/Off button allows you to hide or show the Create Bar. Hiding it will give you more real estate in which to work with other nodes.

◆ ✎ The Clear Graph button clears out any nodes that are in the work area. It doesn't delete them; it just clears the area.

◆ ▦ The Rearrange Graph button will clean up the work area, which tends to get cluttered when you create new nodes.

◆ ▣ Clicking the Graph Materials on Selected Objects button is a quick way to find out what material is assigned to a specific object. Just select the object, then click this button, and the material and everything that is connected to it will show up in the work area.

◆ ▣ The Show Up and Downstream Connections button shows everything that is connected to a node. For example, you can select a material and click this button, and the material will show up in the work area with all of its connections.

◆ ▬▬▣ These buttons (Windows only) let you isolate the Hypershade tabs or the work area. On the left is Show Top Tabs Only. In the middle, Show Bottom Tabs Only. Right, Show Top and Bottom Tabs.

About Materials

There are several different types of materials, including Lambert, Blinn, Phong, and Anisotropic. Each one has some different options and reflects light differently. Lambert has no specular highlight, so it is matte, while Blinn and Phong both look shiny. Anisotropic is also shiny, but unlike Blinn and Phong, it reflects specular light unevenly (**Figure 13.9**).

There are several controls that are common to the basic materials. They include *color, transparency, ambient color, incandescence,* and *bump mapping.* Any of these can have an image mapped to them, and most of them can have a color or luminance value assigned to them. All are accessible in the Attribute Editor for the material (**Figure 13.10**).

Common material attributes

◆ Color simply determines the color of an object. You can pick a color using the Color Chooser, or you can map an image to the color.

◆ Transparency allows you to make a surface see-through. You can use the slider to make it more or less transparent, or map an image to make part of the surface transparent and part of the surface opaque. It only recognizes luminance—that is, how light or dark an image is. White is transparent and black is opaque (**Figure 13.11**).

◆ Ambient color allows you to lighten the color of the material. You can lighten the color of the whole surface evenly by using the slider, or you can map an image to the ambient color to lighten only certain parts of a surface.

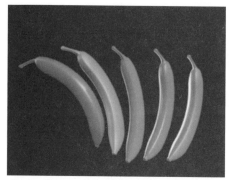

Figure 13.9 Each banana has a different material assigned to it. From left to right; Anisotropic, Blinn, Lambert, Phong, and Phong E.

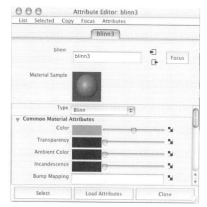

Figure 13.10 This is the Attribute Editor for a Blinn material. It holds most of the controls that determine the look of the surface.

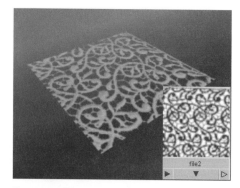

Figure 13.11 The node in the lower-right corner is the texture, which was mapped to the plane as a transparency map. The parts of the image that are white determine the parts of the plane that are transparent.

ABOUT MATERIALS

Figure 13.12 The node in the lower-right corner is the texture, which was mapped to the plane as a bump map. The white areas are higher, the dark areas are lower. You must render to see the results of a bump map.

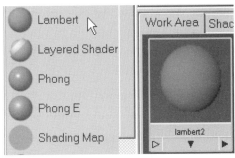

Figure 13.13 This is a portion of the Hypershade. When the Lambert button is clicked, a new material node called lambert2 appears.

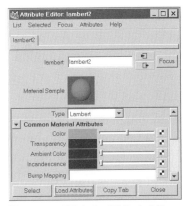

Figure 13.14 This is the Attribute Editor for the material that was just created in the Hypershade.

◆ Incandescence gives a material the appearance of having its own light. In general, you need to have a light in a scene for anything to render out. However, if an object has a material on it with the ambient color turned up, it will render out without any lights in the scene.

◆ Bump mapping creates the look of bumpiness on a surface. It must have an image mapped to it to work. The whitest parts of the image will cause the tallest bumps, and the black parts of the image will cause no bumps (**Figure 13.12**).

To change the color of an object:

1. From the Window menu select Rendering Editors > Hypershade.

2. Select Create Materials, if it is not already selected, from the pull-down menu in the Create Bar.

3. Click Lambert (**Figure 13.13**).

   A new material appears in the work area, which is the lower half of the window.

4. Double–click the new material.

   The Attribute Editor for this material appears (**Figure 13.14**).

continues on next page

ABOUT MATERIALS

5. Click the field next to Color.

The Color Chooser opens (**Figure 13.15**).

6. Choose a color by clicking one of the color swatches at the top of the window or by clicking in the color wheel.

7. Click Accept.

The Color Chooser window closes.

8. Middle mouse button–drag the material from the Hypershade on to the surface.

or

Select the surface, then right mouse button–click the material. From the Marking Menu that appears, select Assign Material To Selection (**Figure 13.16**).

✔ Tip

■ If you assign a shader to a surface by middle mouse button–dragging it from the Hypershade, be sure that the view you drag it into is in shaded mode. If it were in wireframe mode, you would need to drag it precisely onto an isoparm or edge of the surface, which is more difficult.

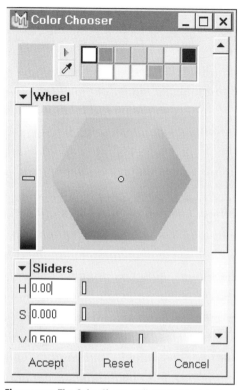

Figure 13.15 The Color Chooser allows you to select a color either from the swatches at the top or from the color wheel.

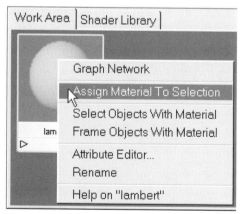

Figure 13.16 When you right-click a material in the Hypershade, a Marking Menu appears that allows you to assign that material to the selected surface. This is a particularly convenient method if you are assigning shaders to multiple surfaces at once.

ABOUT MATERIALS

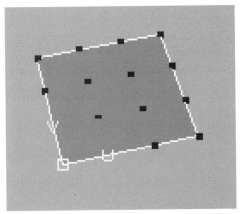

Figure 13.17 On this plane, the CVs are visible, and you can easily see the U and V directions. The square at lower left is the start point; the U is to the right of it and the V is above it. This means that the U direction is from left to right and the V direction is from bottom to top.

Figure 13.18 The same image is assigned to different NURBS surfaces. It gets wrapped around the surface, and its orientation depends on the U and V directions of the surface.

About texture-mapping NURBS surfaces

A NURBS surface is always four-sided. Even a sphere is four-sided—it is pinched at the top and bottom and the other two sides meet. NURBS surfaces have a U and a V direction. In the simple example of a plane, the U direction is from left to right and the V direction is from bottom to top. This makes the lower-left corner the start point (**Figure 13.17**).

Any image you bring in is also four-sided— image files are square or rectangular. The lower-left corner of the image is placed at the start point of the surface. The bottom of the image is mapped on the surface along the U direction, and the left side of the image is wrapped along the V direction (**Figure 13.18**).

Once the image is on the surface, it can be moved, rotated, and repeated. If you want one image to be placed over two or more surfaces, you must use a projection map. Imagine taking a slide projector and pointing it at a surface—that's roughly what a projection map does.

Maya comes with several textures, but you can also use your own images. Maya can accept many different image formats, including JPEG; TIFF; or Maya's own format, IFF.

ABOUT MATERIALS

To assign an image map from the Shader Library to a NURBS object (Windows only):

1. From the Create menu select NURBS Primitive > Plane.

2. From the Panel menu in any pane select Panel > Panel > Hypershade.

3. Click Lambert in the create bar of the Hypershade to create a new material.

   A new Lambert material appears in the Hypershade.

4. Assign the material to the plane by middle mouse button–dragging it to the surface.

5. Click the Shader Library tab, which is in the lower half of the Hypershade window.

6. Click the folder called Textures, which is in the lower half of the Hypershade. Several textures appear to the right (**Figure 13.19**).

7. Middle mouse button–drag a brick texture onto your new Lambert (probably called lambert2) that is in the top half of the Hypershade .

8. From the Marking Menu that appears, select color (**Figure 13.20**).

   The brick texture appears on the Lambert node.

9. Click in the Perspective view, and press 6 to go into textured mode.

   The brick texture shows up on the surface to which it was assigned (**Figure 13.21**).

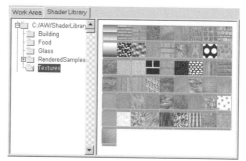

Figure 13.19 The Shader Library provides several textures. They are all repeatable, which means that if they are tiled on a surface, there will be no seams.

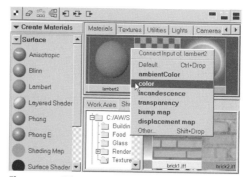

Figure 13.20 When a texture is dragged onto a material, a Marking Menu appears that allows you to choose which attribute you want to map the texture to.

Figure 13.21 The brick texture appears on the plane. This is only visible when you are in textured mode.

ABOUT MATERIALS

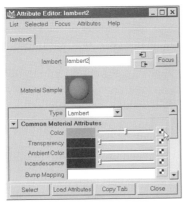

Figure 13.22 By clicking the Map icon, which is little checkerboard to the right of the slider, you can map a texture to the color.

Figure 13.23 In the Create Render Node window, you can choose which texture you want to map to an attribute of a material.

Figure 13.24 An image is mapped to the color of the plane.

To assign your own image map to a NURBS object:

1. From the Create menu select NURBS Primitive > Plane.

2. Open the Hypershade.

3. Click Lambert to create a new material.
   A new Lambert material appears in the Hypershade.

4. Double-click the new Lambert you just created in the Hypershade.
   The Attribute Editor for the Lambert opens.

5. Click the Map icon, which is to the right of the slider for Color (**Figure 13.22**).
   The Create Render Node window opens.

6. Make sure the radio button next to Normal is selected, and then click File in the Create Render Node Window (**Figure 13.23**).
   The Attribute Editor for the File node opens up.

7. Click the Browse button ⅃ next to Image Name.

8. Browse for and open your own image file.

9. Middle mouse button–drag the Lambert you created from the Hypershade onto your surface.

10. Click in the Perspective view, and press ⑥ to go into textured mode.
    The image you chose is now color-mapped to your surface (**Figure 13.24**).

continues on next page

✔ **Tips**

- You can similarly map an image to any of the common material attributes.

- You can also map an image by dragging an existing texture onto the name of an attribute in a material's Attribute Editor (**Figure 13.25**).

When you first map an image on a NURBS surface, it may not be oriented correctly. You can use the place 2d texture node to rotate, move, and scale the image on the surface.

To use place 2d texture:

1. Map a brick texture to a NURBS plane as in the "To assign an image map to a NURBS object from the Shader Library" section above.

2. Select the surface.

3. In the Hypershade, click the Graph Materials on Selected Objects icon ⬚.

   The entire shading network and its connections show up in the work area of the Hypershade (**Figure 13.26**).

4. Double-click the place2dTexture node, which is at the left of the work area.

   The Attribute Editor for the place2dTexture node appears.

5. Click the Interactive Placement button in the Attribute Editor for the place2dTexture node. A red square with a dot in the middle appears on the surface.

6. Middle mouse button–drag, starting from the center point of the interactive placement.

   The texture moves on the surface (**Figure 13.27**).

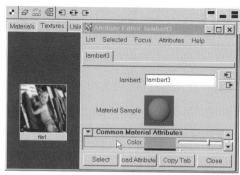

Figure 13.25 The file texture in the Hypershade is being middle mouse button–dragged to the color in the Attribute Editor of a material. This can be a convenient way to make connections quickly.

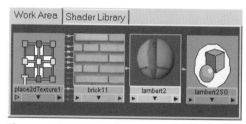

Figure 13.26 In the work area of the Hypershade, we can see all of the nodes that are associated with this material.

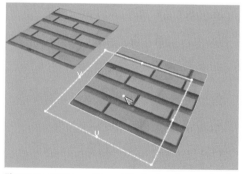

Figure 13.27 The position of the texture is moved using interactive placement. Compare the position of the bricks once they've been moved, in the lower right, with where they were originally, in the upper left.

ABOUT MATERIALS

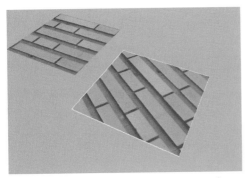

Figure 13.28 The interactive placement was used to rotate the brick texture.

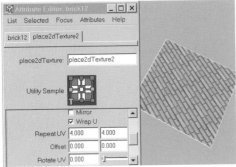

Figure 13.29 By increasing Repeat U and V of the place2dTexture to 4 (in the Attribute Editor on the left), the brick texture is repeated many times on the surface.

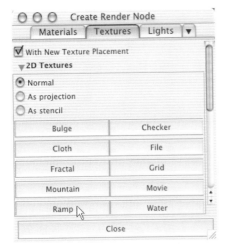

Figure 13.30 When you click Ramp in the Create Render Node window, a new ramp texture is created and mapped to a material.

7. Middle mouse button–drag at the corners of the red square. The texture rotates (**Figure 13.28**).

8. Click in the field next to Repeat UV and type 4. Press Enter.

The bricks are repeated four times in the U direction. The column on the left is for U values; the column on the right is for V values.

9. In the field two columns to the right of Repeat UV, type 4. Press Enter.

The bricks are now also repeated four times in the V direction (**Figure 13.29**).

Procedural textures are built into Maya; they do not rely on an image file. Their color and luminance are determined mathematically. One commonly used procedural texture is a ramp, which is like a gradient.

To assign a ramp texture to a surface:

1. From the Create menu select NURBS Primitive > Sphere.

2. In the Channel Box, type 90 in the field next to Rotate X, and press Enter.

3. In the Hypershade, click Phong E.

A Phong E material shows up in the work area.

4. Double-click the Phong E material in the Hypershade.

The Attribute Editor for the Phong E material appears.

5. In the Attribute Editor for the Phong E, click the map button next to the slider for Color ⬚.

The Create Render Node window opens.

6. Click the Ramp button (**Figure 13.30**).

The Attribute Editor for the ramp appears. A ramp texture node also appears in the Hypershade.

continues on next page

7. Middle mouse button–drag the Phong E from the Hypershade onto the sphere to assign the shader.

If you have trouble finding the Phong E, click the work area of the Hypershade and press ⓐ. This will frame all of the nodes.

8. Click the Perspective view and press ⑥ to see the texture (**Figure 13.31**).

To adjust the ramp texture to make it look like an eyeball:

1. Create a material with a ramp texture, and assign it to a sphere as in the previous section.

2. In the work area of the Hypershade, double-click on the ramp texture.

The Attribute Editor for the ramp appears.

3. In the Attribute Editor for the ramp, change the type to U Ramp.

4. Click and drag the top position indicator down slightly (**Figure 13.32**).

5. Change its color to black by dragging the slider next to Selected Color all the way to the left.

6. Click and drag the middle position indicator, which is green by default, to just below the top one.

7. Click on the ramp about one fifth of the way down from the top.

A new position indicator appears (**Figure 13.33**).

8. Click and drag the bottom position indicator up to just below the new one.

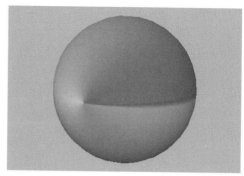

Figure 13.31 This sphere has a ramp textured to its color.

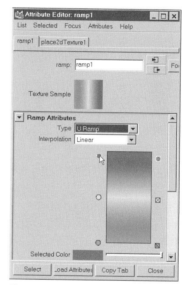

Figure 13.32 The Attribute Editor for the ramp holds the controls for determining the look of the gradient it produces. Position indicators are the circles to the left of the ramp. They determine where a color is positioned within the gradient.

Figure 13.33 When you click in the middle of the ramp, a new position indicator is created. By clicking the square with the X in it to the right of the ramp, you can delete a position indicator.

ABOUT MATERIALS

Figure 13.34 The white swatch is selected in the Color Chooser, which causes the selected position indicator and the ramp below it to become white.

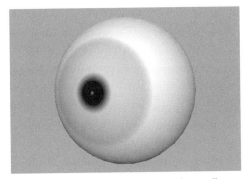

Figure 13.35 The eyeball is complete with a pupil and iris.

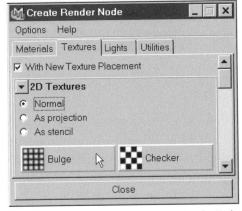

Figure 13.36 Clicking Bulge in the Create Render Node window creates a bulge texture that is mapped to the bump of a material.

9. With the bottom position indicator still selected, click the color swatch next to Selected Color.

   The Color Chooser opens.

10. Click the white swatch at the top of the Color Chooser (**Figure 13.34**).

    The sphere is now textured like an eyeball (**Figure 13.35**).

To assign a bump map to a surface:

1. From the Create menu select NURBS Primitives > Plane.

2. In the Hypershade create a Lambert.

3. Assign the Lambert to the plane by middle mouse button–dragging it from the Hypershade to the plane.

4. Double-click the Lambert in the Hypershade.

   The Attribute Editor for the Lambert appears.

5. Click the Map button next to Bump Mapping ⬛.

   The Create Render Node window appears.

6. Click Bulge (**Figure 13.36**).

   The bulge shows up in the work area of the Hypershade. We'll need to render it to see the resulting bump.

continues on next page

7. From the Create menu select Lights > Directional Light.

Bump maps show up better with a directional source of light than with ambient light.

8. Rotate the light so that it is pointing diagonally at the plane (**Figure 13.37**).

9. Click the Render icon 📸, which is near the top right of the interface.

The image renders out into a new window. The bulge is visible on the surface (**Figure 13.38**).

Figure 13.37 A directional light is created and rotated diagonally to the plane. Directional lights make bumps stand out in greater contrast because the light is coming from only one side.

Figure 13.38 This is a rendered image of a plane with a bulge texture mapped to its bump. You must render to see the bump—it does not show up in the Perspective view.

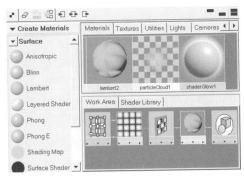

Figure 13.39 All of the nodes associated with the material are visible in the work area of the Hypershade. The utility that controls the height of the bump is in the middle.

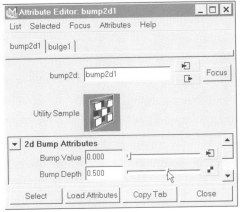

Figure 13.40 The Attribute Editor for the bump2d node contains the bump depth attribute. Bump depth controls the overall height of the bump.

Figure 13.41 The plane on the left has a bump depth of 1, the plane the right has a bump depth of 0.5.

To adjust the height of a bump map:

1. Create a plane with a bulge bump map, as in the previous section.

2. Select the plane.

3. Click the Graph Materials on Selected Objects button 🔲 in the Hypershade.

   The material with all its connections appears in the work area of the Hypershade (**Figure 13.39**).

4. Double-click the bump2d node.

   The Attribute Editor for the bump2d appears.

5. Change the bump depth by moving the slider or typing in a number (**Figure 13.40**).

6. Click the Render icon 🔲.

   The bumps are smaller than in the previous bump map (**Figure 13.41**).

About projection maps

Sometimes you want one image to be mapped across two or more surfaces. For that you can use a projection map. The default projection type is *planar,* which acts like a slide projector pointed at a surface. There are other projection types, such as *spherical* or *cylindrical.* They project an image from a shape that surrounds the surface (**Figure 13.42**).

To map a texture as projection:

1. Create a Lambert material in the Hypershade, and assign it to a NURBS plane and a NURBS sphere (**Figure 13.43**).

2. Double-click the Lambert in the Hypershade.

   The Attribute Editor for the Lambert opens.

3. In the Attribute Editor for the Lambert, click the map button next to the slider for Color ![icon].

   The Create Render Node window appears.

4. Click the radio button next to As Projection (**Figure 13.44**).

5. Click the File button.

   The Attribute Editor for the projection appears. A place3dTexture node appears in the Perspective view.

6. Click the file1 tab at the top of the Attribute Editor.

   The Attribute Editor changes to show the options for the file texture.

7. Click the Folder icon next to Image Name. The file browser appears.

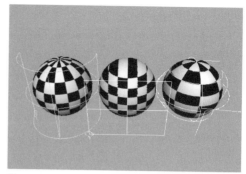

Figure 13.42 A checkered texture is mapped to spheres using three different projection types: from left to right, cylindrical, planar, and spherical.

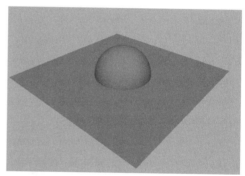

Figure 13.43 A NURBS sphere and a plane.

Figure 13.44 The As Projection radio button has been selected in the Create Render Node window.

ABOUT MATERIALS

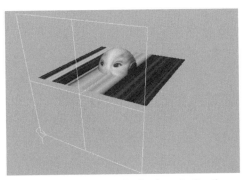

Figure 13.45 The planar projection is projecting the image across the two surfaces from the side. This causes the image to be stretched along the plane.

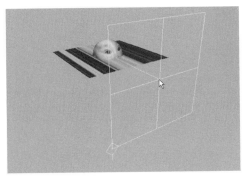

Figure 13.46 The place3dtexture utility has been selected in the Perspective view. This node can be moved, rotated, and scaled the same way you would for any object.

8. Browse for and open an image of your own.

9. Click the Perspective view, and press ⑥ to go into textured mode.

The place3dtexture node is visible in the Perspective view. The image is visible on the surface, but it is stretched out because it is being projected on from the side (**Figure 13.45**).

✔ Tip

■ If you move a surface with a projection texture mapped to it, the surface will appear to be moving through its texture when it is rendered out. To solve this problem, select the surface, and then from the Texturing menu select Create Texture Reference Object.

To adjust a projection:

1. Projection map a texture onto a plane as in the previous section.

2. Select the place3dtexture utility in the Perspective view (**Figure 13.46**).

The line coming out from the center is the direction it is projecting. It is projecting on the side of the plane, and we want it to project on the top.

3. Rotate the plane –90 degrees in the x-axis.

The image is no longer stretched out, but it does not fit precisely on the surface.

4. With the place3dtexture still selected, press Ctrl/Control a to open the Attribute Editor.

The Attribute Editor for the place3dtexture node opens.

continues on next page

ABOUT MATERIALS

5. Click the "Fit to group bbox" button.

The place3dtexture is automatically resized to the size of the plane, and the image now fits (**Figure 13.47**).

✔ Tip

■ If you move or rotate the place3dtexture, the image on the surface will move or rotate. If you scale it up, the image will scale up. If you scale it down, the image will scale down and be tiled (**Figure 13.48**).

Textures often show up blurry in the view, especially projected textures, even though they will render out clearly. However, when placing a texture, you often need the image to appear sharper.

To improve the quality of a texture image in a view:

1. Projection-map a checkered texture onto a sphere (**Figure 13.49**).

The texture on the surface is very blurry.

2. Select the sphere.

3. In the Hypershade, click the Graph Materials on Selected Objects icon 🖼 .

The material with all of its connections appears in the work area of the Hypershade.

4. Double-click the material in the Hypershade.

The Attribute Editor for the material appears.

Figure 13.47 Now that the place3dtexture utility is oriented to the surface, the image is projected across the two surfaces.

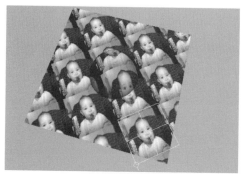

Figure 13.48 The place3dtexture utility has been scaled down, rotated, and moved.

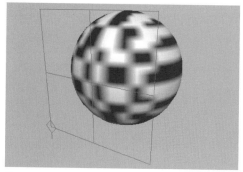

Figure 13.49 A checkered texture is projected onto a sphere. It appears very blurry and does not accurately represent how it will look when it is rendered out.

ABOUT MATERIALS

Figure 13.50 Hardware Texturing options are visible in the Attribute Editor for a material. By increasing the "Texture quality" setting to High, the checkers will become clear.

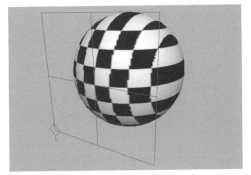

Figure 13.51 The checker texture is much sharper now that the texture quality for the Hardware Texturing has been increased.

5. Under Hardware Texturing in the Attribute Editor, click the arrow to expand the options (**Figure 13.50**).

6. Change the "Texture quality" setting to High.

The blurry checkers on the sphere become sharper (**Figure 13.51**).

✔ Tip

- Making the texture quality high will slow down the interactivity of Maya, especially with a high-resolution image. Once you've completed placing the texture, it is a good idea to reset it to low quality.

About the 3D Paint tool

The 3D Paint tool allows you to paint directly on a surface. You can create a new texture image from scratch with this method, and Maya will create a new image file.

It is important to make sure you've set your project before you begin painting (File > Project > Set), because the current project will determine where this image ends up. When you save the scene after painting, a folder named after your scene is created in the 3dPaintTextures folder of the project you are currently set to. Any images that were created by painting will be put in that folder.

You can also paint on a surface that already has an image file textured on it. This could be used to add dirt or other details to an existing image.

continues on next page

ABOUT MATERIALS

To paint directly on a surface:

1. Create a Lambert material in the Hypershade, and assign it to a NURBS sphere.

2. Select the sphere.

3. From the Texturing menu (Windows) or Lighting/Shading menu (Mac) select the box next to 3D Paint Tool.

   The 3D Paint Tool Settings window opens (**Figure 13.52**).

4. Scroll down until you see File Textures (**Figure 13.53**).

   You can change the Image Format that will be created at this time, if necessary.

5. Click the Assign Textures button.

   The Assign File Textures window appears. You can increase the resolution of the texture here in case you need a highly detailed texture. The default of 256 by 256 will suffice for now (**Figure 13.54**).

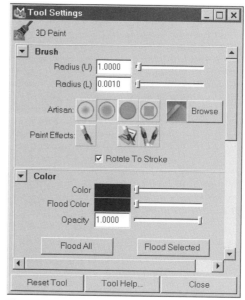

Figure 13.52 The 3D Paint Tool Settings window includes many controls that determine the look of the brush strokes.

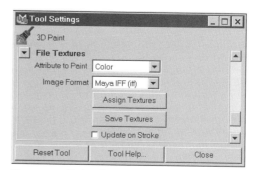

Figure 13.53 Under File Textures in the 3D Paint Tool Settings window you can assign a texture to the material for a selected object. You cannot paint on a surface that does not have a file mapped to its color.

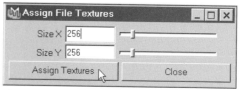

Figure 13.54 Once you click Assign Textures, you can paint, because a file texture has been connected to the material for the object you want to paint.

ABOUT MATERIALS

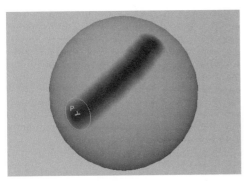

Figure 13.55 The paintbrush has been dragged across the sphere, producing this black mark.

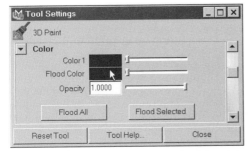

Figure 13.56 You can choose a color to flood the whole object with by clicking the field next to Flood Color.

Figure 13.57 A smiley face has been painted on the sphere with three brush strokes.

6. Click Assign Textures.

   A file texture has now been connected to the material so you can paint.

7. Click in the Perspective view, then hold down B and middle mouse button–drag from right to left to get the brush down to size.

   The red circle, which represents the brush size, should shrink.

8. Click and drag on the surface to paint on it.

   A mark appears on the surface (**Figure 13.55**).

To use the 3D Paint tool:

1. Continue with the sphere from the previous section.

   If the paintbrush is not visible or the tool options are no longer open, select the sphere, and then from the Texturing menu select the box next to 3D Paint Tool.

2. Click the color swatch next to Flood Color in the 3D Paint Tool Settings window (**Figure 13.56**).

   The Color Chooser appears.

3. Choose the yellow swatch at the top of the Color Chooser, and click Accept.

4. Click Flood All.

   The sphere turns yellow.

5. Paint a smiley face by clicking and dragging on the surface (**Figure 13.57**).

   The following steps are only for the Windows version.

6. Click the Get Brush button ⩗ which is to the right of Paint Effects in the 3D Paint Tool Options window.

   The Visor window opens.

continues on next page

ABOUT MATERIALS

7. Scroll down in the Visor, and click the Hair folder.

Several hair types appear (**Figure 13.58**).

8. Click on the hair of your choice.

9. Paint some hair on your smiley face sphere (**Figure 13.59**).

✔ Tips

■ After using a Paint Effects brush, you can return to a normal brush by clicking one of the brush profile buttons next to Artisan in the 3D Paint Tool Settings window (**Figure 13.60**).

■ By decreasing the opacity in the 3D Paint Tool Settings, you paint on a surface but still see the color underneath your brush strokes. This can be helpful if you are trying to make a surface look dirty.

■ One technique for using this tool is to paint out areas roughly to mark out the different parts of a surface. You can then open the image file (that is created once you save the scene) in Adobe Photoshop and paint the details there.

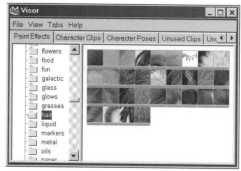

Figure 13.58 You can choose from a variety of different brushes to use with the 3D Paint Tool in the Visor. Here we see the brushes in the Hair folder.

Figure 13.59 Hair has been painted on the sphere by using one of the Paint Effects brushes.

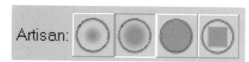

Figure 13.60 To return to a normal brush, choose from one of the profiles of the Artisan brushes.

Figure 13.61 A wrapped gift texture has been mapped to a cube.

Figure 13.62 The white lines in the UV Texture Editor are the edges of the cube. You can see how the cube has been "unwrapped." The image beneath is what the actual image file that is mapped to the surface looks like.

Figure 13.63 Four different textures have been mapped to different parts of the same polygon sphere by assigning them to specific faces of the sphere.

About Texturing Polygons

Anything covered in the chapter so far would work on a polygon primitive. However, these techniques would not necessarily work on a polygon surface that you modeled. NURBS surfaces are always four-sided, but polygon surfaces are made up of many small faces. So the way a texture gets mapped on polygon surfaces is not as simple as it is on NURBS surfaces.

Think of a wrapped present. Imagine carefully removing the wrapping paper and flattening it out. Once it is flattened out, you could easily paint a new image on it (**Figure 13.61**).

This is essentially what you need to do to texture a polygon surface. Before you can successfully texture-map it, you need to "unwrap" the surface. You create a UV map, which you can see in the UV Texture Editor (**Figure 13.62**).

For a complicated character, the UV maps can be very confusing to look at and require a lot of work to be able to use them effectively. Polygon primitives do not need a UV map because they already come with one.

One distinct advantage polygons have over NURBS is that you can assign multiple materials to a single polygon surface, while a NURBS surface can have only one. This is done by selecting polygon faces and assigning the materials to them, not to the object as a whole (**Figure 13.63**).

To create automatic mapping for a polygon texture:

1. Create a polygon telephone (**Figure 13.64**). For detailed steps, see Chapter 8, "To model a SubD telephone receiver, starting with a polygon." Do not convert it to subdivision surfaces. Instead, smooth the polygon with a subdivision level of 3 and a continuity of 0.35.

2. Create a Blinn material, and assign it to the surface.

3. Double-click the Blinn material in the Hypershade.

   The Attribute Editor for the Blinn material opens.

4. Click the Map button next to the Color slider in the Attribute Editor ⬛.

   The Create Render Node window appears.

5. Make sure that the radio button next to Normal is selected, and then click File.

   The Attribute Editor for the file node opens.

6. Click the Browse button ⬛ next to Image Name.

7. Browse for and open your own image file. I've created one especially for the phone, but any image will do. The image will look messed up and stretched out on the phone in the Perspective view (**Figure 13.65**).

8. Select the surface.

9. From the Edit Polygons menu select Texture > Automatic Mapping.

   The image is not stretched out as much, but the different elements are not in place (**Figure 13.66**).

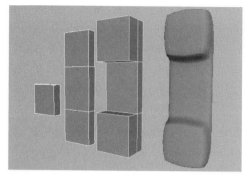

Figure 13.64 By using Extrude Face and Smooth, a phone can be modeled from a cube in a few easy steps.

Figure 13.65 On the left is the file texture that is mapped to the phone. On the right, the texture on the phone is stretched out and in the wrong places.

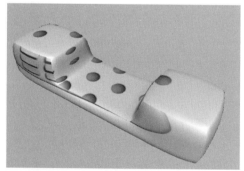

Figure 13.66 Now that a UV map has been created using automatic mapping, the texture is placed on all parts of the surface, but not in the right places.

ABOUT TEXTURING POLYGONS

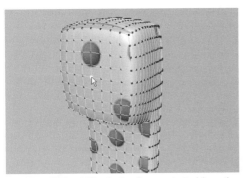

Figure 13.67 One UV point has been selected from the center of the earpiece of the phone.

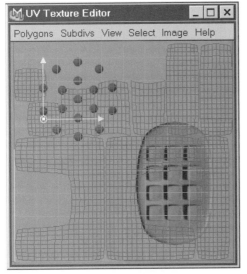

Figure 13.68 In the UV Texture Editor, you can see how the different parts of the surface have been laid out over the image map. The UV point that was selected in the Perspective view is also selected here and is seen with move manipulators on it. This makes it easy to recognize which shell is the phone's earpiece.

Getting around in the UV Texture Editor is the same as getting around in any panel. You can track and dolly just as you do in any view panel. The Move, Rotate, and Scale tools work just as they do in the rest of the program.

The image that is mapped to the surface is tiled in the UV Texture Editor. This allows you to move up different parts of the surface onto the part of the image you want without a lot of messy overlapping.

To use the UV Texture Editor:

1. Continue with the phone from the previous section.

2. Right mouse button–click the surface, and from the Marking Menu select UV.

3. Choose one UV point from the center of the earpiece part of the telephone (**Figure 13.67**).

4. From the Window menu select UV Texture Editor (Texture View on Mac). The UV Texture Editor opens. You can see the image that was assigned to the surface, and on top of that is the wireframe of the different parts of the surface (shells) that have been separated. The one point you picked on the surface is visible and is easy to find because of the transform manipulator on it (**Figure 13.68**).

continues on next page

ABOUT TEXTURING POLYGONS

5. Right mouse button–click the shell, and from the Marking Menu choose Select > Select Shell (**Figure 13.69**).

All the UVs of the shell are selected.

6. Move, scale, and rotate the shell over a recognizable part of the image.

You can watch the image on the selected area of the phone change interactively in the Perspective view (**Figure 13.70**).

7. Repeat steps 3 through 6 for other parts of the phone.

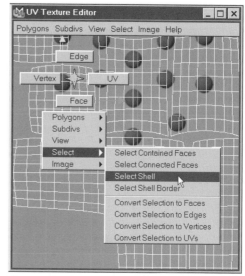

Figure 13.69 Rather than having to carefully select each UV of the shell, you can select the whole shell at once by right mouse button–clicking and choosing Select Shell from the Marking Menu.

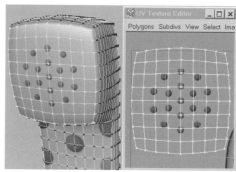

Figure 13.70 While placing the UVs in the Texture view (right), you can see the effects on the surface simultaneously (left).

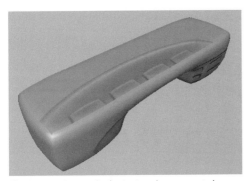

Figure 13.71 A seam in the texture is apparent along the side of the phone.

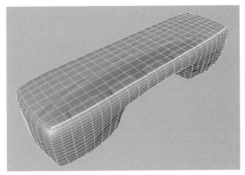

Figure 13.72 All the polygon edges along the edge of the seam have been carefully selected.

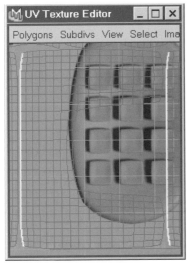

Figure 13.73 The edges of two shells are selected because they are in fact one edge that is shared by the two of them.

Because the surface is in many separate pieces (shells) in the UV Texture View, there are seams on the surface. We can combine two shells and get rid of the seam by using Move and Sew UVs (**Figure 13.71**).

To eliminate a seam in a texture using Move and Sew UVs:

1. Continue with the phone from the previous sections.

2. In the Perspective view, carefully select all the edges along the seam (**Figure 13.72**).

   The corresponding edges are selected in the UV Texture Editor as a result of the selection on the object (**Figure 13.73**).

   continues on next page

ABOUT TEXTURING POLYGONS

3. From the Edit Polygons menu select Texture > Move and Sew UVs.

The seam on the object disappears in the Perspective view (**Figure 13.74**). In the UV Texture Editor, two shells have been combined along that edge (**Figure 13.75**).

Figure 13.74 The seam is now gone because the edges of the two shells have been sewn together, so the texture image goes across both of them.

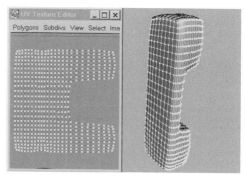

Figure 13.75 What was once two separate shells is now one bigger shell covering a larger portion of the phone.

CAMERAS AND RENDERING

Figure 14.1 Compare a hardware render of a tractor (left) with a software render (right). The software render has a bump map forming the treads of the tires and a transparency map creating the grill in the front.

Figure 14.2 A wineglass is rendered using raytracing. Reflections and refractions on the glass are what make it look real.

Creating quality images in Maya, whether for print or video, depends on rendering. Rendering is the process of creating an image, or sequence of images, from a scene. When you render, you create a two-dimensional image from a specified three-dimensional view of your scene. Maya makes intensive mathematical calculations using laws of physics to realistically create lighting, shadows, reflections, and textures. With a few settings, you can take even a very simple scene and make it look realistic by rendering it.

Rendering lights, shadows, and textures is known as *software rendering*. Maya also performs *hardware rendering*, which is essentially what you have been looking at in your Perspective view. When you press ⁊ for hardware lighting, you are hardware rendering. Maya has a Hardware Render Buffer, which will make a series of screen snapshots and export the images for you. The Hardware Render Buffer also has a few options that can clean up your images (**Figure 14.1**).

Software rendering has two basic categories: the default (known as *A-buffer*) and *raytracing*. The default renderer can create high-quality images with lighting, shadows, texturing, and motion blur. But for added realism you may need reflections and refractions. This is where raytracing comes in. For example, if you want to make a wineglass look real, you need to raytrace (**Figure 14.2**).

About Cameras

One essential part of rendering is your point of view of your scene. Any time you view your scene in Maya, you are looking through a camera. The four views—Top, Front, Side, and Perspective—are actually four different cameras. Most often you render using the Perspective view, but you can use the others as well.

Cameras determine both your view of the scene and the view that gets rendered out. When you are tumbling and tracking in the Perspective view you are essentially just moving and rotating that camera. The four default cameras—Top, Front, Side, and Perspective—cannot be deleted, but you can create new cameras (**Figure 14.3**).

You can also animate a camera just as you would any other object. You can simulate camera motion from real films, such as crane, helicopter, and dolly shots. By animating a camera, you could do a fly-through, which is often done for architectural visualization. You can also simulate camera cuts—the camera can stay at one view for a while, and then jump to another view.

Cameras have a few useful attributes. *Focal length* allows you to adjust the zoom of the lens just as you would on a real camera (this is different from dolly). *Center of interest* allows you to move the point where you want the camera to look. An *image plane* will put an image in the background of the camera view, regardless of how the camera is moved.

To create and adjust a camera:

1. From the Create menu select Cameras > Camera on Windows or select Create > Camera on the Mac.

A new camera appears in the Perspective view (**Figure 14.4**).

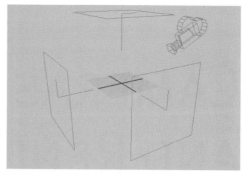

Figure 14.3 The icon that looks like a camera represents the Perspective view. The orthographic views (top, front, and side) are represented by squares with a line extending from the middle.

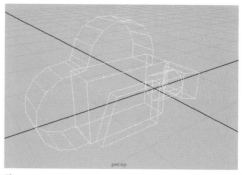

Figure 14.4 When a new camera is created, it appears at the origin.

ABOUT CAMERAS

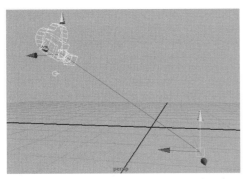

Figure 14.5 The camera itself has been moved, and its center of interest is moved separately; the camera continues to aim at it.

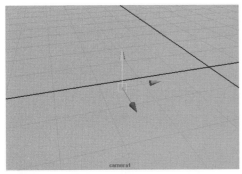

Figure 14.6 This is the view through the new camera that was just created. The manipulator we see is the camera's own center of interest, which is still visible because the camera is still selected.

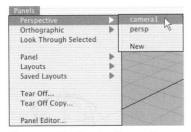

Figure 14.7 The Panels > Perspective menu provides different camera views.

2. With the camera still selected, press t for the Show Manipulator tool.

A Move manipulator appears on the camera and another one appears in front of it. The one in front of it is called the center of interest.

3. Move the camera and the center of interest around.

The camera follows the center of interest—that is, it stays aimed at it (**Figure 14.5**).

4. From the Panels menu in the Perspective view, select Look Through Selected.

The view changes, and you are now looking through the camera that was just created. Note that the camera name at the bottom of the screen has changed from persp to camera1 (**Figure 14.6**).

✔ Tips

■ Another way to choose which camera you are looking through is from the Panels menu in the Perspective view. You'll find the list of available cameras in Panels > Perspective (**Figure 14.7**).

■ You can rotate a camera, which might be useful when doing a camera pan.

■ Scaling the camera does not affect its view but could make it easier to select.

There is a subtle but important difference between creating a regular camera, and a *camera and aim*. The camera and aim has an additional node, which can be keyframed or parented to an object.

To create and adjust a camera and aim:

1. On Windows, from the Create menu select Cameras > Camera and Aim. On Mac, select the box next to Create > Camera to open the camera's option box, and under the Animation Options arrow click two node; press Create to create the two-node camera.

   A new camera appears in the Perspective view. It has a dot in front of it, which is the aim (**Figure 14.8**).

2. From the Window menu select Hypergraph.

   You can see the different nodes associated with the camera group (**Figure 14.9**).

3. From the Hypergraph, select the group node of the camera (probably called camera1_group).

4. Move the camera around.

   The aim and camera move together.

5. In the Perspective view, select and then move the aim.

   The camera stays aimed at it.

6. In the Perspective view, select and then move the camera.

7. The camera moves, but continues to point at the aim (**Figure 14.10**).

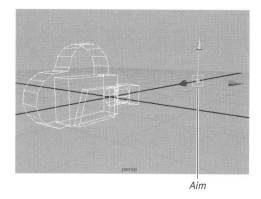

Aim

Figure 14.8 A camera and aim has been created. Note that the aim is represented by a small circle with a dot in the middle.

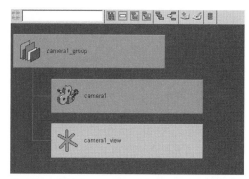

Figure 14.9 This is a camera and aim as represented in the Hypergraph. It has three nodes on Windows, and two nodes on Mac; a regular camera has only one.

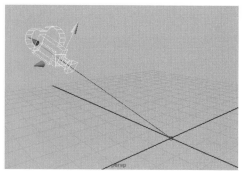

Figure 14.10 The camera has been moved up and away from the origin, but it continues to look at the aim.

ABOUT CAMERAS

Figure 14.11 If you decide that you want a different camera type after you create it, you can change it here, in the Attribute Editor.

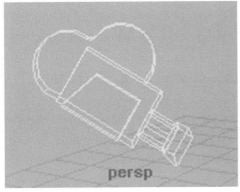

Figure 14.12 At the bottom of the pane, you can see the name of the camera you are currently looking through. In this case it is persp (short for perspective). Note that the camera that is selected is not the perspective (persp) camera.

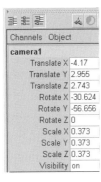

Figure 14.13 In the Channel Box, you can see the name of the camera selected. When you make a new camera, it is named camera1 by default.

✔ Tips

■ You can also create a *camera, aim and up* on Windows, or a three-node camera on the Mac. This is similar to the camera and aim, except that it has one more node that controls the tilt of the camera.

■ You can change whether the camera has an aim and up after it is created. In the Attribute Editor for the camera, there is an option under Camera Attributes called Controls where you can choose from the three different types of cameras, Windows only (**Figure 14.11**).

Animating the camera

Animating a camera is essentially the same as animating anything else. You select it, keyframe it, change the current time, move it, and keyframe it again. However, you do many things differently when you animate a camera.

You might want to do camera cuts, where the camera stays still and then jumps to the next position. Or you might want the aim of the camera to follow an object as it passes through the scene. Cameras can be animated along a path, which could be used for the fly-through of a scene.

One thing to understand before you begin animating is that the camera that is selected is not necessarily the one you are looking through. At the bottom of the view, you can see the name of the camera you are currently looking through (**Figure 14.12**). In the Channel Box you can see the name of the currently selected camera (**Figure 14.13**). One common mistake is to move the view and set keyframes without having that camera selected. You will not end up with any camera animation if you make this mistake.

An easy way to animate the camera is to use tumble, track, and dolly, which you have been using all along to see different parts of your scene.

To animate the camera using tumble, track, and dolly:

1. Create some objects and move them around the scene so you have something to look at.

2. From the View menu in the Perspective view, choose Select Camera (**Figure 14.14**).

   You can see that the camera is selected because the name of the camera, persp, appears at the top of the Channel Box.

3. Press $\boxed{s}$ to keyframe the camera.

4. In the Time Slider, change the current time to 30 by clicking the number 30.

5. Tumble, track, and dolly the camera to change the point of view.

   (See Chapter 2 for more on how to tumble, track, and dolly.)

6. Press $\boxed{s}$ to keyframe the camera again.

7. Rewind and play back the animation by using the playback control buttons in the timeline (**Figure 14.15**).

   The motion of the camera is animated, so the view changes as you play back the animation (**Figure 14.16**).

Figure 14.14
From the View menu in the Perspective view, choose Select Camera. This selects whichever camera you are currently looking through.

Figure 14.15 These are the playback controls. The button all the way on the left is the rewind button. The large triangle pointing to the right is the play button.

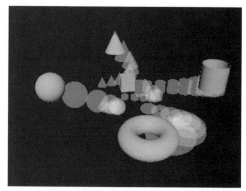

Figure 14.16 This image represents what you would see through the camera once it is animated.

ABOUT CAMERAS

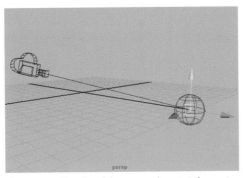

Figure 14.17 The aim of the camera is put at the center of an animated sphere and then parented to it.

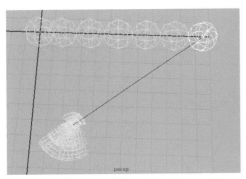

Figure 14.18 The camera follows the sphere as it is animated across the screen.

To make the aim of the camera follow an object:

1. From the Create menu select NURBS Primitives > Sphere.

2. With the sphere still selected, press ⓢ to keyframe the sphere.

3. Change the current time in the timeline to 30.

4. Move the sphere, then press ⓢ to keyframe the sphere again.

    The sphere is now animated.

5. From the Create menu select Cameras > Camera and Aim on Windows. On a Mac select the box next to Create > Camera to open the camera's option box, and under the Animation Options arrow click two node; press Create to create the two-node camera.

6. Select and move the aim of the camera to the center of the sphere (**Figure 14.17**).

7. With the aim still selected, Shift-select the sphere. Press ⓟ to parent the aim to the sphere.

8. Rewind and play back the animation.

    The camera follows the sphere (**Figure 14.18**).

9. Select the camera, and from the Panels menu in the Perspective view choose Look Through Selected.

    The view changes to the camera you just created.

10. Rewind and play back the animation.

    You can see the camera following the sphere from the point of view of the camera.

When modelers want to show off their models, they often do a turntable animation. One way to create this is to place the model at the center of the scene and rotate the camera around it.

To rotate the camera around an object:

1. Place any object at the origin.

2. From the Create menu select Cameras > Camera on Windows, or Create > Camera on Mac.

   A new camera appears in the Perspective view.

3. Move the camera back from the origin.

4. Press [w], then press [Insert]/[Home] to go into Pivot Move mode.

5. Move the pivot point to the origin (**Figure 14.19**). Press [Insert]/[Home] again to get out of Pivot Move mode.

6. Select the camera, and press [s] to keyframe it.

7. Change the current time in the timeline to 30.

8. In the Channel Box, type 360 in the field next to Rotate Y. Press [Enter].

9. Press [s] to keyframe the camera again.

   If you play back the animation now, you will see the camera rotating around the object (**Figure 14.20**).

10. Select the camera, and from the Panels menu in the Perspective view choose Panels > Look Through Selected.

    You are now seeing through the view of the camera. When the animation is played back, it will look like a turntable animation.

✔ Tip

■ To move the Pivot Point to the exact origin of the scene, hold down [x] to snap the Pivot Point to the grid.

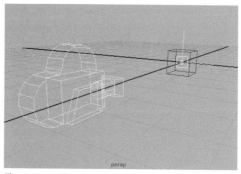

Figure 14.19 The pivot point of a camera is put at the center of an object so it can rotate around that object.

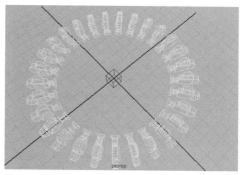

Figure 14.20 The camera is animated to rotate around the object.

ABOUT CAMERAS

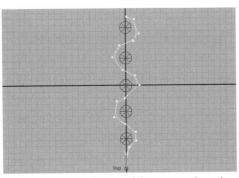

Figure 14.21 A curve is created that weaves through some cones, seen from the top view.

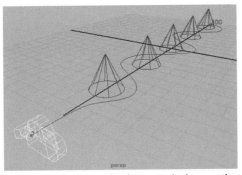

Figure 14.22 The camera has been attached to a motion path, so it jumps to the beginning of the curve. However, it is facing the wrong way.

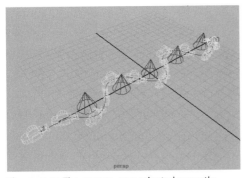

Figure 14.23 The camera, now oriented correctly, follows the curve as the animation is played back.

To animate a camera along a path:

1. Create a row of cones.

2. In the top view, create a NURBS curve that weaves through the cones (**Figure 14.21**).

3. From the Create menu select Cameras > Camera on Windows, or Create > Camera on Mac.

   A new camera appears in the Perspective view.

4. With the camera still selected, (Shift)-select the curve.

5. From the Animate menu select Motion Paths > Attach to Motion Path on Windows, or Animate > Paths > Attach to Path on Mac.

   The camera jumps to the beginning of the path, but it might not be pointing in the right direction (**Figure 14.22**).

6. With the camera still selected, click motionPath1 in the Channel Box.

   Four attributes of the motionPath appear.

7. If the camera is not pointing in the right direction, click Up Twist in the Channel Box, and then middle mouse button–drag in the Perspective view until the camera is pointing down the path correctly.

8. Rewind and play back the animation. The camera travels down the path (**Figure 14.23**).

Focal length

Focal length is an attribute that is similar to the zoom on a real camera. When you increase the focal length, you zoom in. An object appears closer, but zooming in also has the effect of flattening distance. When you decrease focal length, you zoom out. Distances seem exaggerated with a short focal length, and you get a fisheye lens effect.

To adjust the focal length of the camera:

1. Place any surface at the origin (**Figure 14.24**).

2. From the View menu in the Perspective view choose Select Camera.

   The perspective camera becomes selected.

3. In the Channel Box, change the Focal Length to 6.

   The object seems to be farther away (**Figure 14.25**).

4. Dolly the camera in close to the object (see Chapter 2, Navigating and Changing the Interface).

   The object is distorted, as it would be with a fisheye lens on a real camera (**Figure 14.26**).

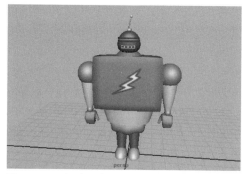

Figure 14.24 A robot character has been placed at the origin. The camera's focal length is set to the default of 35.

Figure 14.25 With the focal length set to 6, the robot seems very far away, even though the camera hasn't moved.

Figure 14.26 The camera has been moved close to the robot with the focal length still set to 6. The result is like what you would get with a fisheye lens—distances are exaggerated.

ABOUT CAMERAS

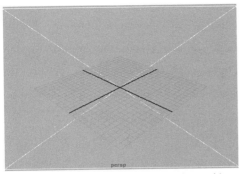

Figure 14.27 When you create an image plane, a big square with an X through it shows up in the view. This is where the image will be once you choose it.

Figure 14.28 The sunrise image appears in the background of the scene. This image will stay in the same place relative to the camera, even if you tumble, track, or dolly.

Image planes

An image plane is a component of the camera that stays in the background of the view regardless of where the camera is moved. This can be useful for having an image to use as a template when modeling a character. Or it can serve as a backdrop to a scene. It renders out with the rest of the scene.

To create an image plane:

1. From the View menu of the Perspective view select Camera Attribute Editor.
   The Attribute Editor for the camera appears.

2. Scroll down in the Attribute Editor, and click the triangle next to Environment.
   This expands the options concerning the camera environment.

3. Click Create next to Image Plane.
   The image plane appears in the Perspective view (**Figure 14.27**), and the Attribute Editor changes to show the options for it.

4. Click the folder icon next to Image Name.

5. Browse for and open your image, then close the Attribute Editor.

6. The image now appears on the image plane (**Figure 14.28**).

✔ Tips

- To select the image plane, the Pick Mask needs to be set to "Select by component type" by clicking that icon ▣ , and the Miscellaneous icon must be selected ? .

- Once the image plane is selected, you can move it by changing the Center X, Y, and Z settings in the Channel Box. It can also be deleted by pressing [Backspace] / [Delete].

- A quick way to hide an image plane is to uncheck Cameras from the Show menu of the view pane you are in. Since it is a component of the camera and you are hiding the camera, the image place also gets hidden.

About Rendering

Rendering is how you output images once you finish modeling, animating, lighting, and texturing your scene. There are many options to set and you will find these in the Render Globals window.

First you decide what your output will be. The resolution of an image is its size in pixels. The size you choose depends on what medium your images will end up on.

If you are making a small image for a Web site, you might use the default resolution of 320 by 240. If you are going to put the images on NTSC video, you'll probably use 720 by 486 (**Figure 14.29**).

If you are going to print, you'll need a much higher resolution to get decent quality. Printing at 300 dots per inch (dpi) will produce a sharp image. If you want to print an image that is 8 by 10 inches, you will need a resolution of 2400 by 3300 pixels. This will take a long time to render.

You can set the resolution quality in the Render Globals window. Lower quality images will render faster, so they are good for tests. Higher quality settings will make for a cleaner, better-looking image and should be used for final output (**Figure 14.30**).

Figure 14.29 The same scene has been rendered out in a variety of resolutions.

Figure 14.30 Compare production quality (left) with preview quality (right). The one on the right renders out much more quickly but looks worse.

ABOUT RENDERING

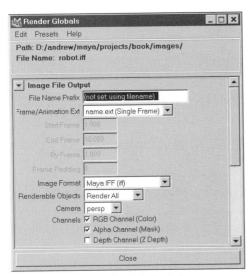

Figure 14.31 In the Render Globals window you can set options such as quality, resolution, image file format, and much more.

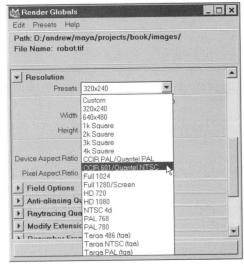

Figure 14.32 Choose a resolution from the list of presets. Resolution determines the size of your image in pixels.

Before you render your scene, you need to save it and set your project. Taking these steps will help you avoid losing images when you render.

To render out a single image:

1. In the Render view click the Render Globals button ▓ (Windows only), or from the Options menu select Render Globals.

   The Render Globals window appears (**Figure 14.31**).

2. Choose an image format.

   Maya IFF is the default, but it won't necessarily open in other programs. You might want to choose something more common, like TIFF or Targa.

3. Choose the camera view you want to render from.

   Even if you've created new cameras, perspective is still the default camera in the Render Globals window. It is a common mistake to overlook this and render out the wrong camera view.

4. Click the triangle next to Resolution.

   The Resolution options are expanded.

5. From the Presets menu choose CCIR 601 (Quantel NTSC, on Windows) (**Figure 14.32**).

   This is a good choice if your image is going to end up on NTSC video.

6. Click the triangle next to Anti-Aliasing Quality.

   The Anti-aliasing options are expanded.

   continues on next page

7. From the Presets menu choose Production Quality (**Figure 14.33**).

This will automatically set several of the options below and is a good choice for most renders.

8. Click the Render button 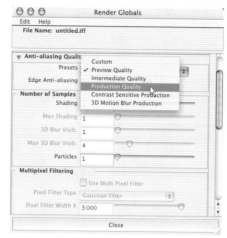.

9. The Render View window appears. The image will take time to render out, depending on the scene's complexity (**Figure 14.34**).

10. From the File menu in the Render View window select Save Image.

You can save the image to any folder and in any format you desire.

To render out a series of images:

1. In the Render view click the Render Globals button (Windows only), or from the Options menu select Render Globals.

The Render Globals window appears.

2. Set the camera, anti-aliasing quality, resolution, and image format options as in the previous section.

3. Change the filename if you want the images to be named something other than the name of the scene file.

When a new name is typed in, the example filename at the top of the window reflects this change (**Figure 14.35**).

4. Choose name.#.ext from the Frame/Animation Ext menu.

The example name changes to reflect this update. You must choose an option that includes # to be able to render animation as opposed to single frames. This is a good choice for the Windows operating system, but for Macintosh or Irix you may want to use either name.# or name.ext.#. The choice mostly depends on the software into which you plan to bring the images.

Figure 14.33 Choose Production Quality from the Presets menu. This is the setting you will want in most cases when you are creating your final image.

Figure 14.34 This image is in the process of rendering in the Render View window. It doesn't appear all at once. The image is broken down into little rectangles that appear gradually.

Figure 14.35 The example filename at the top of the Render Globals window changes when a different filename is typed in.

Path: D:/andrew/maya/projects/book/images/
File Name: billyTheRobot.0001.tif
To: billyTheRobot.0010.tif

Figure 14.36 When Frame Padding is changed to 4, the number of the image becomes four digits long.

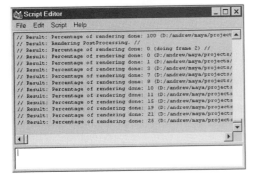

Figure 14.37 You can watch the progress of your render in the Script Editor. It also tells where it is putting the images, with the path, and what they are named.

5. Set the Start Frame and End Frame of your animation.

These should be set to the range of time you want to render out.

6. Change the Frame Padding to 4 and close the Render Globals window.

This will put zeros in front of the numbers in the image name so that they are four digits long. This is helpful because your images will be listed in order when sorted by name (**Figure 14.36**).

7. From the Render menu select Batch Render. On Windows the render will begin, on the Mac a dialog box opens; select a name for the batch file in the Save As field and press OK.

The render begins.

8. Click the Script Editor icon ▤ in the lower right-hand corner of the interface.

The Script Editor opens. You can watch the progress of the render here (**Figure 14.37**).

✔ Tips

- If you choose AVI from the image format, it will just render out a single movie file rather than a series of individual numbered images.

- In Render Globals you can turn on Motion Blur, which causes moving surfaces to blur slightly. This makes them look better because they more closely resemble moving objects captured by a real camera.

ABOUT RENDERING

Maya comes with FCheck, a program that provides an easy way to view images and animations.

To view a render:

1. From the Render menu select Show Batch Render.

   If it is still rendering, the progress of the current frame opens in FCheck (**Figure 14.38**). If it is finished rendering, the last frame opens FCheck.

2. From the File menu in the FCheck window select Open Animation/Open Sequence (**Figure 14.39**).

   A file-browsing window opens.

3. Browse for your rendered image files.

   They should be in the images folder of the project folder you are currently set to.

4. Open the first image in the series.

   The animation will load in slowly and then play back at full speed. It may not ever get to full speed if there are very many images or the resolution is high. It also depends on your computer's hardware.

✔ Tip

- FCheck has some hotkeys that make it easy to use:

  Spacebar starts and stops the playback of animation.

  ← goes back one frame.

  → goes forward one frame.

  Click and drag from left to right to scroll through the animation.

Figure 14.38 Since the batch render still has not completed, the progress of the current frame shows up in FCheck. It will not update in this view as the render continues.

Figure 14.39 You can open an animation in the FCheck window, which can play back all of the frames you rendered out.

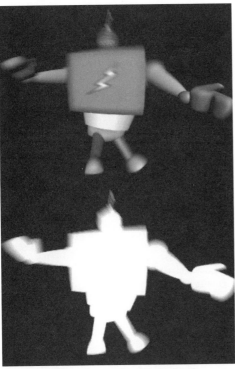

Figure 14.40 The robot was rendered using the Hardware Render Buffer with motion blur turned on. In the bottom, you can see the alpha channel created for this image; it can be used for compositing.

Figure 14.41 This robot was software rendered. Note the bump map on the arms, the glow on the visor, and the reflectivity of the chest.

Using the Hardware Render Buffer

Software rendering can take a very long time. If you want to make a preview of your animation without having to software-render it, you can hardware-render it. It is kind of a middle ground between a playblast and a software render. Hardware rendering is essentially a series of screen snapshots of your scene.

Hardware rendering does a few things that playblast cannot. It can anti-alias the edges of your surfaces and create motion blur so that the animation looks smoother. It can also create an alpha channel, so you can easily composite with other images (**Figure 14.40**). One technique is to hardware render some elements of your scene and composite them with a software-rendered background.

On the other hand, there are a number of things that hardware rendering does not do that software rendering does. It cannot create shadows, reflections, or refractions. It doesn't do as good a job with textures and lights. Special effects like glow do not work, and you can't see bump maps or many other things (**Figure 14.41**).

To use the Hardware Render Buffer:

1. Open or create a scene with some animation in it.

2. From the Window menu select Rendering Editors > Hardware Render Buffer.

   The Hardware Render Buffer appears.

3. From the Cameras menu in the Hardware Render Buffer select the camera view you want to render out (**Figure 14.42**).

   To adjust the view, you can tumble, track, and dolly inside the Hardware Render Buffer.

4. From the Render menu in the Hardware Render Buffer select Attributes.

   The Attribute Editor for the Hardware Render Globals opens (**Figure 14.43**). The Hardware Render Globals is the collection of settings for the output of your image files using the Hardware Render Buffer. Note that this is not the same as Render Globals, which is for software rendering only.

5. Set the filename, extension, start frame, end frame, image format, and resolution as desired.

   See "To render out a single image" and "To render out a series of images" earlier in this chapter for more information on these. All the same issues apply for hardware rendering.

6. From the Render menu in the Hardware Render Buffer select Render Sequence.

   The sequence quickly renders out. The image files are put in the Images folder of the project you are currently set to.

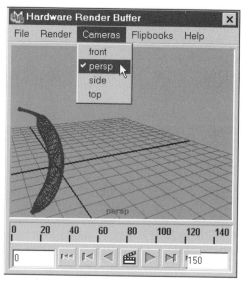

Figure 14.42 Choose a camera view from the Cameras menu in the Hardware Render Buffer.

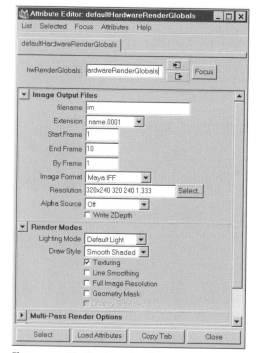

Figure 14.43 The Hardware Render Globals window controls the filename, resolution, range of frames, and many other attributes concerning the render.

ABOUT RENDERING

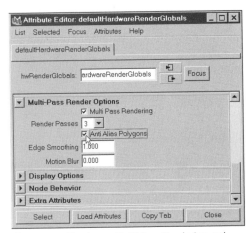

Figure 14.44 Turning on Multi Pass Rendering and Anti Alias Polygons will improve the look of your render by smoothing aliased (stair-stepped) edges.

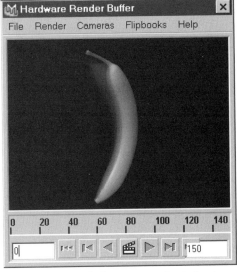

Figure 14.45 Since the banana was animated and Motion Blur was turned on in the Hardware Render Globals, you can see some blur in the resulting image.

To adjust hardware-render quality:

1. From the Window menu select Rendering Editors > Hardware Render Buffer.
   The Hardware Render Buffer appears.

2. Set up the hardware-render attributes as in the previous section.

3. Scroll down to Multi-Pass Render Options. Select Multi Pass Rendering and Anti Alias Polygons (**Figure 14.44**).

4. Click the Test Render button in the Hardware Render Buffer to see the result 🎬.
   Three passes of the image are done and then composited together automatically. The edges of the surfaces are anti-aliased.

5. Change Render Passes to 5 and Motion Blur to 1.

6. Click the Test Render button in the Hardware Render Buffer to see the result.

7. Five passes of the image are done. With the Motion Blur set to 1, the passes are done over the duration of one frame (**Figure 14.45**).

About Raytracing

Achieving realistic renders often requires reflections and refractions. Raytracing must be turned on to achieve these effects. It can make renders take significantly longer, but they look much more realistic.

When an object has other objects visible in its reflection, the light rays bounce off one surface, and then bounce off another surface and into your eyes or a camera lens. You need other objects in the scene in order to see a reflection of them; the object has to have something to reflect (**Figure 14.46**).

Refraction is the bending of light as it travels through a dense, transparent material such as glass or liquid. Without it, glass doesn't look real. You can set a refraction index, which controls how much the light bends as it passes through the surface (**Figure 14.47**).

To create reflections:

1. Create a scene with a large plane, a sphere, many cubes, and some lights (**Figure 14.48**).

2. Assign a Phong material that is red to the cubes, a Phong material with a checker color to the plane, and a Phong material to the sphere.

3. In the Render View click the Render Globals button 🖼 (Windows only), or from the Options menu select Render Globals.

   The Render Globals window appears.

4. Change the Anti-Aliasing Quality Preset to Production Quality.

5. Scroll down and click the triangle next to Raytracing Quality.

   The Raytracing Quality options are expanded.

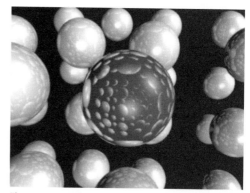

Figure 14.46 This is a scene made up of only spheres. They reflect each other because raytracing is turned on.

Figure 14.47 Each transparent sphere has a different refraction index: left, 1.0; middle, 1.333; right, 2.0.

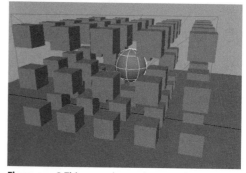

Figure 14.48 This scene has a plane, a sphere surrounded by many cubes, a directional light, and an area light.

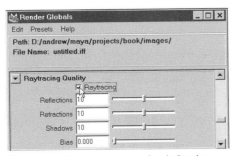

Figure 14.49 Raytracing is turned on in Render Globals. Reflections and refractions do not render out unless this is selected.

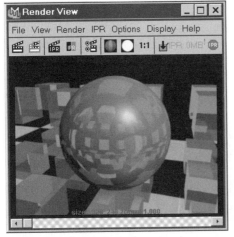

Figure 14.50 When the scene is rendered, you can see the cubes reflected in the sphere.

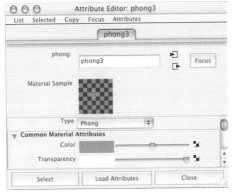

Figure 14.51 The Transparency slider is dragged to the right, which makes the color field white. White is transparent and black is opaque in Maya.

6. Select Raytracing (**Figure 14.49**).

7. Frame the sphere in the Perspective view, then click the Render button.

8. The Render view appears, and the image renders with reflections (**Figure 14.50**).

To create refraction:

1. Continue with the scene from the previous section.

2. Select the sphere.

3. Click the Graph Materials on Selected Items button in the Hypershade.

The material for the sphere appears in the work area of the Hypershade.

4. Double-click the Phong material that is assigned to the sphere.

The Attribute Editor for the Phong material opens.

5. Drag the slider for Transparency all the way to the right.

The color field next to Transparency becomes white (**Figure 14.51**).

continues on next page

ABOUT RAYTRACING

6. Scroll down in the Attribute Editor, and click the arrow next to Raytrace Options.

The Raytrace Options are expanded.

7. Select Refractions.

8. Change Refractive Index to 1.333 (**Figure 14.52**).

9. Click the Render button 🎬.

The Render View window appears, and the scene renders out. The sphere refracts the light, which causes the objects seen through it to appear warped (**Figure 14.53**).

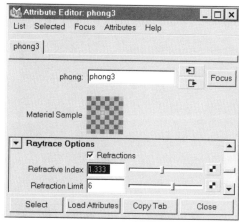

Figure 14.52 Refractions are turned on, and the Refractive Index is set to 1.333. If you do not do this, reflections will render but refractions will not.

Figure 14.53 The transparent sphere is rendered out and refracts light. It is dark because the scene surrounding it is dark.

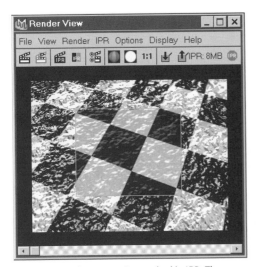

Figure 14.54 A bump map is tweaked in IPR. The selected area updates when the bump depth for this surface is changed from 1.0 to 0.1.

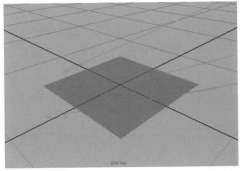

Figure 14.55 A plane is created with a bump map and a directional light pointed at it.

About Interactive Photorealistic Rendering (IPR)

Every time you make a change to a material or a light you need to render it out again. This makes tweaking things like lights or bump maps time-consuming because of the wait for render time.

To address this problem, Maya has Interactive Photorealistic Rendering, known as IPR. If you render out using IPR, you can select a region of the render, and the changes you make will update interactively (**Figure 14.54**).

There are some limitations to IPR. It won't update the positions of objects or changes to the camera. It won't update the position of a shadow. It doesn't do any raytracing, which means no reflections or refractions. It always does low-quality anti-aliasing.

However, it will update most changes to materials and lights. This alone can save you a great deal of time.

To use IPR:

1. Create a plane, assign a material with a bump map to it, and create a directional light pointed diagonally to the plane (**Figure 14.55**).

   See "To assign a bump map to a surface" in Chapter 13 for more on bump maps.

2. Click the IPR button 📇.

   The Render View appears, and the scene renders out. You will see the prompt "Select a region to begin tuning" at the bottom of the Render View.

   continues on next page

3. Select a region in the Render View (**Figure 14.56**).

4. Select the plane.

5. Click the Graph Materials on Selected Items button in the Hypershade ⬚.

The nodes for the shader appear in the work area of the Hypershade.

6. Double-click the bump2d utility in the Hypershade.

The Attribute Editor for the bump2d opens.

7. Change the Bump Depth to 2.

The selected region of the Render view updates the change quickly (**Figure 14.57**). Try updating other things, such as the intensity and color of lights, or the color or type of material.

✔ Tip

■ If IPR is not updating, it may be because Raytracing is on. Turn Raytracing off in Render Globals and try IPR again.

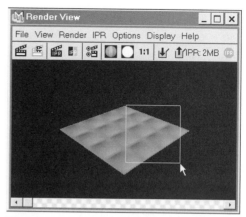

Figure 14.56 After being prompted in the Render View, select a region. Only this region will update when you make changes, but you can select the whole image as the region if you want.

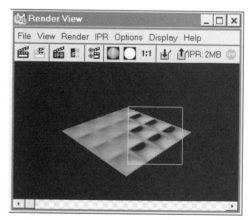

Figure 14.57 When the bump depth is changed, it updates interactively in the Render view.

Index

point, 243, 251–252
reflected, 264, 312–313
refraction, 312, 313–314
rendering and, 241–242
scenes, 238
setting mood, 238
shadows, 255–261
specular highlights, 264
spotlights, 243, 252–254
types of, 243–245
Lights panel, 240
linear tangent type, 228
local coordinates, 3
Loft command, 148
lofting, 56, 75

M

main menu bars, 4, 42
main menus, 4, 59, 68
Make Planar command, 150
manipulator axes, 100
manipulator tools, 99–107
manipulators, 5, 25–26
Marking Menus
changing menu sets, 45
described, 5, 45
hiding, 47
Hotbox and, 9–11
illustrated, 5
manipulation tools, 103
objects, 47
shortcuts, 5
showing, 47
marquee, 83, 84, 86, 122–123
masks, Pick, 4, 81–96
masks, selection, 10
materials, 268–286
3D Paint tool, 283–286
attributes, 268–269
color, 268
described, 264, 265
NURBS surfaces, 271–279
projection maps, 280–283
texture-mapping, 271–279
texturing polygons, 287–292
UV Texture Editor, 289–292
Maya
basics, 1–30
described, 2
help features, 29–30
interface, 4–17, 31–52
manual for, 29
preferences, 24–27
Maya IFF format, 305
Maya Unlimited, ix, 158
Maya versions, ix
menu bars, 42

menu sets, 4, 45, 46, 47
menus, 10
minor sweep attribute, 63
mirroring joints, 192
mirroring objects, 108–114
Modify Boundary options, 132, 134
Modify Position options, 132, 133
Modify Tangent options, 134
motion, objects, 277. *See also* animation
Move tool, 99, 100, 101, 102–103
movies, 306–307. *See also* animation
Multiple Knots option, 132

N

nodes
animated, 13
connections, 2, 12, 14
dependencies, 13
described, 2
grouping and, 121–123
hierarchies, 12, 13
icons, 12
showing, 12, 13
non-uniform rational B-spline. *See* NURBS
NURBS components, 56, 136, 138
NURBS curves. *See also* curves
components, 138
creating, 135, 137–146
degrees and, 55
described, 135, 136
NURBS degrees, 55
NURBS (non-uniform rational B-spline)
described, 56
overview, 55–56
subdivision surface modeling, 172
vs. polygons, 287
NURBS objects, 135–156
assigning image maps to, 272–274
components of, 56, 136, 138
creating, 56
described, 55, 136
uses for, 55
NURBS planes, 280
NURBS primitives, 57–64
attributes, 57, 61–64
creating, 56, 58–60
described, 54
radius of, 61–62, 63
types of, 54
NURBS spheres, 280
NURBS surfaces
converting to subdivisions, 182
degrees and, 55
described, 135, 136
texture-mapping, 271–279
uses for, 135

INDEX